THE HISTORY

OF THE

CHRISTIAN RELIGION AND CHURCH,

DURING

THE THREE FIRST CENTURIES.

BY DR. AUGUSTUS NEANDER.

TRANSLATED FROM THE GERMAN,
BY HENRY JOHN ROSE, B.D.
RECTOR OF HOUGHTON CONQUEST, AND LATE FELLOW OF ST. JOHN'S COLLEGE, CAMBRIDGE.

IN ONE VOLUME,

CONTAINING

THE CHIEF FATHERS OF THE CHURCH.

FIFTH EDITION.

Philadelphia:
...MES M. CAMPBELL, 98 CHESTNUT STREET.
NEW YORK: SAXTON & MILES, 205 BROADWAY.
Stereotyped by C. W. Murray & Co.

1844.

**The History of the Christian Religion and
Church During the First Three Centuries
ISBN 1-58509-077-8**

©2000
THE BOOK TREE
All Rights Reserved

Published by
**The Book Tree
Post Office Box 724
Escondido, CA 92033**

We provide controversial and educational products to help awaken the public to new ideas and information that would not be available otherwise. We carry over 1100 Books, Booklets, Audio, Video, and other products on Alchemy, Alternative Medicine, Ancient America, Ancient Astronauts, Ancient Civilizations, Ancient Mysteries, Ancient Religion and Worship, Angels, Anthropology, Anti-Gravity, Archaeology, Area 51, Assyria, Astrology, Atlantis, Babylonia, Townsend Brown, Christianity, Cold Fusion, Colloidal Silver, Comparative Religions, Crop Circles, The Dead Sea Scrolls, Early History, Electromagnetics, Electro-Gravity, Egypt, Electromagnetic Smog, Michael Faraday, Fatima, Fluoride, Free Energy, Freemasonry, Global Manipulation, The Gnostics, God, Gravity, The Great Pyramid, Gyroscopic Anti-Gravity, Healing Electromagnetics, Health Issues, Hinduism, Human Origins, Jehovah, Jesus, Jordan Maxwell, John Keely, Lemuria, Lost Cities, Lost Continents, Magick, Masonry, Mercury Poisoning, Metaphysics, Mythology, Occultism, Paganism, Pesticide Pollution, Personal Growth, The Philadelphia Experiement, Philosophy, Powerlines, Prophecy, Psychic Research, Pyramids, Rare Books, Religion, Religious Controversy, Roswell, Walter Russell, Scalar Waves, SDI, John Searle, Secret Societies, Sex Worship, Sitchin Studies, Smart Cards, Joseph Smith, Solar Power, Sovereignty, Space Travel, Spirituality, Stonehenge, Sumeria, Sun Myths, Symbolism, Tachyon Fields, Templars, Tesla, Theology, Time Travel, The Treasury, UFOs, Underground Bases, World Control, The World Grid, Zero Point Energy, and much more. Call **(800) 700-TREE** for our *FREE BOOK TREE CATALOG* or visit our website at www.thebooktree.com for more information.

INTRODUCTION

Augustus Neander was without a doubt one of the greatest religious historians to have ever lived. In this abbreviated version of a larger work, he covers the current of Gnostic ideas during the formation of Christianity. This topic is important because it outlines all of the competitive beliefs that were at work at the time and how they effected the Christian struggle in both positive and negative ways.

Neander's contribution is valuable because he does not seem to have an agenda or any biases—he reports things in a factual manner and allows the reader in many cases to form his own opinions.

What can be observed is that Christianity was a multi-faceted belief structure with many mystical factions. Mystics who achieve their own personal bliss always experience this in a variety of ways, none of which could be "standardized" in the way Christianity was trying to develop. In sorting through these competitive strains, Christianity became organized—but it took three hundred years. This is highly revealing. Three hundred years is a long time. A lot happened here that should be looked at and studied closely by each and every Christian who *really* wants to know about the origins of their own faith.

A great deal of information found in this book is not found elsewhere, making this a fascinating study. Neander's reputation is a great one, and he is always mentioned at the top of the list of respected Christian scholars—but his books have all but disappeared and are incredibly difficult to find. With this modest work, we hope to at least start bridging that gap and make his work available once again.

In exploring this work, we also recommend one other of great importance called *The History of the Christian Religion to the Year 200*, by Charles B. Waite, available from The Book Tree at the time of this writing, but in limited supply. The two of these books together will provide one with immense knowledge of what really occurred during such an important time in history. With the help of these important works, one will become aware of so many important facts that they will certainly come away with a deeper understanding of how Christianity is structured in its truest sense. Such a compelling view will, in many cases, shake the very foundations of the reader's beliefs, in both positive and negative ways. This book may cause one to never look at Christianity in quite the same way again, due to its immense scholarship and interesting array of facts.

Paul Tice

CONTENTS

THE GNOSTIC SECTS 5
*General remarks on their origin,
Character, and differences.*

THE INDIVIDUAL SECTS 21
1) *The Gnostics, whose system was
engrafted on Judaism.*
a) *Cerinthus* 21
b) *Basilides* 24
c) *Valentinus and his School* 32
d) *Distinguished Men of the
School of Vanentinus* 42

2) *The Gnostic sects, which denied the* 47
*connection between the Old and New
Testaments, and between the visible and
invisible world.*
a) *The Ophites* 47
b) *Pseudo-Basilidians* 50
c) *Sethites and Cainites* 51
d) *Saturninus* 51
e) *Tatian and the Encratites* 52
f) *Eclectic Antinomian Gnostics;* 54
*Carpocrates and Epiphanes, Prodicians,
Antitacti, Nicolaitans, Simonians.*
g) *Marcion and his School.* 58

Marcionite Sects   66

ADDITIONAL REMARKS   67
On the Cultus of the Gnostics

Manes and the Manichees   69

THE ALEXANDRIANS   85
Includes Basic Philosophy, Clement of Alexandria, Platonism, Origen, Tertullian, Hermogenes, Patripassians, and Noetus

The Sects which arose from the mixture of the oriental Theosophy with Christianity.

1. *The Gnostic Sects.*

General remarks on their origin, character, and differences.

We pass from the Judaizing sects to the Gnostics, who, proceeding from *one* common stock with the former, developed themselves afterwards in a manner which set the two parties in a constantly increasing opposition. If we contemplate the characteristics of both dispositions pushed to the extreme, we cannot conceive a stronger opposition than that between the narrow and carnal disposition of Judaism, which cleaves to outward things, and comprehends every thing only after the senses,—and the spirit of Gnosticism, which gives itself up to unbridled license in its speculation on Divine matters, despising the letter, idealizing every thing, and striving to reach beyond the limits of earthly existence and the material world; and yet, just as one is often led to observe, that dispositions, which in our conceptions are widely opposed, really are connected together in the outward world* by various means, and unite together by many points of communication, so the following considerations will verify such an observation in regard to *this very difference.*

At the time of the first propagation of Christianity, the name γνωσις, [*gnosis,* knowledge,] in the widely extended phraseology of the Jewish divines of Alexandria, denoted a deeper insight into the nature and the inward connection of the various doctrines of religion. As far as the word denotes *only this general idea,* it might be used in regard to Christianity, without prejudice to the peculiar nature of Christian faith. Nay, even here, in conjunction with other *charismata* more immediately connected with what is *practical,* there might be a *charisma* of Gnosis, which, setting out from its own peculiar position, might exert a general and beneficial effect on the development of the Christian life; and, in fact, St. Paul mentions such a thing in the first Epistle to the Corinthians. Thus the name Gnosis, in the epistle ascribed to Barnabas, betokens that deep insight into the spirit of the Old Testament, and the object of the economy of the Old Testament, which was afforded by Christianity.

Although this idea was applied in an arbitrary, and therefore, in a false manner, —as, for instance, in that very letter, (see below)—yet, considered in itself, and by itself, it contains nothing repugnant to the simple nature of the Gospel, because that Gospel, in its very simplicity, is destined to imbue and appropriate to itself all the powers and dispositions of human nature, even those that are spiritual, and in its very simplicity it opens the inexhaustible depths of Divine wisdom in the eye of the Spirit. Among the *mystical sects of the Jews* and *their philosophical teachers of religion at Alexandria,* we have already remarked the germ of a Gnosis, conceived under an entirely different notion. Here, under the name of "the *Religion of the Perfect,* an esoteric system of doctrines, containing only *pure ideas,* which could be comprehended only by a small number of initiated persons, consisting of men distinguished for their high intellectual gifts of perception, and their high spiritual nature, (the πνυματικοι,)—was opposed to the *faith founded* *on authority,* and entertained by the sense-bound multitude, who held fast only the symbolic covering of these pure ideas, and were utterly incapable of understanding them in their real meaning. (These were the ψυχικοι, the πολλοι.) Such an opposition, although necessarily grounded on the very nature of the religion that preceded Christianity, would entirely overthrow the fundamental characteristics of Christianity, because Christianity pulled down every such partition wall between man and man, and Greek and barbarian, educated and uneducated, were to become one in Christ, and one source of Divine life and inward illumination was to be present in one common faith; this illumination was to develope itself in proportion to their advances in holiness, and Christian views were not to be made dependent on intellectual powers, bestowed only on a certain class of men, but were to proceed, in all, out of their inward Christian life, and out of their own inward experience, although, nevertheless, peculiar depth or clearness of view might be a particular *charisma.* Christ, indeed, thanks his heavenly Father for having revealed to children what he had hidden from the wise; and St. Paul requires that those who are wise in this world should become fools that they might receive Divine wisdom. But then, such Gnostics as these were unable to comprehend these truths and to become children, in order to enter into the kingdom of heaven, and *to be poor* with the rest of mankind, and to be rich only in Christ: they wished to have precedence of the multitude of the believers by means of a pretended higher kind of wisdom.

Another disposition belonging to this Gnosis, which is at variance with the peculiar nature of the gospel, is closely connected with that of which we have just treated. It was because Christianity presented religion in its independence and elevation above every thing earthly, that it was able to find entrance and extend itself among all the different habits of life which mankind adopts, and form a Church differing in its constitution from all other social unions among men, and independent of them; and thus also it presented religion, considered in a doctrinal point of view, in a substantial form, entirely independent of all speculations as well as of all mythology, and in a form adapted to all the various degrees of advancement which are found in human nature, and all

---

* ["Erscheinungswelt." Lit. World of Appearances, or phenomena.—Tr.]

the various periods of its progress. That Gnosis, on the contrary, brought the doctrines of religion into connection again with all the inquiries which can occupy a speculative reason, as was the case in the old Oriental systems of religion, such as those of Zoroaster, of Brahma, and the Buddhists. A speculative cosmogony, desirous of explaining what is incomprehensible, and a theosophy, which would anticipate the views reserved for a higher state of being, were made the basis of the doctrines of religion, and these would, therefore, be unintelligible to the greater mass of mankind, and, *in consequence of this,* an opposition would necessarily follow between the esoteric and the exoteric religion. This mixture of religion and speculation would besides necessarily be dangerous to the essentially *practical character* of Christianity, in virtue of which all is made to turn on the acknowledgment of sin, the application of the redemption provided for man, and the sanctification which proceeds out of it by means of faith working by love.

It appears, then, that the VIEW *of religion* on which this Gnosis was founded, was the *old Oriental* system, to which also the Platonic joined itself, as well as the *new Platonic.* It might happen that men who were altogether devoted to some such Oriental theosophy would constantly find themselves attracted on one side or the other by Christianity, which is calculated to lay hold on human nature from so many different sides, while yet they might be unable to conquer themselves so far as to sacrifice their former habits of thought entirely to Christianity; and hence they endeavoured to form for themselves a theosophistical Christianity of their own, and a theosophic Christ of their own, after their own manner. And thus also, if the Gospel were now to make its way powerfully among the Persians, the Brahmins, and the Hindoos, it is most probable that similar phenomena would take place again; the real and genuine Christians would be accompanied by converts who would endeavour to amalgamate Suphism, Buddhism, and Brahminism with Christianity; and in fact we find traces of such an attempt here and there even now.*

In order to perceive clearly the formation of *those Gnostic systems,* one must put oneself into that remarkable time of ferment from which they proceeded. A lively intercourse and an unusual interchange of ideas was then taking place between the nations of the western and the eastern world, which are otherwise so widely separated by their situation and by their differences in their peculiarities of character; an intercourse that arose from the overgrown empire of Rome, which embraced within it all these nations, or at least brought their boundaries into close connection with each other. The spirit, which sighed after new revelations from heaven, and after some new excitement of the spiritual life, unsatisfied alike by the Hellenic mythology and by the dicta of philosophical systems among the Greeks (Hellenes,) mingled together all these various elements of religion, and endeavoured to put together out of them the fragments of a system of truth which had been lost. The comparison of different systems of religion would of course open many resemblances to their view, which to the surprised inquirer would seem as evidences of truth; for the religious development of human nature is a mirror which reflects partly, the *original revelation* of a Divine Being who draws man to him,—a revelation which has been variously propagated by tradition, either more or less corrupted: partly, the needs, desires, and wishes that arise from the religious nature of man; and partly also, that speculative reason which mixes itself up in all religious contemplations, which has its own fundamental principles that constantly recur under different forms, and which is forever wearying itself in vain to pass over that line, which the limits of human knowledge draw around it. At Alexandria, and in different parts of Asia, even Jewish theologians were unconsciously carried away by this religious eclecticism.

Accordingly, in the Gnostic systems the elements of the old Oriental systems of religion, (especially the Persian, but certainly the East Indian also,) of Jewish theology, and of Platonic philosophy, may be found melted down together, and a more extensive acquaintance with the different religious systems of the interior of Asia might, perhaps, give us a great many new disclosures as to the connection between these systems; but then at the

---

* The English Missionary reports from the East Indies, and the conversations of that genuine evangelical missionary, Martyn, with the Persian Suphi, in the very instructive biography of that person, will give proofs of this assertion.

same time we must carefully guard ourselves against immediately concluding that an outward communication has at some time or other taken place solely from finding an agreement which may arise from an inward source, namely, in the selfsame essential dispositions of human nature, from which similar phenomena will result under similar circumstances.

This Gnosis opposed Judaism as a religion too carnal, too earthly, too narrow, and too little theosophical; for how little spiritual, how cold, how little, and empty must Judaism appear to men of this disposition, when they compared it with the old colossal systems of religion in Asia, although to one who knows what purpose religion is to serve for man, the very comparison which led them to despise Judaism would be the first thing which would lead him to recognise its full value for the religious development of human nature. Those old religions, in their enigmatic form, in which men are inclined to look for lofty wisdom rather than in a simple one, appeared to promise far more decisions on the *questions* which exercised *their inquiries*. Mere Platonism appeared to them too jejune* and too measured;† it appeared to them constantly to confine itself entirely to the narrow limits of finite reason, and to have no sense and perception of higher intercourse with the spiritual world. Gnosis was desirous, by means of the new ideas opened to it by intercourse with the East, of obtaining higher and more recondite conclusions about the nature of things, their origin and development, than Platonism had to offer. Had this Gnosis been consistent in its disposition, and had it not been carried away by the mighty attracting power of that which is Divine in Christianity, it might have come in good earnest into controversy with Christianity as a religion of too practical and human a nature, and as a religion that did not raise itself enough into the supernatural regions. The selfsame character of mind which in the Christian Gnostics opposed only the *ecclesiastical* disposition, and a faith that would set limits to speculation, would have opposed Christianity in general, had it been carried to extremes, and had it been clearly aware of its own principles; and, indeed, the traces of an unchristian, and also of an openly antichristian Gnosis are to be found, perhaps, in a certain class of the Ophites (see below), in the Jewish Cabbalists, and in the Zabians, or the disciples of John.

Although the Gnostic systems contained elements selected out of various old systems of religion, yet they can never be entirely explained from the supposition of an intermixture and joining together of these alone; there is *a soul and spirit of a peculiar kind,** which animates most of these collections. In the first place, the time in which they originated, has impressed upon them a wholly peculiar character, just as it often happens in times of great ferment, that certain dispositions communicate themselves to a whole series of spiritual phenomena, even without any outward connection or intercourse. Now the prevailing tone† in most serious minds of that time, was the feeling of disunion, and of being unsatisfied by the existing world; a longing which would overclimb the limits of the earth; a desire after a new and higher order of things. This tone of feeling pervades also the Gnostic systems, and Christianity worked in an especial manner on this tone; and without Christianity, the Christian Gnostic systems would have become an utterly and entirely different thing. The idea of *redemption* was that which formed the peculiar nature of Christianity; and this idea suited that peculiar tone of feeling prevalent among those systems, although it could be embraced by them only in a partial manner, and not in its whole extent, and all the consequences deducible from it. The ideas of restoring an harmonious tone to a world in which it had been broken, of restoring a degraded creation to its original state, of restoring the lost connection between heaven and earth, of the revelation of a mighty and Divine life in man, elevated above the limits of human nature, as well as the notion of a new course of development, which had entered into the whole economy of the world;—these

---

* Zu nüchtern.—Germ. Perhaps it may mean too sober, too temperate.

† Zu besonnen.—Germ. Too ratiocinative, too much the result of deliberative meditation.

[I add the German words here that those of my readers who understand that language may draw their own conclusions as to what Neander intends here; for I am not aware of any expressions in English, which are entirely synonymous with his. —H. J. R.]

* [Ein eigenthümliches beseelendes Princip.— Germ. Literally, a peculiar animating principle.]

† [Grundton, key-note. The word translated disunion is zwiespalt, which expresses division, in consequence of a violent rent.]

were the ideas which communicated a new and imposing character to Gnosis altogether.

Those theosophists busied themselves with the investigation of the great inquiry, the answer to which has always been the highest problem of human speculation; but in answering which human reason must always recognise its own insufficiency; or, if it will explain that which is incomprehensible, must always deceive itself with mere phrases, or with the fictions of fancy. These Gnostics, as Oriental theosophists, in whom, at least for the most part, the Oriental element predominated over the Hellenic, must in no manner or degree whatever be compared with the thinking people of the Western world; they engaged themselves far more in representations and visible images, than in abstract ideas.* Where the thinking man of the west would have formed to himself only an abstract conception, with them a living appearance, a living personality stood before their souls, for them absolutely to look upon in reality. They disregarded the abstract notions of the mind as a lifeless sort of thing; every thing hypostasized itself in their eyes, where nothing but abstract ideas were presented to the thinkers of the Western world. The image, and that which was represented by the image, were so constantly joined together in their modes of thought, that they were unable to separate the one from the other. They were far rather carried away unconsciously by the ideas that floated before their minds, or that inspirited them, from one mental picture to another,† from image to image, so that they were not in a condition to develope these ideas with any thing like a clear consciousness of their nature. The inquiries which chiefly occupied them were these: How is the transition from infinite to finite? How can man imagine to himself the beginning of a creation? How can he think of God as the original projector of a material world so foreign to his own nature? Whence come those wide differences of nature among men, from the man of truly godly disposition, down to those who appear given up entirely to blind desires, in whom no trace of the rational and the moral creature can be found?*

Now it was exactly here that Christianity made religious faith independent of speculation, and cut off at once all that could lead to those speculative cosmogonies, by which the element of pure religious faith was only troubled, and the confusion between the ideas of God and nature furthered, inasmuch as it (Christianity) directed the eye of the spirit beyond the whole extent of the visible world, where, in the chain of cause and effect, one thing is constantly unfolding itself out of another, to an Almighty work of creation performed by God, by which the worlds were produced, and in virtue of which the visible did NOT spring out of that which appears. Heb. xi. 3. Creation is received here as an incomprehensible fact, under the constraint of a faith, that raises itself above the position occupied by the understanding, which wishes constantly to deduce one thing from another, and to explain every thing, while it denies all that is immediate.† This, which is the only real point of practical importance, the doctrine of the Church endeavoured to maintain in its conception of the creation out of nothing; opposing itself thus to the old methods of‡ representation, which limits the creation of God by supposing matter already in existence, and represents him, after an anthropopathical manner, not as an independent original Creator, but as a being who acted on and formed pre-existing matter. Gnosis would not acknowledge any such limits to speculation; she wished to explain and represent to the mind *how* God is the foundation and the source of all existence.

---

* Sie bewegten sich viel mehr in *Anschauungen* und *Bildern*, als in *Begriffen*.—Germ.
 [It is difficult to render these words exactly. Anschauung, (*intuitio*) *looking upon*, in its *original* sense, means the representation or image of an object conveyed to the mind by the *sight*; and it is used also *secondarily* of the notices conveyed by other senses. It is here used of *visible representations* or *images*, as opposed to *Begriffe* or *abstract* ideas. For some further remarks on these words, see the Preface.—H. J. R.]

† [From *anschauung* to *anschäuung*.—See last note.]

---

* On this portion of the subject, see the 5th Book of Beausobre's Histoire du Manich isme. Vol. ii. especially p. 205, &c.—H. J. R.]

† [Alles unmittelbare.—Germ. I understand by this all immediate acts of the Divinity, such as creation. The word translated *understanding*, is *verstand*, and we must bear in mind the distinction usually made in Germany between verstand and *vernunft*, the understanding and the *reason*. See Coleridge's Aids to Spiritual Development.—H. J. R.]

‡ [Anschauungsweise.—Germ. I suppose this word to mean a habit of considering these subjects, where all the operations of the Divinity are presented to the view of the mind in a palpable form or image. See Preface.—H. J. R.]

As it misunderstood the *negative* import of the creation out of nothing, it opposed to it the old principle, "out of nothing comes nothing." Instead of this it presented to its imagination the idea of an outflowing of all Being, from the highest Being of the Divinity. This idea of an emanation would allow itself to be conceived under a variety of images: under the form, for instance, of a numerical development from an original unity; of an outstreaming of light from an original light; of an unfolding of spiritual powers or ideas, which obtained substantiality, and of an utterance of a series of syllables and sounds, till they were re-echoed.

The idea of such an emanation corresponds to a feeling deeply rooted in the human mind, and found in it something to fasten itself upon; but at the same time, it gave occasion to many speculations by which men might easily be led away forever, farther from that which is of practical importance for religious belief, and indeed, might lose it altogether.

In this mode of representation God appeared as the incomprehensible original source of all perfection,* and shut up within himself; and no means of transition between this incomprehensible Being of God, and finite existence could be imagined. *Self-limitation, a letting down,* is the first beginning of a communication of life on the part of God, the *first revealing* of the hidden God, from which every other revelation of God, which unfolds itself further, proceeds.† Now from forth of this first member of the chain of life there develope themselves, first, the manifold powers or attributes, which dwell in the very Being of God, which, up to that first time of his letting himself down had been shut up in the abyss of his Being, every one of which represents the whole Divine existence, in some one particular point of view, and to which, in this point of view, the names that belong to the Deity were transferred.* These Divine powers, therefore, unfolding themselves into substantiality, are the seeds and elements of all other developments of life. The life contained in them developes and individualizes itself constantly more and more, and in such a manner also, that the degrees of this development of life constantly go lower down, and the spirits constantly become weaker, the more distant these developments are from the first link of the chain. We must remark that a Gnosis which, in its endeavour to explain the incomprehensible, was forever falling into anthropopathism, has here unconsciously attributed the relations of time to the Eternal.

Granting now that the existence of a pure spiritual world, akin to God, was fairly to be explained, men could represent to themselves the development of different degrees of perfection; but how was it possible to explain the origin of the *material world** by means of an emanation from God? and how the *origin of evil?* Even in respect to the latter,—a problem on which speculation has made shipwreck so often, to the prejudice of God's holiness, and the freedom of man, a being gifted with reason, and destined for morality; even in regard to this point, Gnosis would not allow any limits to be put to speculation. If God gave freewill to man, and if this freewill is the cause of evil, then the origin of evil, said the Gnostics, falls back *on God himself.* They would not hear of a difference between a permission, and an actual originating cause, on the part of God.‡ Now whosoever does not follow the necessities of his moral nature, and the law inscribed upon his inmost conscience, and with immovable certainty of faith, and with the assurance of inward moral experience, firmly hold, that evil can be founded in nothing else, and be explained from nothing else, but can only be comprehended as the act of a *wilfulness, that falls away from God's holy law, and a self-seeking which opposes itself to the will of God,*—he must necessarily either prejudice the holiness of God, and take away the objective importance of the opposition between good and evil, and therefore, utterly remove in its foundations

---

* The unfathomable Βυθος, according to Valentinus, the Being raised above all description, of whom nothing can be suitably (eigentlich) predicated; the ἀκατονομαστος of Basilidas, the ὢν of Philo.

† Ἡ πρώτη καταληψις ἑαυτου: the πρωτον καταληπτον του Θεου hypostatically embodied (hypostasirt, hypostasized) in a νους or Λογος.

‡ Hence comes the difference in the use of the word αἰων among the Gnostics; according to its etymological meaning, namely, *eternity,* it sometimes denotes *the eternal,* as a distinctive predicate of the Supreme Being; sometimes it denotes those Divine original energies, and sometimes the whole world of emanations, πληρωμα, in opposition to the *temporal* world. It occurs in the latter sense in Heracleon ap. Origen. 7, xiii. in Joh. c. 11.

† [*Sinnliche,* that which is the object of the senses. The *external,* or material world.]

* Το μη κωλυον αἰτιον ἐστιν—was their usual motto in opposing the church doctrine.

the idea of moral good and evil, considered in themselves, because he throws back the origination of the latter upon God,—or else he must prejudice the omnipotence of God, because he establishes an absolute evil, and an independent foundation of that evil beyond God, by which also, in fact, he fundamentally removes the idea of evil in a moral point of view, because he deduces it from without, and makes of it an independent nature, which operates necessarily, by which means he involves himself at the same time in a contradiction with himself, through the idea of an independent being besides God, of a God who is not God, who is not good. The Gnostics, avoiding the first rock, made shipwreck on the second.

They united a Dualism with their system of emanations, and endeavoured to explain the origin of this whole earthly world, in which good and evil are mingled together, and which does not answer to the ideal of the spirit, from the intermixture of two opposite principles and their mutual operations; and this endeavour to explain, opened a wide space to their speculation and their formation of fantastic theories. There now developed themselves here two modes of viewing these matters,[*] which, however, in those days, of religious and philosophic eclecticisms did not always come into sharp opposition, but came into connection with each other by the amalgamation of various intermediate members, while the same idea, in fact, forms the foundation of both these modes of view, only that it was conceived in the one case after a more *speculative* fashion, in the other after a more *mythical*. In the one mode of conception the element of *Grecian speculation* more prevails, in the other the element of *Oriental imagery* [anschauung,] and hence these two modes of view make the difference between an Alexandrian Gnosis and a Syrian Gnosis, (the latter being determined particularly by the *influence* of *Parsism*,) as far as we can oppose, in abstracts, these two kinds of Gnosis to each other, without regard to the intermixture of them together, which we find in the phenomena of those times.

In *the first* the *Platonic notion of an* ὑλη *prevails*; this is dead and lifeless matter; the boundary of which from without, limits the development of life, that proceeds by regular gradations, in virtue of which imperfect beings develope themselves out of the perfect, each more imperfect than the preceeding; and this ὑλη again is represented under various forms—as the Darkness that stands by the side of the Light—as Emptiness (κένωμα, κενον) in opposition to the Fulness of the Life of God—as the Shade that stands beside the Light—and as Chaos and the dark stagnant water. This matter of itself being lifeless, has by its nature no impulse; every kind of life is foreign to it, and of itself it makes no attack on the Divine being; but inasmuch as the Divine developments of life, (the beings that proceed from the preceding emanation,) the farther they are removed from their first member, become always weaker and weaker, because their connection with that first member is always less close, there arises in the last grade of the development an imperfect work, which cannot maintain itself in connection with the divine chain of life, which sinks from out of the world of Æons into that Chaos, or else—which is the same representation a little differently modified—something froths over out of the fulness of the Divine life into the neighbouring chaos.[*]

Lifeless matter now receives, by means of its intermixture with the Living Being, that of which it was in want, a quickening;[†] but then the Divine Being, the Living Being, is also injured by means of its intermixture with the chaotic. Being multiplies itself; a subordinate, deficient life arises; ground is taken for a new world, and a creation forms itself beyond the bounds of the emanation-world; but, as the chaotic principle of matter on the other hand, has obtained a spirit of life, a *clear, active* opposition to the Divine nature now comes forward, a blind, undivine natural power, of an entirely negative character, which opposes itself hostilely to all formation through the Divine Being; and thence come as the works of the spirit of the ὑλη (the πνευμα ὑλικον)—Satan, evil spirits, and wicked men, in all of whom no reasonable, no moral principle, no principle of freewill prevails, but only blind desires. As Dualism carries in itself a self-contradiction, it cannot maintain its ground with any clear speculative thinker, who is conscious of the course of his reasoning. The more Gnosis inclined to this side, and became clearly conscious

---

* [Anschauungsweise.]

* According to the representations (anschauungsweise) of the Ophites, and of Bardesanes.
† [Eine Beseelung—Germ. Literally a quickening, an animation, the infusion of a soul of life. H. J. R.]

to itself of this disposition, which to say the truth rarely happened, because of the prevalence of oriental imagination over occidental abstract comprehension, in all Gnostic systems,—the more must it have endeavoured to lead back this Dualism to a higher unity. It then declared expressly what the Cabbala and the Neo-Platonism taught,—that *Matter is nothing else than the necessary limit* between existence*, which can be conceived as any thing having an independent existence, only by the power of abstraction :† it is the opposition to being, which arises as a necessary limit on every development of life from out of the Deity.‡ In such a manner *Dualism* might finally resolve itself into *Pantheism*.

The other mode of viewing these matters engrafted itself more upon the *Parsic* doctrine of an Ahriman and his kingdom, which it would be an obvious course for the Gnostic sects, especially those which were formed in Syria, to appropriate to themselves. This mode of view supposed an active, wildly-raging dominion of evil or darkness, which by means of its attack on the empire of light, introduced a mixture of light and darkness, of the divine and that which opposes it. Different as these two modes of conception may appear in their way of representation, yet the selfsame fundamental idea may be recognised in them.

When the latter mode of view takes a somewhat more speculative turn, it passes into the first, of which we shall find traces in the views of Manicheeism, which bears upon it far more than all Gnostic systems the mark of Parsism (see below;) and where the first mode of view takes a more poetical character, and endeavours to picture itself upon the imagination, it passes over involuntarily into the last.§

Even among the Platonists there were some, who supposed that from the very beginning, together with an unorganic, dead matter, as the materials for the *bodily world*, there existed also a *blind, unbridled, moving power*, an undivine soul, as the originally-moving and active principle. Thus, while that unorganic matter was organized into the bodily world by the formative power of the Deity, that formative power communicated also law and reason to that wild, tumultuous, and reason-opposing soul. Thus the chaos of the ὕλη was formed into an organized body of the world, and that blind power into a reasonable principle of the soul of the world, that animates the universe. Thus, while all reasonable spiritual life in human nature descends from this last, all that is contrary to reason comes from the other: all that is impelled by desire and passion; all evil spirits are its productions. One sees easily how the idea of this ψυχη αλογος, floating over the chaos, might fall in with the idea of a Satan, who originally presided over the kingdom of darkness.*

In the system of the *Zabians* or *disciples of John*, which is undoubtedly connected in its origin with the Syrian Gnosis, although there appears an independent kingdom of darkness with its own peculiar powers, yet this has no influence on the higher kingdom of light.† It was the thought of one of the genii of the kingdom of light, to tear himself loose from the source which every thing ought to glorify, and to form an independent world that should exist for itself——it

---

* It was thus also called the exterior rind of existence, קְלִיפָּה.

† By means of a νοθος λογος according to the Neo-Platonists.

‡ Thus the Gnostics in Irenæus, (ii. 4,) expressly defend themselves against the reproach of Dualism. 'Continere omnia Patrem omnium et extra Pleroma esse nihil et id quod extra et quod intus, dicere eos secundum agnitionem et ignorantiam, sed non secundum localem distantiam." The lower creation was contained in the Pleroma veluti in tunica maculam.

§ Thus, for example, where Plotinus paints matter as seized with a longing after light or the soul, and speaks of it as darkening the light, while it endeavours to embrace it, Plotin. Enneas I. lib. viii., c. 14. Τἡν παρουσα πρωαιτω, και οιον ενοχλω, και εις το εισω παρελθων εθελω, την δε αλλαμψιν και το εκωθεν φως ισκοτωσι τη μιξει.

* See Plutarch de Animæ Procreat. e Timæo. especially c. 9. Opera Ed. Hutten. t. xiii. p. 296.

† This sect of Zabians, (βαπτισται, from צָבַע,) Nazarenes, Mandæans, (according to Norberg, from יְדַע, μαθηται or γνωστικοι,) clearly derives its origin from those disciples of John the Baptist, who, contrary to his spirit and feeling, after his martyrdom took up an hostile disposition towards Christianity. Traces of such persons are to be found in the Clementine, and the Recognitiones Clementis, and perhaps, also in the ἡμεροβαπτισται γαλιλαιοι of Hegesippus. See F. Walch, de Sabæis comment. Soc. Reg. Gott. t. iv., Part. Philolog. From these a sect afterwards formed itself, whose system being formed out of the elements of older Oriental theosophy, is of great importance for the history of Gnosticism. A critical treatise on their most important religious book, the Liber Adami, would contribute much to this object. See the critique of that work by Gesenius, in the Literatur Zeitung of Jena. Jena. 1817, No. 48—51, and (Kleuker's?) critique on it in the Anzeigen of Gottingen.

was this thought that first became the cause of a mixture between the two kingdoms, the first foundation of this visible world, built upon an earth won from the kingdom of darkness; i. e. from chaos, which world the powers of darkness at once endeavour to seize upon or to destroy, because they will not suffer any strange rule in their domain. Now, while this genius, *Abatur*, who formed the third stage in the development of life, was looking into the dark water of chaos, there arose out of his reflection in it an imperfect genius, formed from a mixture of this form of light with the being of darkness, and to be ennobled by degrees hereafter, namely, *Fetahil*, the former of the world, from whose imperfection all the defects of this world are derived.* In the system of the Syrian Bardesanes also, matter appears as the mother of Satan.†

This sufficiently shows how the modes of view of the Syrian and the Alexandrian Gnosis pass into each other on this side. It may, indeed, very fairly be asked, whether one is justified in speaking of a Gnosis as originally Alexandrian, or whether Syria be not the birthplace of all Gnosis, whence it was only transplanted to Alexandria, and received a peculiar stamp at this latter place in consequence of the Platonizing, Hellenizing disposition, which prevailed there? In Alexandria, such a Gnosis would probably find much to engraft itself upon in certain Jewish idealistic philosophy of religion, already in existence there; but in this the platonic and occidental element, which keeps itself more on the pure idealistic point of view, and does not immediately hypostasize ideas, and make representations of them, was two predominant to suffer the peculiar character of Gnosis to proceed forth from it, without the influence of the pure Orientalism from Syria.

One might imagine that this double mode of view would have produced a peculiar distinction in the practical spirit of these two systems. As the Syrian mode of view supposed an active empire of evil, which was destroyed with the empire of matter, one might be led to imagine that it made the avoidance of this abominable matter and its hostile productions, and the strictest asceticism, the chief object of morality. As, on the contrary, the Alexandrian Gnosis considered matter as unorganized materials for formation, and the *Divine Being* as the *formative principle*, one would think that it would re-recognise no such negative system of morality, but would establish a more active formation and improvement of the world, by the power of the Divine principle as the foundation of the moral system. This supposition might, perhaps, appear still more probable on a comparison of many Alexandrian and Syrian systems.

And yet on a more accurate investigation, it appears that such a difference in the practical influence of these two systems is by no means necessary. Even a system, in which the *Parsic Dualism* prevailed to the utmost extent, might recognise in the whole universe a higher life, which was only bound prisoner in the bonds of matter, and might recommend co-operation towards the freeing of that life, by victory over the empire of darkness, by means of a practical forming and improving influence over nature. And so, in fact, Parsism commanded an outward activity, because it represented all formative influence upon the outward world, especially agriculture, as a struggle against the destroying and order-opposing power of Ahriman, and as an activity which was employed in the service of Ormuzd. And therefore, the dualistic Manicheeism furthered a *great reverence towards nature*, and by no means an *enthusiastic and ascetic contempt* of it; although on another ground this system led to a strict asceticism: and certainly it cannot be denied, that the prevailing feeling of Oriental notions, as we may even now see from the people of the East, in general shone forth in highly prizing an ascetic and contemplative disposition, which elevated itself above the ordinary earthly life. But this disposition had also spread itself already in the district, where a Grecian spirit prevailed, and had found reception particularly in Alexandria. The *pure Platonic doctrine of gross matter*, as being the source of blind desires, and of the guilt contracted by the soul in a former life, might become a point for a strict asceticism to fix itself upon; as in fact it did to many Platonists.

The most *essential* difference between the different Gnostic systems, the influence of which was very great on the reli-

---

* Lichtnatur, Being of light.—Germ.
† This idea is entirely to be compared with the ophiomorphos of the ophitish system, (see below,) although in the ophitish system this appears of a lower kind; and the ophitish system, in its speculative notions, is yet akin to the Alexandrian system of Valentinus in many respects.

gious and spiritual character of these sects, concerns their different view of the relation of the temporal, earthly system of the world, to that higher and invisible one, of the relation of Christianity to the whole development of human nature, (whether they supposed a gradual development of the theocracy, as an organically-connected whole; or whether they made Christianity out to be a fragment which appeared all on a sudden, without previous preparation,) and of the relation of Christianity to Judaism. All these considerations are closely connected together.

All Gnostics agree in this, that they suppose, as we have above remarked, a world in which there is a pure development of life out of God; a creation, which is nothing but a pure unfolding of the Divine Being,* as being elevated far above that creation which was produced from without by means of the formative power of God, and was limited by matter previously existing;—and they agreed in *this* also, that they did not allow the Father of that higher emanation-world to be the immediate Former of *this lower* creation; but they brought down the Former of the world, (the δημιουργος,) far below that higher system and its Father, because he (the δημιουργος) was connected with the universe, which was formed and governed by him. But the difference among them was this; namely, that though they agreed as to the existence of this inferiority, they were at variance as to the mode of it. One party, setting out from views which had already long been prevalent among the Alexandrian Jews, supposed that the Supreme God had produced, and still governed this world, by means of the angels, who were his ministering spirits. At the head of these angels stood one, who guided and ruled every thing, and on that account was especially called the Former and the Governor of the world. They compared this Demiurgos with the spirit that formed and animated the world, after the system of Plato and the Platonists, which also (according to the Timæus of Plato, endeavoured to form the image of the Divine reason in that which was "Becoming to be."† This angel is a representative of

the Supreme God on this lower stage of existence; he does not act independently but only according to the ideas given to him by the Supreme God, as the world-forming soul of the Platonists creates every thing after the ideas imparted to him by the supreme νους:* but these ideas are elevated above his own limited being; he is unable to understand them; he is only their unconscious instrument, and is, therefore, unable himself to understand the meaning of the whole work wrought by him: as an instrument guided by a higher inspiration, he reveals what is above his own comprehension. Here, therefore, they grafted themselves on the current ideas of the Jews, in supposing that the Supreme God had revealed himself to their ancestors through the medium of an angel that served him as the organ of his will; and that the Mosaic legislation was derived from such an angel. And they considered the Demiurgos as the representative of the Supreme God in this respect also; just as the rest of the nations of the world were partitioned among the other angels, as their guides, so the Jewish people, as the peculiar people of Jehovah, that is, the Supreme God, were committed to the care of the Demiurgos, as his representative.† He also revealed here in the establishment of their religion, as well as in the creation of the world, those higher ideas which he himself could not understand in their

---

* עולם אצילות.

† [As Neander has only referred generally to the Timæus, I have taken this phrase from the translation by Taylor. I add the original of

---

Neander: Das ideal der göttlichen vernunft in dem *werdenden*, zeitlichen darzustellen strebt. We have no word that answers to *werdenden*, which expresses the *beginning of existence*, the *becoming*, not the actually *being*.—H. J. R.]

[Since the above note was written a friend lent me "Bockshammer on the Freedom of the Will; translated by A. Kaufman, of Andover, 1835;" in which the word 'becoming' is used substantively, e. g. p. 75: "Yet this connecting love, according to the representation of the above named treatise, is rather *an originated becoming*, man, an original being:" and a note referring to Neander is added by the translator, to this effect: "The idea of a secondary Being, without beginning, anfängslosen werdens, an originated becoming in opposition to an unoriginated Being, (eternal generation,) was somewhat refined, was somewhat incomprehensible; nay, it appeared even contradictory to Arius, who had but little of the speculative or intuitive, &c. Neander," &c.—H. J. R.]

* The ὁ εστι ζων (in opposition to the γνωτα, or the ὁως γνωτα of Plato,) the παραδειγμα of the Divine reason hypostasized.

† According to the Alexandrian version of Deuteron. xxxii. 8, 9, ὁτι διεμεριζεν ὁ ὑψιστος ἐθνη, ὡς διεσπειρεν υἱους Αδαμ, εστησεν ὁρια εθνων κατα αριθμον αγγελων Θεου και εγενηθη μερις κυριου λαος αυτου Ιακωβ.

true meaning. The old Testament, like the whole creation, was the *veiled symbol of a higher system.*

But in the Jewish people itself they made a complete distinction, after the Alexandrian fashion, between the great multitude, which is only a representative type of the people of God (the Israelites according to the flesh, the 'Ισραηλ αισθητος, κατα σαρκα,) and the small number of those who become really conscious to themselves of the destination of the people of God. (The souls of this number are the spiritual men of Philo, the 'Ισραηλ πνευματικος, νοητος; the generation consecrated to God which really lived in the contemplation of God, the ανηρ ορων τον Θεον, the πνευματικοι, γνωστικοι, in opposition to the ψυχικοι or πιστικοι.) The latter (the ψυχικοι) with their fleshly thoughts kept fast to that which was outward only; they did not observe that *this* was merely a symbol, and therefore, they did not recognise the intention of that symbol.* Those sensuous-minded men did not recognise the angel through whom God *revealed* himself in all the appearances of God (the Theophanies) in the Old Testament, that is to say, the Demiurgos, in his just relation to the hidden Supreme God, who never reveals himself in the world of sense; they confused form and prototype, symbol and idea.† They did not elevate themselves above the Demiurgos, but considered him as the Supreme God himself. Those spiritual men, on the contrary, have clearly recognised the ideas which were wrapped up in Judaism, or at least have a presentiment of them; they have raised themselves up beyond the Demiurgos to recognise the Supreme God, and thence they become peculiarly his true worshippers (θεραπευται.) The religion of the former class was solely founded on a faith which they took upon authority, while these latter lived in the contemplation of Divine things. The former required to be educated by the Demiurgos by rewards and punishments, and the means of terror; but these latter required no such means of discipline; they raised themselves up by the force of their spirit to the Supreme God, who is a source of blessing only to those who are capable of communion with him, and they love him for his own sake.

Now, when these Jewish theosophists of Alexandria had embraced Christianity, and interwoven their former notions with it, they saw the spirit of the Old Testament entirely unveiled in Christianity, and the highest ideas of the whole creation brought clearly before the light; and now for the first time the object of the whole creation, and of the whole development of human nature became clear. As far as the highest Æon,† who appeared in the person of Christ, was elevated above the angels and the Demiurgos, so far is Christianity elevated above Judaism and the whole earthly creation. The Demiurgos himself now recognises a revelation which entered into his kingdom, and from henceforth serves it as its instrument, conscious that he was only an instrument.‡

The *other party of the Gnostics* consisted especially of persons who had *not* been attached to the Mosaic religion before their conversion to Christianity, but had formed to themselves in former times an Oriental Gnosis opposed to Judaism as well as to all national religions, a kind of system of which we find some traces in the books of the Zabians, and which is constantly found in the East among the Persians and the Hindoos. They did not, like the former, consider the Demiurgos and his angels merely as subordinate and limited beings, but as beings entirely hostile to the Supreme God. The Demiurgos and his angels wished to establish themselves in their limited condition as independent beings and would suffer no foreign sovereignty in their dominion. Whatever of a higher nature comes down into their sphere they endeavour to keep

---

* Thus a moderate Gnostic, who had not reached that refined Gnosticism formed by the mixture of Alexandrian idealism with Syrian theosophy, determines (in the letter ascribed to Barnabas,) that the Jews had entirely misunderstood the whole ceremonial law, by observing it outwardly, instead of seeing in it only an allegorical representation of general religious and moral truths. It was Gnosis, which first opened this true sense of it.

† [The form, and the original form represented by it; the symbol, and the idea symbolized. The German is, sie verwechselten auch hier bild und urbild, symbol und idee.]

† Νους or λογος.

‡ We see easily how these Gnostics might use the passages of the New Testament where the λογος λαληθεις δια του Υιου is compared with the λογος λαληθεις δι' αγγελων, (see *e. g.* Heb. ii. and Ephes. iii. 10,) in order to form their artificial superstructure of doctrines, by means of their fanciful and idle speculation, on the foundation of a Jew, hints only thrown out, *en passant*, by the apostle.

imprisoned there, that it may never be able to raise itself above their narrow limits. In this system it is probable that the empire of the world-forming angels coincided for the most part with that of the deceiving spirits of the stars, which are hostile to man's freedom and exercise a tyrannic sway over the affairs of this world.* The Demiurgos (according to this system,) is a limited and limiting being, proud, envious, and revengeful, and this his character declares itself in the Old Testament which is derived from him. As these Gnostics were unable, from want of the requisite exegetic and hermeneutic knowledge, as well as of the proper pædagogo-historical† point of view, to understand the Old Testament, which was so opposite to their system, and were yet, nevertheless, accustomed to give their judgment upon every thing, they attributed all the errors which arose from a gross and sensuous anthropopathical view of the Old Testament among the common sort of Jews, to the *Old Testament itself*. But, according to their view, the error of the Jews consisted solely in this, that they considered the Demiurgos who reveals himself such as he is, in the Old Testament, to be the Supreme God, who differs from him infinitely. The Demiurgos is (according to them,) really such a being as that which the Jews represented to themselves under the notion of the Supreme God. These Gnostics believed that they recognised the form of that hateful Demiurgos in the Old Testament, and also in nature, which they judged with the same dogmatical human rashness. The Supreme God, the God of holiness and love, who stands in no connection with the world of sense, has not revealed himself in this earthly creation by any thing, except by some Divine seeds of life which are scattered abroad in human nature, and whose unfolding the Demiurgos endeavours to stop and to overwhelm. He can be acknowledged and honoured in the highest degree only in the mysteries, by the few who are spiritual men; and now (according to them,) this God has let himself down all at once, without previous preparation, to this system of the world by means of his *highest Æon*, in order to draw up to himself the higher spiritual natures akin to himself which are imprisoned there.— Christianity can find no point in all creation to attach itself upon, except in some mysteries and philosophical schools, in which a higher kind of wisdom is propagated as their common doctrine.

This difference between the Gnostic systems was of the greatest importance in a theoretical and practical point of view. As the Gnostics of the first class recognised in the Demiurgos the instrument of the Supreme God and his representative, who formed nature according to the ideas of the Supreme God, and conducted the development of the kingdom of God, in history, they might, in accordance with their principles, search for the revelation of the Divinity in nature and in history; they needed not of necessity to be entangled in *an unchristian hatred of the world*. They might acknowledge that the Divinity might be revealed under earthly relations, and that every thing earthly might by this means become ennobled. They might, therefore, be very moderate in an ascetic point of view, as in fact we find was the case with many of this class, although the practically injurious disposition of deducing evil only from the existence of objects of sense, must easily have arisen from their notion of the ὕλη; and although their overprizing of a contemplative Gnosis must have been in danger of becoming prejudicial to the spirit of active love.

On the contrary, the other sort of Gnosis, which considered the Creator of the world as a being entirely at enmity with the Supreme God and his system, would naturally produce a wild, dark hatred of the world, entirely at variance with the spirit of Christianity. This exhibited itself outwardly in two ways; it either showed itself with nobler and more rational men in an extravagantly strict asceticism, and an anxious avoiding of all intercourse with the world,—on which, however the Christian is bound to exert a forming influence, and then, at all events, morality would be a thing merely of a negative kind; nothing, in short, but a way of purification as a preparation for

---

* Thus the seven star spirits, and the twelve star spirits of the zodiac, which were produced by the evil connection with the deceived Fetahil with the spirit of darkness, in the Zabian system, play an important part in all that is evil. It is from their deceitful artifices that Judaism and Christianity, which are so hateful to the Zabians, are produced.

† [I suppose Neander here considers the Jewish history as affording an instructive lesson to man, as containing the Divine mode of education for human nature; but as I am not certain that this is his view, I have only put the German compound word into literal English; pädagogisch-geschichtliche gesichtspunckt.—H. J. R.]

contemplation,—or else it showed itself in men of an impure nature, and inclined to wild fancies, and in men of ungoverned passions, in a *licentious contempt for all moral laws.* When once these Gnostics set out from this principle,—' this whole world is the work of a limited ungodly spirit, it is utterly incapable of all revelation of the Divinity, and we higher natures, who belong to a far higher world, are imprisoned in it,'—this conclusion would immediately follow; ' Every thing outward is utterly and entirely indifferent to the inward man; nothing of an higher nature can here be expressed, and the outward man may give himself up to every kind of lust, provided the inward man be not thereby disturbed in the tranquillity of his contemplation. The very means by which we must prove our contempt and our defiance of this wretched and hostile world, is by not suffering ourselves to be affected by it in any condition whatever. The means by which we must extinguish the empire of our senses, is by remaining undisturbed in our tranquillity of spirit, while we give ourselves up to every kind of desire. " We must struggle against our lusts by the indulgence of them," said these freethinkers; " for there is nothing great in abstaining from pleasure, if we have never tried it; but it argues greatness when a man finds himself in the midst of pleasure, and yet is not overcome by it."* The heathen philosopher Plotinus makes a very striking remark against these men, which all, who view the matter even from the ground of Christianity, must recognise as true, namely, that while they venture with *more boldness* than Epicurus, who denied any overruling Providence of this world, to throw out the same accusations that he did, they must necessarily bring men to *the same result*, in regard to morals; which result would be this: " That nothing is left for us here, except to give ourselves up to our desires, and to despise all the laws of this world, and all morals, for there is nothing good to be found in this abominable world."*

This difference is also shown in the consideration of individual moral relations. The Gnostics of the latter class either prescribed celibacy and abhorred marriage, as something unclean and profane, or else, according to the principle that every thing relating to the senses is entirely indifferent, and that people here must only defy the Demiurgos by contempt of his limiting laws—they justified the indulgence of every desire. Those of the former class, on the contrary, honoured marriage as an holy state, by which the natural state of man was to be ennobled. And the *Valentinian* Gnosis, in fact, as it universally considered the lower world as a symbol and mirror of the higher, and as it sought for the revelation of the highest law of that higher system in the different stages of existence in manifold degrees,—so also it recognised, in the marriage connection, the image of a higher connection, which runs through all stages of existence, from the very highest link of the whole chain. (See below.) Besides, the influence of the *originally Jewish notions*, which were inclined to prize the marriage condition highly, is also shown here.

The difference between these two classes of Gnosis is still farther brought prominently forward in their different mode of considering the *person* of Christ. *All Gnostics*, however, in a certain respect agree in this, that, as they separated the God of heaven and the God of nature from each other, and as they, therefore, severed also the invisible and the visible system, the Divine and the human, too widely from each other; so also they would not recognise the union of the Divine and the human in the person of Christ. And yet, just as we have observed a remarkable difference in regard to the first of these matters, between the two chief divisions of the Gnostic system, we shall also be able to remark such a difference in regard to the latter of them. We shall find here also an essential gradation in the views entertained of the relation between the Divine and the human in Christ. The one party, indeed, recognised the manhood of Christ as real, and also conceded to it a certain dignity, although, as they made two Gods out of the one God of heaven and of nature, and

---

* Clemens, Stromata, lib. ii. p. 411. Porphyry de Abstinentia Carnis, lib. i. § 40, &c., paints the notions of these men in a manner quite accordant with that of Clemens. " It is only some little standing water," say they, " which can be defiled by receiving into it something unclean; not the ocean, which receives every thing, because it knows its own greatness. So also little men may be overpowered by what they feed upon, but not he who is an ocean of power (ἐξουσία, apparently an expression peculiar to them, founded on a misuse of that of St. Paul in 1 Cor. viii. 9; vi. 12.) which receives all things into itself, and becomes not defiled."

* See the excellent argument in Plotinus, Ennead. ii. lib. ix. c. 15.

allowed the Creator of the latter to be only the instrument of the former, they also divided the one Christ into two Christs, a higher and a lower, a heavenly and an earthly one, in such a manner, that the latter was merely the instrument of the former; and these two they held were not originally indissolubly bound together, but the former had united himself to the latter, for the first time, at the baptism in the river Jordan. But the other class of Gnostics, as they denied the connection of Christianity with Judaism, and with all historical development of God's kingdom among mankind, and as they made out of the God of Christ and of the Gospel a different God from that of nature and of history, so also they rejected the connection of the appearance of Christ with nature and with history. Christ did not here, (according to them,) enter into nature, nor into the historical development of human nature. The view, which suited the fantastic disposition of the East, and had long since been spread abroad among the Jews, namely, that a higher Spirit might represent itself to the eye of sense in a multitude of delusive forms,* which appeared to the senses, but had no reality, —this notion was applied to Christ, and one whole essential part of his earthly existence and his personality, was thus argued away; *the whole of his human nature was denied; the whole human appearance of Christ was made a mere deceptive appearance, a mere vision*—and this was *Docetism*, the direct contrary to mere *Ebionitism*, which would recognise nothing but the human in Christ. And this view might, at last, be carried so far—as it was among the more fanciful *Basilidians* —as exactly to despise the most holy points in the human life of Jesus in the most profane manner.

The Gnostic systems will also admit of a very natural division into two classes by means of their most essential and influential differences. *The first class*, consisting of those sects *which acknowledge the connection between the visible and the invisible world,—between the relation of God in nature, in history, and in Christianity, and the connection between the Old and the New Testament, as the development of one whole theocratical scheme— and the second class, of those which tear asunder these connections, and which make*

Christianity only an insulated fragment in the history of man; or, as we may explain it more shortly, the sects *which founded their views on Judaism,* and those which set themselves *entirely at enmity against it.** It is, we avow, natural enough, that between these opposite extremes many intermediate opinions should be found, which do not, however, invalidate the correctness of the division.

It is peculiarly instructive to consider the mode and manner by which these Gnostics were able to come to the persuasion, that their doctrines, so foreign to the simple Gospel, could have been delivered by Christ and the apostles, and how they endeavoured to prove this. We find here the same phenomena, which, arising out of causes that lie in the very inmost nature of man, were often repeated in following centuries. With a ready-formed Theosophic system, based on its own fundamental principles, they went to the Holy Scriptures, and sought to find in them something to hang their system upon. And this they might easily find, because they were wholly unacquainted with the rules of grammatical and logical interpretation,† and despised attention to such matters as carnal;‡ for their inward intuition was to open every thing. But they were punished for the pride, which, trusting to a certain inward light, only granted to higher natures of a certain class, despised the usual human means of knowledge. Therefore, they were given up to every kind of error which can arise from *the want of considering the occasion and the connection in which any thing is said, from the confusion between different meanings*

---

* This division has this circumstance in it. favour, that it is only in this manner that the peculiar system of Marcion—which, however, is necessarily connected with the Gnostic systems only *from one side,*—can find its proper place among them. Clement of Alexandria in a certain degree confirms this division, when he calls Valentinus the κορυφαιος των πρεσβευοντων την κοινοτητα. (Strom. lib. vi. 641,)—the leader of those who maintain *a common source of the revelation of the Divinity among men,* and do not deny the connection of Christianity with all earlier revelations of God. The πρεσβευοντες το ιδιον των χριστιανισμων, who would not acknowledge any such κοινοτης between Christianity and any other revelation whatever on Divine truth, according to him, also, would be the contrast to this class.

† Origen (Philocal. c. 14,) shows how much strengthened in their errors the Gnostics were by their αγνοια των λογικων in their interpretation of the Bible.

‡ Only fit for the ψυχικοι.

---

* My readers may remember the Indian Maja, and many other Indian Myths.

of a word,* from the want of distinguishing between *metaphorical and proper expressions*, and from the arbitrary application of single traits in comparison, *without regard to that which constitutes the real points of comparison*. The *subjective caprice* of the imaginative faculty, of the feelings, and of speculation, without an objective law, proceeding from the application of the rules of thought and language, might find whatever it chose in the Scriptures and introduce it into them. The Parables, for the simplicity and practical depth of which they had no feeling, were, therefore, peculiarly acceptable to them, because an arbitrary interpretation, when they had once put the real point of comparison out of their view, had the freest play here. But contention against the arbitrary biblical interpretation of the Gnostics had also the advantageous effect, that it made their opponents attentive to the necessity of a more accurate grammatical and logical interpretation of the Bible, and induced them to the establishment of the first Hermeneutic Canons, as we may observe from various proofs in the writings of Irenæus, Tertullian, Clemens, and Origen.

The bolder among the Gnostics used a theory of interpretation likely to lead to arbitrary principles of criticism. They said,—Christ and the apostles spoke according to the different conditions and views of the man to whom they spoke; they took these different positions themselves. With the ψυχικοι—those who were in the condition of a blind unintellectual faith (those who were fettered by Jewish prejudices)—they spoke only of a Demiurgos, because their limited natures could not understand any thing higher. (The Gnostics are the fathers of *the theory of an accommodation as used in the Christian Church*, in an exegetical point of view, although of itself the theory of an accommodation is as old as the difference between an esoteric and an exoteric religious system.) The higher truths from the world of Æons, and those above that world, they (i. e. Chirst and the apostles,) had (according to this view,) communicated only to a small circle of initiated men, who were capable of receiving such truths in virtue of their higher spiritual natures (as πνυματικοι,) and these truths *they indicated* only in detached images and hints, which could be understood by none but such natures. That higher wisdom they had delivered (as St. Paul says, 1 Cor. ii. 6,) only orally among the perfect, and only orally was it forever to be propagated in the narrow circle of the initiated.

The knowledge of this secret tradition, therefore, first gives the true key of the deeper interpretation of the Scriptures. Irenæus says, on the contrary,* " For the apostles, who were sent forth to find the wandering, and to give sight to those who saw not, and to heal the sick, did not address them in language suited to their then notions, but according to the revelation of truth. . . . . . For what physician who wishes to heal the sick, would act according to the desires of the sick man, and not according to that which is proper to cure him? . . . . †The apostles, who are the disciples of the truth, are far from all lies; for a lie has nothing in common with the truth, any more than darkness with light. . . . . Our Lord, who is the truth, lied not."

Or else they said, " From the account of the apostles itself, we cannot learn the pure doctrine of Christ, for the apostles were fettered by psychical, and Jewish opinions; and the Pneumaticus (i. e. the spiritual man,) must separate the psychical from the pneumatical in their writings." Or they even ventured to separate, in *the very discourses of Christ himself*, what the psychical Christ spoke in him by the inspiration of the Demiurgos,—what the Divine wisdom, still hovering between the dominion of the Demiurgos and the Pleroma, and not yet arrived at its full perfection,‡—and what the highest νους, uttered from out the Pleroma.§

If these Gnostics had been thinkers of the same sort with the people of the western world, they would have separated in their composite (construirten) Christ what he said under the influence of immediate inspiration, out of an intuition elevating itself above all that belongs to

---

* As, for example, where they found the word "world" used with blame in the New Testament, these passages served them for a proof, that this whole creation is something imperfect, and could not come from the supreme and perfect God; for it never entered into their heads, that the word "world" might be used in the New Testament in a different sense.

* Contra Hæres. iii. 5.
† [This passage, in the original, precedes the rest of the quotation.—H. J. R.]
‡ " Sophia," or "Achamoth." See below.
§ See Irenæus, lib. iii. c. 2.

time; and what he said speaking from a reflection disturbed by ideas belonging to time; but they would only have been expressing the same notions in different language.

These Gnostics were, in part, not thoroughly resolved to break from the rest of the Church, and to found separate communities. They were, indeed, persuaded that the ψυχικοι, as they were conditioned, could receive Christianity in no other than the churchly form; that they could arrive at no higher degree than that of faith upon authority, that their faculty for the higher spiritual intuition was utterly gone, and therefore, they wished not to disturb these men,* whose views were more of the common ecclesiastical kind, in their tranquil faith,—but they wished, after grafting themselves upon the common Church assemblies, to found, in connection with them, a kind of theosophic schools, and of Christian mysteries, into which all those in whom they believed they could observe that higher faculty, not conceded to all, might be received. They made complaints also that men would not suffer them to remain in the communion of the Church, and called them heretics, whereas they entirely agreed with the doctrine of the Church.†

But what would have become of the Church, if this intention of theirs,‡ of extending themselves in the Church by this distinction of two different stages of religion, had succeeded? How deeply would it have injured the simplicity, the confidence, and the clearness, of the Christian faith, the practical spirit of Christianity, the bond of Christian communion that unites all hearts, and reason also which attains the development due to its nature in the light of Christianity, while it is conscious to itself of its natural limits,—limits which a presumptuous intellectual intuition pretended to pass over.§ But the spirit of Christianity, as we shall see when we come to consider the theological development of spiritual knowledge in the Church, awakened two different dispositions, which, uniting in this warfare, opposed Gnosticism.

That which procured an entrance for Gnosticism, was a pride (founded, we confess, on one side in human nature,) which has always especially contributed to further those dispositions which are not willing to content themselves with that which is simple, but are always anxious to have something of their own, which sets them above others, a pride which finds it very hard to let itself down so far, as *simply to receive and accept*, together with the rest of mankind. Irenæus and Plotinus, two men of such thoroughly different characters, both point out to us how the pride of human nature is flattered by the phantasies of the Gnostics. The former says,* "He who has given himself up to them becomes instantly puffed up; he believes himself to be neither in heaven nor on earth, but to have entered into the Pleroma, and carries himself most proudly." And Plotinus says, "Irrational men are at once caught by such speeches as these: 'Thou shalt become better, not only than *all men* but than *all Gods* also," for great is the pride of men. The man who was before humble and discreet, now hears with pleasure—'Thou art a son of God,† but the rest, whom thou lookest up to with admiration, are no sons of God; thou art also higher than heaven, without doing any thing for that purpose.'"

On the other hand, as it usually happens that every prevailing error of any age has its opposite in another error, by which it has been called forth, and the combating of which lends it a plausible appearance; and as, for the most part, it happens that whenever any false tendency spreads itself abroad among one part of mankind, it has

---

* Τους κοινους ἐκκλησιαστικους.

† Queruntur de nobis, quod cum similia nobiscum sentiant, sine causa abstineamus nos a communicatione eorum, et cum eadem dicant et eandem habeant doctrinam, vocemus illos hereticos. Iren. lib. iii. c. 15.

‡ In which they themselves were conscious of no impropriety, because this sort of proceeding was founded on the entire view which they entertained of religion.

§ The doctrine of Plotinus,—το δε ὑπερ νουν, ηδη ἐστιν ἐξω του νου το πνευν,—is quite just, in as far as it opposes the Gnostics, who spoke of a higher *organ* than reason for the *knowledge* of the Divine nature, that is to say, the πνευματικον, a faculty which resided only in certain natures. But *this*

---

proposition is false when it is used, as in the notions of Plotinus it might be, to oppose Christianity in general, which gave us an objective *source of knowledge* of Divine things, elevated above human reason, in a revelation of God, from which reason, as an organ (or instrument) is to draw (its knowledge) under the illumination of a higher Spirit.

* Lib. iii. c. 15. [This passage is paraphrased, but not translated, by Neander; in fact, the first part of it almost baffles translation. We must remember that part of Irenæus has descended to us only in a Latin translation.—H. J. R.]

† A πνευματικος, who alone could descend immediately from the Supreme God.

for its foundation some truth, which is misunderstood, and partially conceived, and some want of human nature, which, *in itself*, and of itself, is real, but has been led astray,—so it happened here also. It was opposition against a gross and sensuous conception of Divine things, among the Jews and Christians, which called forth Gnosticism; and it furthered its propagation the more, because Christianity had awakened also new spiritual wants, which could find no satisfaction in a mere faith founded on authority, which despised every thing ideal, cast away from it all higher contemplation and intuition, and abruptly rejected all speculation. If the Gnostics did imagine faith so mean a thing, and if they did not attain to a knowledge of what it is in vital Christianity, and in the ideas of St. Paul, they may have been induced to such a course by their opposition to men, who either did not in their lives manifest the true power of faith, by showing that it was an animating principle of life, or at least did not understand how to show, in its full development, the truth, that faith is something more than a mere belief on the strength of authority, and than a mere subjection to outward authority, that it is an *inward living disposition* and an *inward principle of life*, the source of a *new life within*.

Many have been led to Gnosticism by an unsatisfied desire after a deeper Christian knowledge, and after a knowledge of the inward organic connection of the doctrines of Christianity.* The Gnostics made the first attempt to develope the Christian doctrine as a whole, and in its individual parts, according to their interior connection, and to form out of Christianity a continued and connected mode of viewing divine and human things. The desire and endeavour after an inward connection and an inward unity of knowledge, is not to be mistaken among them; although we acknowledge this endeavour of theirs, which in one point of view was right, was sadly led astray, and took a false and destructive turn, because they would not know Christianity from its own peculiar and essential nature, because they mixed heterogeneous elements with Christianity, which is complete and sufficient in itself, because they did not regard the natural limits of human knowledge, and because they were unable to perceive the limits which belong to religion, and those which belong to knowledge. Their tremendous errors stand in history as an instructive warning and example.

After these general reflections, we now proceed to the individual Gnostic sects, and, according to the division which has appeared the most suitable, we shall first speak of those *Gnostic sects which, engrafting themselves on Judaism, supposed a gradual development of the theocracy to take place in mankind, proceeding from one original foundation.*

(β.) *The individual sects.*

(1.) *The Gnostics, whose system was engrafted on Judaism.*

(a.) *Cerinthus.*

As the doctrine of this Gnostic shows us clearly how Gnosis formed itself out of Judaism, he forms the natural transition-point from the Judaizing sects to the Gnostics. In the accounts which remain to us of his opinions, we find contradictions and difficulties which can only be explained by taking a just view of the manner in which Gnosticism was deduced from Judaism. Cerinthus, according to an old tradition which we have no valid reason to doubt, lived at Ephesus at the same time with St. John. He lived in those regions, where corruptions of Christianity had already in early times threatened Christianity; which were, however, different corruptions from those* with which Christianity had to contend in its very birth, and which proceeded from a Pharisaical Judaism, while these rather arose from a mixture of Jewish theosophy with Christianity.

The most striking contradiction between the accounts of the doctrines of Cerinthus appears to lie in this; that Irenæus makes him out a complete *Gnostic*, while the Presbyter Caius of Rome, who wrote *at the end of the second century*, and Dionysius, bishop of Alexandria, after the middle of the third century,

---

* As Ambrosius, of whom and to whom the great Origen (who converted him from the errors of Gnosticism,) said: " From want of persons who preach the better truths, while you could not, out of your love to Jesus, bear an unreasonable and ignorant faith (αὐτος γοῦν ἀπορια των πρεσβευοντων τα κρειττονα, μη φερων την ἀλογον και ἰδιωτικην πιστιν, δια την προς τον Ἰησουν ἀγαπην,) you gave yourself up formerly to doctrines which afterwards, using the understanding bestowed upon you rightly, you knew to be erroneous, and cast away."—Origen. T. v. Joh. towards the end.

* See Acts xx. 29. Comp. 1, and 2, Epistles to Timothy, and the Epistle to the Colossians.

ascribe to him a gross sensual Chiliasm, which bears upon it the garb of the carnal notions of Judaism. We might, however, bring these two accounts nearer to each other, if we were at liberty to subtract a little from each. It may easily have happened to Irenæus, that, where he found a few traits resembling Gnosticism, he made out of them a whole Gnostic system. To the Presbyter Caius, as a zealous opponent of Chiliasm, every thing was welcome which could serve to place Chiliasm in an unfavourable point of view; and certainly he was not inclined to explain the expressions of a system which he detested, in the mildest manner; and was the less likely to do so, because these expressions might easily be misunderstood by a person not accustomed to the Jewish-Oriental mode of speaking allegorically. And besides, it was natural that Irenæus, in whose persuasion a belief in Chiliasm was necessary to a perfect orthodoxy, should not quote such a view among the peculiar opinions of a Gnostic, whom he hated. We shall now endeavour, from the fragments which we can gather from the above cited reports, compared with the account of Epiphanius, to put together a whole.

According to Irenæus,* Cerinthus taught that the world was created by a power† quite subordinate to the highest God, which did not even so much as know this God who was elevated above every thing. According to Epiphanius,‡ he held that the world was created by angels. The Jewish element, which is the foundation of all this, is here easily recognised; he thought that the God,§ who was elevated above all contact with material things, and who came not forth from the hidden recesses of his incomprehensible nature, had created this world by means of ministering angels. He supposed, in accordance with the Jewish theories, different ranks and degrees in the higher world of spirits, and ascribed to the angels or powers, through which God had created earthly things, a lower stage in this gradation; just as he chose to place earthly things, without denying their divine origin, yet far below heavenly things.

Perhaps he did not teach, that those angels did not know the Supreme God; but only that they had a very imperfect knowledge of God, and of the highest heavens, and not the perfect knowledge which was first to be communicated by the revelation of the Divine Logos. At the head of these angels, Cerinthus (according to Irenæus) placed a power, which was taken from among them, and presided over them. He maintained also, according to the apparently common representation of the Jews, that the Mosaic law had been revealed by means of this angel.* While he said this, he still desired strictly to bring forward and elevate the dignity of the Mosaic law, as compared with all human systems, and all other national religions: but then when compared with the revelation of the Messiah, he desired to sink this same law as low as the angels are below the highest Logos. In his doctrine as to the person of the Messiah, he was in some respects entirely inclined to cling to the usual Jewish notion. (See above.) The man Jesus was (in this view) a son of Joseph and Mary, begotten in the natural way, provided with no sort of miraculous gifts, who had distinguished himself from the rest of the Jews only by a superior degree of obedience to the law† and wisdom. By these qualities he made himself worthy of being chosen‡ from among all mankind as the Messiah. He himself knew nothing of this destination appointed for him; this was first revealed to him in his baptism by John, at the time destined to his consecration for the office of Messiah, and at the same time he was furnished with the powers necessary to him for the fulfilment of this destination. That Supreme Logos or Spirit of God§ appeared and descended from the heavens which opened above Jesus, in the radiant form of a dove, and it sunk down into the heart of Jesus. The narrative given in an Ebionite recension of the Εὐαγγέλιον καθ' Ἑβραίους, where it is said,‖ "While the people were being

---

* The passage which is most to be used for this purpose, being that in which Irenæus mixes up Cerinthus less than elsewhere, with other Gnostics, is lib. i. 26.

† Virtus, *δυναμις*, גְּבוּרָה, a *terminus technicus* of Jewish theology.

‡ Hæres. 8, or 28.

§ The of Philo.

* According to Epiphanius, by *one* of those, perhaps the presiding one, to whom, as the representative of the Supreme God on this stage of being, the guidance of the people consecrated to God, was especially confided.

† By *δικαιοσυνη* in its usual Jewish sense.

‡ τῃ ἐκλογῃ Χριστος.

§ It is quite allowable to suppose that Cerinthus, like many Jewish theologians, considered the πνευμα ἁγιον and the λογος as identical.

‖ [This extract is taken from Epiphanius Hæres. xxx. Ebion. § 19, and is printed in Grabe Spicilegium Patrum Sæculi I. p. 27.—H. J. R.]

baptized, Jesus came and suffered himself to be baptized by John," (probably without being conscious that he was different from the rest of those baptized by John, or that any thing peculiar would take place in regard to him,) "and when he came forth from the water, the heavens were opened, and he saw the Holy Spirit of God, in the form of a dove, descending and entering into him."* (The luminous form descended visibly upon his head, and entered into him. It now disappeared; a proof that the Holy Spirit or Logos had wholly united itself with his person.) "And there was a voice from heaven which said, 'Thou art my beloved Son, in thee I am well pleased;" and again, "this day have I begotten thee;"† that is to say, I have brought thee to the dignity of a Son, that is of the Messiah, by means of the connection with this Spirit of God; "and immediately there shone around a great light."‡ By means of a connection with this Supreme Spirit, Jesus now first attained to a rank, a power, and a wisdom, elevated above this whole world, and the angels that preside over it. He now first attained to the perfect knowledge of the Supreme God, and of heavenly things. Now the angels themselves might learn from his revelations; and now he performs miracles by the Divine power of this Spirit which is united to him. This is that which used him as its instrument in every thing; this is the πνευμα του Χριστου, the Messiah himself, in the highest sense of the word.§ The idea of a Messiah, who should redeem by means of his sufferings, did not suit the notions of a Cerinthus, who had no feeling for the Divine nature in the form of a servant, and who was attached to the imposing grandeur of a magical and theosophic system.‖ In union with the mighty Spirit of God, Jesus could not have suffered: by this union he must necessarily have triumphed over all his enemies. The very fact of suffering is of itself a proof that the Spirit of God which was united with him, had been beforehand separated from him, and had gone up again to the Father. To the suffering of the man, now left to himself, Cerinthus apparently ascribed no part of the redemption.*

According to Epiphanius, this theosophist, who arranged every thing anew so as to suit his own notions, denied the resurrection of Jesus Christ. In pursuance of this idea he may have supposed that the Divine Logos would unite itself again to the man Jesus, only when it was about to appoint him the victorious king of the Messiah's kingdom, and to raise up all the faithful with him to take their share in that kingdom. The account of Epiphanius, however, is not entirely to be relied on; because as he proceeded on the supposition that St. Paul was contending in every place against the followers of Cerinthus, he may have attributed to Cerinthus a doctrine which he did not hold, in consequence of the passage in 1 Cor. xv.

Cerinthus further agreed with the Ebionites in holding the perpetual obligation of the Mosaic law, in a certain sense, upon Christians. He might well suppose that the highest meaning of Judaism, which was not clearly known even to the lawgiving angel himself, the Ιουδαισμος πνευματικος, the heavenly Judaism, which was shadowed forth by the earthly, had been first revealed by the revelation of the Logos, and that yet that earthly and shadowy form was still to last till the triumphant approach of the kingdom of the Messiah, or to the beginning of a new and heavenly order of things. But as Epiphanius says of him, that he *partly*† held fast to Judaism, and it is not likely that the latter should have invented any thing of this sort; we may conclude from it, that Cerinthus did not look on every thing in Judaism as equally divine; and that in some degree, like the author of the Clementine, and many other mystic sects of the Jews, he made a distinction between an original Judaism, and the latter corruptions of it; and that he insisted on the continued obligation only of that part of the ceremonial law which he considered as among the genuine parts of it. As a sort of middle and transition point from the earthly system of the world to the new, eternal, heavenly

---

* Ειδε το πνευμα του Θεου το αγιον, εν ειδει περιστερας καταβαινσης και εισιρχομενης εις αυτον.

† εγω σημερον γεγεννηκα σε.

‡ [I have distinguished the parts which occur in the Greek text by inverted commas; the rest is the interpretation put upon it by Neander, which is hardly distinguished enough in the German. It contains his view of the interpretation the Gnostics put upon this passage.—H. J. R.]

§ The ανω Χριστος, the Χριστος επουρανιος, of whom Jesus was only the human instrument, the κατω Χριστος.

‖ [*Literally*, who loved magic-theosophic grandeur.—H. J. R.]

---

* See next §, under the head Basilides.
† Προσιχων τω Ιουδαισμω απο μερους.

system, Cerinthus, with many Jewish theologists, supposed a thousand-year season of happiness, under the government of the Messiah rendered triumphant through the power of the Logos, which was to take place in Jerusalem as the centre point of the ennobled earth. A too literal interpretation of the passage in Ps. xc. 4, led people to suppose, that as a thousand years in the sight of God are but as one day, the world would last in its present state six thousand years; and then at the conclusion of the earthly course, a Sabbath (a time of undisturbed blessing) of a thousand years would take place on earth for the pious, now delivered from all struggles. We are certainly inclined to ask, whether he made to himself so gross and carnal a representation of the blessings of this thousand-years' Sabbath, as Caius and Dionysius accuse him of, which does not appear to harmonize well with the general character of his opinions. He spoke of a marriage feast, which was at that time an image commonly used to represent the happy union of the Messiah with his own people;* but those who explained his words with a feeling of bitterness against him, might misinterpret such images. Dionysius says, that when he spoke of fasts and sacrifices, he was only endeavouring to gloss over his gross and carnal representations. But what was there to justify him in this declaration?†

(b.) *Basilides.*

We pass now from Cerinthus to Basilides, who wrote in the first half of the second century. It is most probable that Alexandria was the sphere of his activity; the stamp of an Alexandrian Jewish education cannot be mistaken in him and in his son Isidore, whose name points out his Egyptian birth. But the account of Epiphanius, that Syria, the general birthplace of Gnostic systems, was also the native land of Basilides, is not in itself improbable, although it is on the other hand not a sufficient proof. The doctrines of emanation and dualism were the foundation of his system; at the fountain head of these emanations he placed the hidden God, elevated above all representations and images.* The middle point between this incomprehensible origin and all following developments of life, is the unfolding of that Being in his several powers which individualize themselves, and become in fact, so many names of the unnameable Being. Man can only think on God after the analogy of *his own spirit*; and an objective truth forms the foundation of that analogy, inasmuch as the spirit of man is the image of God. He can form to himself no representation of the most perfect Being, without breaking the idea of the most perfect, which resides within his spirit, into the several parts of which it consists; and he feels himself compelled to distinguish the several attributes of this most perfect Being, in order to make this idea comprehensible to himself: but a deep thinker is well convinced, that this is merely a necessary expedient to assist human imperfection, and knows how to distinguish that which is objective, from that which is subjective. And yet the Gnostic was not capable of entering into this distinction: what is necessary to *human conceptions*, he attributed to the objective development of existence; as thus:—in order to bring forth life out of himself, the Being which contains all perfection within himself, must first unfold himself into the several qualities which the idea of absolute perfection contains; and then, instead of the abstract conception of attributes, that suits not with Oriental habits of thought, there come *living, personified* [hypostasirte] *powers, which continue working in independent activity;* as, for instance, first, the *intellectual* powers, the Spirit, (νους,) Reason, (λογος,) Thought, (φρονησις,) Wisdom, (σοφια,) and then Power, (δυναμις,) by which God puts the resolves of his wisdom into execution; and, lastly, the *moral attributes*, without which God's almighty power never shows itself active; namely, *holiness or moral perfection*, (δικαιοσυνη,)† a word which must be understood according to the Hellenistic and Hebrew phraseology, and not in the narrow sense of the German word, gerechtigkeit, unless people will under-

---

* The Gnostics also pictured the happiness of the πνευματικοι received into the Pleroma, under the image of a marriage festival, a marriage between the σωτηρ and the σοφια; between the spiritual natures and the angels. (See below.) So in Heracleon ap. Origen. t. x. Joh. § 14, we find αναπαυσις η εν γαμω.

† Euseb. Hist. Eccles. iii. 28.

* Ὁ ἀκατονομαστος, ἀρρητος.

† It is remarkable that Basilides used the word δικαιοσυνη according to its Hebrew and Hellenistic sense, to denote moral perfection, while other Gnostics, especially those of the second class, used it only to denote a more imperfect moral condition; an idea *of righteousness* (gerechtigkeitsbegriff) in a more confined sense.

ABRAXAS.—DUALISM.—PROCESS OF PURIFICATION.

stand this German word in its original etymological sense,) and then, after moral perfection, follows inward tranquillity, *peace* (εἰρήνη,) which, as Basilides justly acknowledged, can only be there where holiness is; and this tranquillity is the characteristic of the Divine life: and this forms the close of this inward Divine development of life.* The number seven was a holy number to Basilides, as well as to many theosophists of these times; and thus, in his system, these seven δυναμεις, together with the first original, which had unfolded himself into them, formed the πρώτη ὀγδοας, and the root of all existence. From thence the spiritual life went on developing itself, constantly farther and farther into manifold degrees of existence, every lower one being always the impression, the resembling image (ἀν-τίτυπος) of the higher. If we may draw conclusions as to the doctrines of the original school from what we find of the later Basilidians in Irenæus, and from the gems and amulets of the Basilidians, as Basilides, in accordance with the seven days of the week, always supposed seven similar beings in every stage of the spiritual world,—so also, in consideration of the days of the year, he supposed there were three hundred and sixty-five such regions, or stages, in the spiritual world. This is expressed in the mystical word ἀβραξας (which was a symbol of his sect) when it is interpreted by the usual method of reckoning Greek letters numerically.†

Within this *emanation-world* every thing was that which it ought to be in its own proper position: but out of an union between the Divine and the undivine there arose a disharmony, which was to be brought again into harmony.

There is, alas! in this place, an hiatus in our accounts of the Basilidian system. It is a matter of question whether Basilides followed the mode of conception in use with those who supposed the intermixture to take place by the falling down of some of the Divine seed of life into the chaos bordering upon it; or of those, who imagined an empire of evil, which was active by its own energy, and supposed the intermixture to have taken place by an aggressive assault of this empire upon the Empire of Light. In a fragment* which is still extant, Basilides quotes the opinion of the Persians on the two opposite empires of Ormuzd and Ahriman; but as the passage which follows has not been preserved to us, we cannot with certainty conclude whether he quoted this doctrine in approbation or disapprobation. If we remember that he belonged to those who wished to complete the propositions of the Grecian, that is, the Platonic philosophy, by means of the profounder wisdom of the East, the first of these suppositions will appear the most probable. Also, when he spoke of a confusion and intermixture of principles,† this might very naturally lead to such a conclusion. The accusation made by Clemens of Alexandria against Basilides, that he deified the devil,‡ leads also to the supposition that Basilides gave occasion to this accusation by his representation of a substantial evil Being.§ And, besides, the Basilidian doctrines have much that is akin to the Parsic and Manichæan.‖

But howsoever this intermixture of Light and Darkness, of the Divine and the undivine, might have arisen, it would nevertheless, according to this system, necessarily be subservient to the glorification of the Divine Being, to the fulfilling of the ideas of the Supreme Wisdom, and of the law of all the development of life; because the empire of evil is of itself naturally nothing worth. The empire of the Divine Being is the real empire, and that which is naturally victorious.

Light, Life, Soul, Good; on one side:—*Darkness, Death, Matter, Evil,* on the other—these in the system of Basilides, were the members which answered to each other, and maintained the opposition which he supposed to exist

---

* Iren. lib. i. c. 24, lib. ii. c. 16. Clem. Strom. lib. iv. 539.

† [α = 1 + β = 2 + ρ = 100 + α = 1 + ξ = 60 + α = 1 + ς = 200.—H. J. R.]
It may be that this name, which designates the whole emanation-world as development of the Supreme Being, had also another meaning; but all attempts at an explanation of it will forever be merely arbitrary ones, for there are no sure grounds in existence from which one could argue about it.

---

* Disputat. Archel. et Mani. opp. Hippolyt. ed. Fabricii. lib. iii. p. 193.

† ταραχης και συγχυσις ἀρχικη. Clem. l. ii. f. 408.

‡ Clemens Strom. lib. iv. p. 507. πως οὐκ ἀθέως, θεαζων τον διαβολον.

§ Διαβολος, Ahriman.

‖ If Basilides, l. c. in the Dissertation of Archelaus, speaks in his own person of a *pauperis natura, sine radice et sine loco rebus superveniens,* must not these enigmatic words be taken to express the doctrine of an empire of evil, without beginning, which, in its poverty, is smitten with desire after the treasures of the kingdom of Light; and penetrating into the light, would wish to seize these, and carry them off for itself.

throughout the whole course of the universe. In general, just as rust fastens itself from without on iron, so *Darkness* and *Death* cleave to the fallen seed of *Light* and *Life*, *Evil* cleaves to *Good*, and the *undivine* to the *Divine*, without, however, effecting the annihilation of the original Being; it must only by degrees purify itself from every thing foreign to it, in order to attain to its original splendour, just as iron must be cleansed from rust in order to obtain again a higher polish.* Such a process of purification the whole course of *this world* affords to the fallen being, as a system which was formed for the perfection of this purification, in order to separate that which is Divine from that which is foreign to its nature, and to conduct it again to what is akin to it, and to a reunion with its original source.

One would be inclined to think that a system in which a *moral retribution* was the prevailing idea, might, perhaps, admit the notion of a passage of the soul into *various human bodies*, according to the measure of its deserts in a former state of existence, so that it might be placed, according to its *deserts*, in a different human body, and in different circumstances, and a different situation, and so that it might have to expiate by penitence the guilt contracted in its former state, although only conscious of it in a mysterious and general manner. But the doctrine of a banishment of the soul into the bodies of animals does not appear to suit so well the prevailing moral notion of the system, as one cannot imagine any penitence taking place where there is no moral consciousness at all. And yet, in all systems of this nature, the moral element is not purely and abstractedly conceived, but is always mixed with physical considerations. We have, therefore, no reason to doubt an account which makes Basilides introduce such a metempsychosis in his own words; as it is a doctrine which, by means of the intermixture of Orientalism, Platonism, and Judaism, was certainly at that time widely diffused even among many Jewish sects.

Two modes, however, of viewing this doctrine may now be thought of; the one, when the notion of *moral retribution* is constantly kept steadfastly in view, and the soul is supposed to be banished into the bodies of animals, only as a mode of *punishment*: the other, when it is conceived under the more *physical notion* of a gradual development of the spiritual seed of life, which constantly becomes more freed from matter, which keeps it prisoner, and constantly attains more and more to consciousness, and to the development of its original nature. Basilides appears in one passage to favour this latter notion, and appears to be declaring how the soul struggles itself into *consciousness*, in the *body of an animal out of an unconscious state*. The words in Rom. vii. 9, about a life without the law, he understands as relating to such a life in the body of an animal, whether that of a quadruped, or that of a bird; where no law for the soul could exist.* The view, that the soul might be still more imprisoned and hemmed in by matter, in yet lower degrees of existence, would easily engraft itself on this interpretation; and also that in plants, and in stones, there is a soul, only more imprisoned, which, by degrees, freeing itself more and more, developes itself from stone to plant, from plant to animal, and from animal to man. This mode of representation suits also with his whole system; because he considers matter not as any thing that lives, but only as that dead stuff, which has joined itself with that which is living. And beside, there is with him no such thing as a *dead nature*; but in all nature there is a life which is held prisoner by matter, and striving to set itself free. And thus he might well say, that all existence is connected together one part with the other; and that, according to the will of God, man must love all that exists, in virtue of this mutual connection.†

Two different views were here also united together: the one was, a gradual development from the lowest to the highest, from which that *original intermixture* and *that original fall* had proceeded; and the other, a voluntarily-incurred degradation into a lower state of being. And yet, one is inclined to ask, whether Basilides really supposed that the being of light (lichtnatur) or soul, which had once attained to humanity, in the process of its

---

* Basilides speaks thus in general terms about the *sufferings* of all fallen Beings of Light; "Trouble and anxiety naturally fall on things, as rust on iron." Ὁ πονος και ὁ φοβος ἐπισυμβαινει τοις πραγμασιν ὡς ὁ ἰος τῳ σιδηρῳ Clemens Alex. Strom. lib. iv. p. 509. *a*.

* See Origen Commentar. in Ep. ad Rom. vol. iv. Opp. p. 549.

† Ἐν μερει ἐκ του λεγομενου θελημματος του Θεου ὑπειλη φαμεν το ἠγαπηκεναι ἀπαντα, ὁτι λογον ἀποσωζουσι προς το παν ἀπαντα. Strom. lib. iv. fol 509

purification and development, could ever sink back into the body of an animal; or whether he did not, on the contrary, confine the process of purification for a nature which had once attained to this point, entirely within the limits of human nature.

To the whole earthly system, or to this whole purifying process of nature and history, Basilides assigned such a Creator (of whose place in the Gnostic systems we have already spoken in the introductory remarks,) as he called by the name of the Ruler, or the angel that has the government of this world, (ὁ ἄρχων,) and yet, according to the doctrine of Basilides, this Archon does not act independently and by his own power in the conducting of the universe; all at last proceeds from the providence of the Supreme God, which presides over every thing.

In the first place, all beings develope themselves according to the law implanted in their peculiar individual natures; which law, together with their nature, proceeds from the Supreme God. The Archon only gives the first impulse to this natural course of development, and then he himself becomes guided in his whole conduct by the ideas of the Supreme God, who animates every thing, without being able to comprehend them.* We cannot, therefore, in any way accuse Basilides of an unchristian contempt of the world, a denial of a revelation of God in the universe, or an unchristian dualism, which does not recognise the God of grace as the God of creation, and which tears asunder the harmonious connection between revelation and nature; such a violent dualism can by no means be laid to his charge. It was rather that he made it a matter of great consequence to set forth the law of unity which bound every thing together, from the highest to the lowest; " the world is only one, and is the temple of God." (See below.) It was a great object to him to justify Providence against every reproach. His conclusion always was, " I will rather say any thing whatever, than cast the slightest imputation on Providence."*

With regard to the relation of Judaism to the revelation of the loftiest truth and to Christianity, it is in the highest degree probable that Basilides thought in a manner analogous to the Alexandrian Jewish notions on this point, and to his own notions as to the relation between the earthly world and the loftiest system of the universe. He supposed that the Archon, in the conduct of the Jewish people, as well as in the conduct of the universe, had served the Supreme God as an instrument, which was not itself conscious of the ideas which were implanted in it, and that the Archon had been taken by the great mass of the Jewish people for the Supreme God himself, whom he was to represent. It was only those higher natures, which were to be found dispersed among the Jewish people; it was only the " people of God," in its true sense; the πνευματικὸς Ἰσραηλ, that had been able to raise themselves above the Archon himself, to a recognition of the Supreme God represented by him, and thus, above the sensuous covering of Judaism to the contemplation of those ideas, which were contained under this covering, but not understood by the Archon himself. An example of his allegorical notions is found in the following saying, " The one temple of Jerusalem is the type of the one world, which is the temple of God."†

But he supposed also the existence of written documents, in which the higher wisdom was brought forward, perhaps more unreservedly than in the writings of the Canon of the Old Testament. In accordance with an idea then widely spread, he traced the tradition of such a philosophical secret doctrine up to the Patriarchs in particular; and it would appear to him hardly any thing else than natural, that the great mass of the sensuous-minded Jews should not receive those writings, of which they could understand

---

* Clem. Strom. lib. iv. p. 509. Ἡ πρόνοια, ει και ἀπο του ἄρχοντος κινεισθαι δέχεται, ἀλλ᾽ ἡ κατεσπάρη ταις οὐσίαις συν και τῃ των ὅλων γενέσει πρὸς του των ὅλων Θεοῦ. Thus, also, in Plotinus (Ennead. iii. lib. ii.,) on the subject of πρόνοια as a natural development in virtue of an indwelling eternal law of reason, we find the following remark: των πρόνοιαν τῳ παντὶ εἶναι, τὸ κατὰ νοῦν αὐτὸ εἶναι. There is, however, this difference, that in Basilides there is a more Christian consideration brought forward; because he supposes, in co-operation with the law of nature, a personal God, who acts independently, and guides the development of that law of nature; and, by means of the act of redemption, brings to perfection higher results, than could proceed from the mere development of the law of nature.

* Clem. Strom. lib. iv. p. 506. c. Παντ᾽ ἐρῶ γὰρ μᾶλλον, ἢ κακὸν τὸ πρόνοιαν ἐρω.
† Clem. Strom. lib. v. p. 583. D. Ἕνα νέων ἱδρυσαμένος του Θεοῦ (ὁ Μωσῆς) μονογενῆ τε κόσμον κ τ η ͅ θ αι. Similarly also, Philo says, περὶ μονογενές, lib. ii., τὸ μὲν ἀνώτατω καὶ πρὸς ἀλήθειαν ἱερὸν Θεοῦ νομίζειν τον σύμπαντα χρη κόσμον εἶναι, τὸ δὲ χειρικμητον. This idea is still farther carried into particulars both by Philo and Josephus.

nothing, as canonical. According to the Alexandrian fashion, he deduced all the traces of truth found in the best Greek philosophers,* which he eagerly hunted after, from that original tradition. "Let no one believe," says Isidorus, the son of Basilides, "that that which we call a peculiar possession of the elect, was earlier said by some philosophers; for it is not their discovery, but they have taken it out of the Prophets, and attributed it to their pretended sages (or to their false wisdom.")† It certainly deserves to be remarked (as Gieseler has remarked,) that Basilides supposed even Ham to have been among those who handed down this higher wisdom, and perhaps, he deduced peculiarly from him the φιλοσοφια Βαρβαρος,‡ which he probably, as a recogniser of the higher wisdom, set above the Greeks.§

The fundamental Christian doctrine of a redeeming grace had its essential place in the system of Basilides, as the Supreme God was to manifest himself to human nature, and communicate to it a life akin to his own, in order to raise it above the limits of the mundane system, or the world of the archon, to communion with himself, and to the higher world of spirits. It is clear that *this* operation of the Supreme God, according to the system of Basilides, could only relate to those spiritual natures which were destined by their very constitution for a higher world, but which found themselves prisoners in a lower one. These might, through the progressive development of the metempsychosis raise themselves from one stage to another in the kingdom of the Archon; but they could not, in compliance with the desire implanted in them, attain beyond this kingdom and the Archon himself, to communion with the highest system of the world, and to clear knowledge, as well as to the free exercise of their higher nature, unless the Supreme God himself brought his Divine life near to their kindred seed of life, and thereby first set this into activity. And while spiritual natures, by the act of redemption, are raised to the highest position, the influence of redemption at the same time extends itself also to the subordinate stages of being; harmony becomes universally re-established, and every class of being attains the condition which is conformable to its nature. But although Basilides on the one side brought forward an element in the doctrine of redemption, which was entirely foreign to the fleshly Judaism that clung to earth,—he was on the other side, like Cerinthus, altogether *Ebionitish*, inasmuch as he supposed a sudden entrance of the Divine nature into the life of Jesus, and did not recognise any God-man, in whom the Divine and the human natures had been inseparably united from the first. He supposed, as his fundamental position, a redeeming *God*, but no redeeming *God-man*.

The man Jesus was not to him the Redeemer, he was distinguished from other men only in degree; and Basilides does not appear ever to have ascribed *absolute* unsinfulness to him. He was, in the notions of Basilides, only the instrument which the redeeming God chose, in order to reveal himself in human nature, and to seize on that nature so as to work upon it. With him the Redeemer, in the peculiar and highest sense of the word, was the highest Æon,* who was sent down from the Supreme God for the fulfilment of the work of redemption; this Being united himself with the man Jesus at his baptism in the Jordan. From this point the whole work of redemption set forth: from that time the man Jesus spoke things which were far beyond the reach of this lower creation.

The Archon himself, as well as John the Baptist (who was, in the name of the Archon, to consecrate Jesus to the office of Messiah, in the subordinate sense in which the Archon wished, and had promised a Messiah,) was surprised, and seized with astonishment, when he saw the Νους descend, and when he heard at the same time the voice that sounded from heaven, and perceived the accompanying appearances,† and heard this Jesus, whom he had supposed a man of his own kingdom, announce such extraordinary things. He now himself, for the first time, recog-

---

* As with Plato and Aristotle.
† Clem. Strom. vi. 641. Και μη τις οιεσθαι, ο φαμεν ιδιον ειναι των εκλεκτων, τουτο προειρημενον υπερχειν υπο τινων φιλοσοφων, ου γαρ εστιν αυτων ευρημα, των δε προφητων σφετερισαμενοι, προσεθηκαν τω μη υπαρχοντι κατ' αυτους σοφω. It appears to me now, that this passage requires no emendation, if we may take the word σοφω either as masculine or neuter. The expression that follows, οι προσποιουμενοι φιλοσοφων, confirms this explanation of it.
‡ The traces of the higher wisdom, to be found among the Persians and Hindoos.
§ Ἑλληνες de παιδες.

* Or νους, which is called διακονος, as serving to the salvation of mankind.
† Which Basilides apparently learned from an apocryphal Gospel.

nises the Supreme God, and the highest system of the world, to both of which he had involuntarily served, till now, as an unconscious instrument, which believed that it acted independently. He now submits himself willingly to a higher Power, imploring it with astonishment; and from this moment he works freely and consciously, as the instrument of that higher Power. He now recognises the truth, that even *in the kingdom* in which he had hitherto believed himself to be supreme, there are beings imprisoned, which are elevated above himself and his world, and which the Νους will free from these bounds, as well as the man Jesus, and raise them to the higher system of the world; he recognises the essential distinction between the natures that belong to him of right and are akin to him,* and those which, by their kind, belong to a higher kingdom, and are capable of communion with the Νους; he separates each from the other, and lets the latter go free out of his kingdom, without putting any impediment in the way of their elevation. We shall now quote the very words of this man, who conceived every thing under his own peculiar imagery: " When the ruler of the world heard the words of the Redeeming Spirit,† he became astonished at that which he heard and saw, as he heard unexpectedly the glorious message; and his astonishment was called fear." The words, " The fear of God is the beginning of wisdom," are thus to be understood; they mean that the fear of *this* God is the beginning of wisdom, which separates the different kinds of beings from one another, allows them to come to perfection, and leads them all to the stage of existence for which they are destined; for he that rules over all does not separate merely those which belong to the world, but even the elect, and suffers them to depart freely from his dominion.‡

We see here how Basilides conceived and painted after his own eccentric manner, that which Christianity effects, as a divinely animating, freeing and enlightening principle, as the matter which sets human nature in fermentation. These effects, partly judging by the deep penetration of his own mind, and applying its inward operations to outward things, he traced to some fundamental law of Christianity, and partly from observation of the phenomena of his own time. That which Christianity effected generally, in reference to the history of human nature, Basilides represented as an impression made on the Archon which represented that nature.

Like Cerinthus, he also attributed the whole work of redemption to the redeeming heavenly Genius, and most probably coincided with him in the supposition that this Genius had left the man, whom he had hitherto made use of as his instrument, to himself at the time of his suffering. According to his system, the suffering of Christ could have nothing to do with the work of redemption; for, according to his narrow views of justice, it was not consonant to the Divine justice that one, who deserved it not, should suffer for others; and it was required, that all evil should be atoned for by suffering. He considered not merely suffering in general, but also every suffering *in particular*, as a punishment for sin. He

---

* The κοσμος,—the κτισις,—the κοσμικοι,—the κλητοι.

† Also in the Ευαγγελιον καθ' Εβραιους, which Jerome had received from the Nazarenes, the words which sounded from heaven, are ascribed to the "fons omnis Spiritus Sancti, qui requievit super Christum," who descended from heaven.

‡ Clemens, Stromat. lib. ii. p. 375, των Άρχοντα επακυσαντα την φασιν του διακονουμενου πνευματος, εκπλαγηναι τω τε ακουσματι και τω θεαματι και την εκπληξιν αυτου φοβον κληθηναι αρχην γενομεν σοφιας φυλοκριτικης τε και διακριτικης και τελεωτικης και αποκαταστατικης, ου γαρ μονον τον κοσμον, αλλα και την εκλογην διακρινας, ο επι πασι προπεμπει. We must here add a few remarks. The explanation of the

words of Ps. cxi. 10, or of Eccles. i. 16, according to the Basilidian system, gives a remarkable example of the caprice of a theosophical exegesis, which, without regard to the context in which the words stand, lets them, according to this system, mean any thing which they can possibly mean in any context whatever. If the announcement of the heavenly διακονος is called an ευαγγελιον for the αρχον, then it is clear (they conclude,) that he did not merely submit himself by compulsion to the higher powers, but that his first astonishment passed into a mingled feeling of delight and reverence. The prospect, as soon as the elect natures should have attained the glory destined for them, of becoming freed from the tiresome regimen of this world, and of entering into rest with his own people, (to which expectation of the Demiurgos the Gnostics referred, Rom. viii. 20, 21, according to Origen, t. i. in Joh. p. 24,) must assuredly have been a joyful one for him. Comp. Didascal. anatol. opp. Clem. p. 796 D., where the fact that the Demiurgos established the Sabbath, is adduced as a proof how disagreeable labour is to him. Perhaps it may occur to some persons, that we ought to read τω επι πασι instead of ο επι πασι, so that it would mean that the Archon freely leads the elect natures out of his kingdom to the God who is above all, to whom it is their last destination to elevate themselves.

held the theory against which Christ spoke in John ix. 3. Luke xiii. 2. Every one suffers for his actual sins, or for the evil present in his nature,—evil which he brought with him out of a former state of existence, and which, nevertheless, had not yet come into a state of activity.* And thus, by reference to evil of this kind, he justified Providence in the sufferings inflicted on children. If any one made an objection to him from the sufferings of *acknowledged* good men, he had a fair right to answer by an appeal to the general fact of the presence of sinfulness in human nature, and to say,—"Be the man you show me what he may, he is still a man, and God only is holy; who will find harmony among those, where there is no harmony?"† Job xiv. 4.

But then the case was different, where this proposition was applied to the Redeemer, who, as sure as he is the Redeemer, must be free from sin. Clemens of Alexandria expressly blames Basilides because he went so far in the extension of this proposition. But in *those words* of his which Clemens quotes, this is not necessarily implied; he says only,— "But if you, leaving this whole inquiry on one side, come to this, that you put me into a difficulty by *particular persons*, if you say, for instance,—'Then *he* has sinned because *he* has suffered.'"—It may be said that Basilides here speaks only of certain persons held in particular reverence, and in great fame for holiness; and that Clemens has allowed himself to draw an inference. But, *in the first place*, the reproach which Basilides here suffers to be made against his proposition, would lose its proper force and signification, if it were not so understood; and *in the second*, the extension of this proposition thus far, altogether coheres also with his theory of the relation of suffering to sin, and with his theory of the Divine justice, and of the process of purification, to which every nature belonging to the kingdom of the Archon is subject. The Jesus which belonged to this kingdom required redemption even himself, and could be made partaker of it only by his connection with that heavenly redeeming Spirit (the διακονος.) In order to become worthy of being redeemed before all others who needed redemption, and being used as an instrument to extend farther the operations of the redeeming Spirit to others, it was sufficient if he, as the most excellent and purest man, and the most advanced in the process of purification, had merely the minimum of sinfulness. We must here observe that the Basilidian system, which at any rate supposed a proportion between the sin and the degree of punishment, was certainly liable to the following objection: "How does so great suffering consist with the smallest degree of sinfulness?" But, apparently he was not at a loss for an answer here, if we may judge from what he says on the subject of martyrdom. He says, "The consciousness of serving as an instrument for the highest and holiest things of human nature, and of *suffering* in this office, (perhaps also, a prospect of the glory into which he should enter by means of his suffering,) sweetened his sufferings to him so much, that it was to him as if *he did not suffer at all*.

According to the same principle, he also consistently acknowledged no justification in the sense indicated by St. Paul, no objective justification before God; no forgiveness of sin as a release from sin and the punishment of sin. According to his doctrine, every sin, whether before or after faith in the Redeemer, or baptism, must be alike atoned for by suffering. That is a necessary law of the system of the world, which nothing can annul. The only exception he makes is in the case of sins proceeding from ignorance, or involuntary sins:* but it is a pity that his explanation of this very indefinite expression has not been preserved to us. But if, on the contrary, under the term justification (δικαιωσις, δικαιοσυνη,) be understood an inward subjective making just, a sanctification through the communication of Divine life, then such a doctrine would hold a very necessary place in the system of Basilides.

Among the religious and moral notions of the Basilidian school, there is much that deserves attention, which we are desirous of bringing forward particularly.

In regard to the idea of *Faith*, the Basilidian school distinguished itself by this:

---

* Sufferings,—the penances and purifications of ἁμαρτια, or ἁμαρτητικον.—Stromat. iv. 506. [Sylburg, p. 217. Potter, p. 600. Klotz, vol. ii. p. 322.]

† [Germ. "Wer will eine Stimme finden bei denen, da keine Stimme ist?" The Hebrew of the passage, however, is different from this, and exactly agrees with our English translation.—H. J. R.]

* Μετας τας ακουσιας και κατ' ἀγνοιαν ἀμαρτϑαι. Strom. iv. 536. [Sylb. p. 229. Potter, p. 633-4. Klotz, vol. ii. p. 362.]

that they expressly opposed the usual Jewish and Jewish-Christian notion of Faith, as another kind of *opus operatum*, an acknowledgment of certain religious truths, which exists as something individual in the soul of man, and operates no farther on the whole inward life, a mere outwardly existing traditional belief, which brings forth no fruits in the life of man—and also that they, with a deeper penetration into the spirit of St. Paul's doctrines, represented Faith as an inward thing, an entire bent of the inward life, an entrance of the Spirit into a higher sphere, and a *real communion with that higher system*. But, on the other hand, he receded from the genuine notion of St. Paul, because, like all Gnostics (except Marcion) he considered religion in its contemplative, more than in its practical, character; and also, in his notion of Faith, made the contemplative element more prominent than the practical. With him Faith is a certain kind of view,* which includes in itself a certain intellectual appropriation of that which is beheld, and a new spiritual life also in it. On the contrary, according to the genuine Christian idea of St. Paul, Faith is a *practical* appropriation of Divine things, by a *devotion* of the will, a practical entrance into a new relation with God, given by a peculiar revelation from him, from which an entirely new direction and employment of the inward life proceeds. From this we acknowledge, as the whole spiritual life is formed anew from this foundation, an entirely new kind of religious view must develope itself. When, therefore, Basilides supposed different degrees in *this* view [anschauung] (in respect of purity, clearness, elevation and depth,) no objection could lie against him on that account, on any genuine Christian grounds, had he only recognised the common foundation of faith in all Christians, and deduced every thing only from the different degrees in which the influence of that faith developed itself on the spiritual life. But he, confounding between faith and sight,† supposed, instead of one and the same life in a Faith, which is the same in all Christians, *different kinds* of Faith, according to the different sorts of natures. That is to say, just as men, according to their nature, belonged to a higher or a lower grade of the spiritual world, so also they were capable of a higher or a lower kind of view. Those higher ideas need no proof, but they prove themselves through themselves, to those higher spiritual natures which are akin to them, and which become involuntarily attracted by the revelation of the higher world, which is their proper home. Therefore, Basilides says, " The faith of the elect finds out doctrines without any demonstration by means of a spiritual comprehension" (an intellectual sight;)* and in this sense he gives this definition of faith; " an assent of the soul to something which does not act upon the senses, because it is not present."† That is to say,—although the elect live in this world as strangers, nevertheless, by the influence of faith, they recognise, as real, those things of the higher world which beam upon them from afar. And hence he supposes the degree of faith to which a person can elevate himself as a stranger in this world, to correspond to *that* grade of the spiritual world to which he belongs.‡

From the principles of Basilides, his *moral doctrines* must have been of a *severe* nature. In his morality the ruling principle must have been *this*, that man should free himself from that foreign admixture, which having attached itself to his original nature, disturbs and controls it, and that he should constantly attain more and more to a free development and exercise of that original nature. According to this system, man is a little world ; just as, according to his spirit, he may be akin to the different natures of the higher spiritual world, so also, in accordance with his lower nature, he bears within himself that which is akin to the different grades and natures of the lower earthly world. He has within himself many admixtures§ of a foreign nature, wherein the different qualities of the world of animals, of vegetables, and of minerals, are reflected:

---

* [Anschauung. See the former notes on this word, and the Preface.—H. J. R.]

† [Anschauung. Between faith and that faculty, by which Basilides supposed a view, an image or visible representation, to be present to the mind of the believer. See Preface.—H. J. R.]

* Clem. Strom. ii. 363, ἡ πιστις της ἐκλογης τα μαθηματα ἀνατιδικτως εὑρισκουσα καταλήψει νοητικη. [Sylb. p. 156. Potter, p. 433-4. Klotz, vol. ii. p. 128.

† Clem. Strom. ii. 371. ψυχης συγκαταθεσις πρὸς τι των μη κινουντων αἰσθησιν, διὰ το μη παρειναι. [Sylb. p. 159. Potter, p. 443. Klotz, vol. ii. p. 139.]

‡ Clem. Strom. ii. 363, πιστις και ἐκλογη οἰκεια καθ' ἑκαστον διαστημα· ἐπακολουθημα της ἐκλογης της ὑπερκοσμιου ἡ κοσμικη πιστις.

§ Appendages of matter, προσαρτηματα.

and thence come the desires, passions, and affections corresponding to these (as, for example, the imitative and pranksome nature of the ape, the murderous propensities of the wolf, the hardness of the diamond;) and the collection of all these influences of the world of animals, plants, and minerals, forms the blind unreasonable soul,[*] which always opposes the operations of that part of man's nature which is akin to God. It seemed of importance to Isidorus, the son of Basilides, to guard this doctrine from the objection, or the misunderstanding, which would represent it as endangering moral freedom, and holding out an excuse for every wickedness, as if it proceeded from the irresistible influences of these foreign admixtures. He appealed to the superior power of the Divine nature: "Since we have so much vantage-ground by means of our reason, we must, therefore, appear as conquerors over the lower creature in us."[†] He says also, " Let a man *only desire* to do good, and he will attain it."[‡] It is already to be deduced from the whole connection of the Basilidian scheme, that while he placed the power of the will so high, yet he by no means ascribed to it an independent self-sufficiency, nor at all denied the necessity of the assistance of grace from a higher power. According to his theory of redemption, he acknowledged it as necessary that the Divine in man should receive power from its connection with a higher source in order to give it a just activity. How far men were admonished by him of their need of help, is shown by the advice which Isidorus gives to him who is suffering under temptations: "Let him only," he says, "not withdraw himself from the brethren; let him only confide in his communion with the body of saints; let him say, ' I am entered into the sanctuary, nothing evil can happen to me.'"[§] It is also proved by the distinction which he made, of the two conditions of the inward life, the one, where a man in temptations prays for strength to conquer, and the other, where he gives thanks for the victory, which he has obtained by the support of the Divine power.[*] I grant that the doctrine of certain higher natures, which are elevated above the weaknesses of other men, might always easily create dangerous self-deceits of pride, because it is irreconcilable with the existence of Christian humility. There were later Basilidians, who corrupted this doctrine in a most pernicious manner, and thence deduced the freedom of the saints, which was to be bound by no law.[†] (See below.) The doctrine of matter might have led to an exaggerated and partial ascetic tendency in morality: but the acknowledgment of the communication and the interlacing which exists between the visible and the invisible world, as well as the recognition of the Divine nature as a victorious forming-principle for all creation, had here a counter-balancing effect, as we have already observed in regard to this whole class of Gnostics. Basilides considers marriage as a holy state, in no way inconsistent with the existence of Christian perfection; and, under certain circumstances, as a means of guarding against evil propensities. And it was only under certain circumstances that he allowed celibacy to be efficacious, as a means of attending to Divine things, with less interruption from earthly cares.[‡]

(c.) *Valentinus and his School.*

NEXT to Basilides we place Valentinus, who was contemporary with him, although a little later. If we judge from his Hellenistic expressions, and the Aramaic names, which appear in his system, he was of Jewish origin. He was born an Egyptian,[§] and most probably he owes his education likewise to Alexandria. He travelled thence to Rome, where he appears to have passed the latter part of his life; and this gave him an opportunity of making his doctrines more known, and propagating them in these regions also. In his fundamental notions he agreed with Basilides; it was only in the manner of explaining them, and in the representation of the images in which he developed his ideas, that he differed from him. But as people did not carefully distinguish from one another, the doctrines of the founders of Gnostic schools, and

---

[*] The ψυχη πϱοσφυης αλογος.
[†] Δια δε το λογιστικῳ κϱειττονας γινομενους, της ελαττονος εν ἡμιν κτισεως φανηναι κρατουντας.
[‡] Strom. iii. 427, ϑελησατω μονον απαρτισαι το καλον και επιτευξεται. [Sylb. p. 183. Potter, p. 510. Klotz, vol. ii. p. 213.]
[§] Strom. iii. 427. [See the last note for references.]

[*] Strom. l. c. ὁταν δε ἡ ευχαριστια σου εις αιτησιν ὑποπεση.
[†] Strom. iii. 427. [See note first column.]
[‡] Strom. lib. iii., from the beginning.
[§] According to the account given by Epiphanius

those of their later followers, by whom these doctrines had only been modified in a peculiar manner, and as they joined with the Valentinian system many kindred doctrines, which flowed from one common source, it is difficult, from the representations which have come down to us, to determine with certainty what doctrines properly belonged to Valentinus himself, as the founder of the school.

What the δυναμεις were with Basilides, the Æons* were with Valentinus; but the *following notion* is peculiar to him, namely, that as the veil (or covering) of all life resides in the original source of all existence, (the Bythos,) but is not yet unfolded, together with the development of life that proceeds from that first source, members which mutually supply the defects of each other form themselves, that is to say Æons, both male and female, one of which is *chiefly generative*, the other *receptive*;† and that by the mutual communication of these Æons the chain of that development of life constantly goes on. The female is the supplement of the male, το πληρωμα,‡ and the perfect line of Æons is now considered as a whole, as the fulness of the Divine life streaming out of the Bythos, which must again be constantly rendered fruitful, as it were, by it, (the Divine life,) and it is called, in relation to him, the female, the Pleroma! The *hidden being* of God cannot be known by any one; it is the absolutely ἀγνωστον; it only in as far as he has revealed himself in the unfolding of his powers or Æons, that he can be recognised. All individual Æons, in their varied modes of revelation, are called forms and names of that Being,§ who, in his secret existence is inconceivable, not-to-be-named, and elevated above conceptions and images, just as the Monogenes, that first self-revelation of the hidden Being, is called peculiarly the INVISIBLE NAME *of the Bythos*. It is an idea deeply rooted in the Valentinian system, that since all existence has its foundation in the self-limitation of the Bythos, so also the existence of all created being depends on *limitation*. When every thing remains within the limits of its peculiar sphere, and is that which it ought to be according to its assigned position in the development of life, then every thing can dovetail together well, and a just harmony exist in the chain of the development of life. As soon as any being endeavours to overpass these limits,—as soon as ever a being, instead of recognising God in the revelation which he makes of himself to that being, according to his position,—emboldens himself so as to wish to penetrate into His hidden Being, it runs a risk of sinking into annihilation. Instead of laying hold of that which is real, it loses itself in that which is without existence. The Horos (ὁρος,) the Genius of limitation, of bounding, (the power of truth personified, which assigns and sets fast the boundaries of each individual being, which watches over those boundaries, and when they are broken restores them,) therefore, takes an important place in the system of Valentinus. Gnosis is here, as it were, giving testimony against itself. The ideas of the Horos and the Redeemer must have been much akin to each other in the Valentinian system, and in fact the Horos was called by many the λυτρωτης and σωτηρ, the *Redeemer* and *Saviour*; and we find traces which indicate that he was meant to represent only one mode of operation of the one redeeming Spirit,—that Spirit which, according to the different places of his operations, that extend themselves throughout all the stages of existence, and according to his different modes of operation, is betokened by different names, and by others is divided into different persons, (Hypostases.) The Valentinians ascribe two modes of operation to this Horos; *the one* of a negative kind, by means of which he lays down the limits for all existence, and separates and removes from it all that is foreign to it;* and in virtue of this power he is *properly* called ὁρος; and *the other* is that operation, by means of which he sets fast and establishes, in their peculiar sphere and forms, all those beings who are purified from that, which, being foreign to their nature, troubles their existence;† and in virtue of this power he is called σταυρος, a word which is used both for a cross, and a stake or bulwark; to both of which meanings the Valentinians here made allusion. Their remarks on those

---

* See the explanation of this word, p. 26.
† Just as in all the rest of the creation, which represents an image of that higher world, this twofold line of agents is to be found.
‡ Πληρωμα. These Theosophs, who certainly did not scrupulously adhere to the strict grammatical meaning of terms, perhaps understood this word both in an active and a passive sense at the same time, and applied it both to το πληρουν and το πληρουμενον.
§ The Æons are μορφαι του Θεου, ὀνοματα του ἀνονομαστου.

* The ἐνεργεια μεριστικη και διοριστικη.
† The ἐνεργεια ἑδραστικη και στηριστικη.

sayings of the Redeemer in which they thought they recognised the Horos, make their ideas on the subject plain. Thus they referred Luke xiv. 27, to the *establishing* power of the Horos,* and Matthew x. 34, and Mark x. 21, to *his separating power*.† In the first of these passages, according to them, our Saviour means that only those persons can be his disciples who bear his cross, *i. e.* who give themselves up to that Divine power of the Redeemer which is symbolically represented by the cross, and suffer themselves to be formed and firmly established by it in his own peculiar way. In the second passage our Saviour hints at his Divine purifying power, by which he clears that which is akin to God from the admixture of the ungodly, and produces the annihilation of the latter.‡ Both are intimately connected together, the *clearance* from the foreign admixture of the ὑλη, from intermixture with which this irregular, indefinite, and unquiet vacillation between existence and non-existence proceeds, and a firm establishment in a definite, peculiar, Divine existence, unmingled with any thing else.

If Basilides deduced the intermixture of the Divine with matter from an assault of the kingdom of darkness upon the kingdom of light, on the contrary, Valentinus deduced it from a commotion that arose in the Pleroma, and a descent of the Divine seed of life from the Pleroma into matter, consequent upon that commotion. He acknowledged, as well as Basilides, a Divine wisdom, which revealed itself in the world; but here, also, in his view, the lower is only *an image* of the higher. It is not the Divine wisdom itself, not the Æon σοφια herself, but the untimely fruit of her travail, which is to unfold itself and arrive at its maturity only by degrees. He distinguishes between an ανω and a κατω σοφια (Achamoth :)§ this latter is the soul of the world, from the admixture of which with the ὑλη all living existence is produced, and is in different stages, higher, in proportion as it can keep itself clearer from connection with the ὑλη, and lower, in proportion as it is attracted and affected by matter. There exist, therefore, these *three* stages of being.

1. The φυσεις πνευματικαι, or those Divine seeds of life, which are elevated above matter by their nature, and which are akin to σοφια, to the soul of the world, and to the Pleroma.

2. The φυσεις ψυχικαι, or such natures as proceeded from the life that had been divided by admixture with the ὑλη; and an entirely new stage of being begins with these natures, an image of the higher world, but in a subordinate position.

3. The ungodly, which is opposed to all improvement; the being which can only disturb, and is entirely the slave of blind desires and passions.

There is only a *difference of degree* between all, which proceeds from the unfolding of the Divine life (which flows forth from the Bythos through the Æons,) from the Pleroma downwards to its seed, which has fallen down into human nature —that seed which, being sown, must attain its ripeness in the earthly world; but between those three classes of being there is an *essential* difference *of nature*. Each one, therefore, of these classes must have its own independent principle which predominates in it, although every process of improvement and development leads back in the end to the Bythos, which works on every thing by means of various organs in the various grades of being, and whose law is the only ruling one. He cannot, however, himself enter into any immediate connection with that which is foreign to him, and, therefore, in that subordinate grade of being which lies between the perfect or Divine, and the ungodly or material, there must exist a Being as the image of the Most High,* which, while it thinks that it acts independently, must yet serve the universal law, from which nothing is exempt, for the realization of the ideas of the Supreme even to the very extreme limits of matter. This Being is in the psychical world, what the Bythos is in the higher world, only with this difference, that it involuntarily acts as the organ of the former; and this being is the Demiurgos of Valentinus. The *Hyle* also has its principle, which represents it, and through which it operates; but by its very nature it is not of a forming and creative, but of a *destructive* kind: this is Satan.

1. The nature of the πνευματικον is that which is essentially akin to God (the ὁμοουσιον τω Θεω.) and thence comes simple and undivided existence,† the life of unity or oneness (ουσια ἑνικη μονοειδης.)

---

* The ἐνεργεια στηριστικη και ἱδριστικη
† The ἐνεργεια μεριστικη και διοριστικη.
‡ Irenæus i. c. 3. § 5.
§ חכימות

* The μεριστης.
† ['The German is here "das Leben der Einheit." I think in English the same idea would be better rendered 'oneness of existence.'—H. J. R.]

2. The Being of the ψυχικον, divided into number and variety, but still submitting itself to a higher unity, and allowing itself to be guided by that unity, at first unconsciously, afterwards consciously.

3. The Being of Satan and his whole kingdom: mere opposition to all unity; the Being divided and distracted in itself, without any capability for unity, or any point for unity to begin from; and with all this, an endeavour to destroy all unity, to spread its *own* indwelling distraction over every thing, and to distract every thing.*

In that first grade of being, the life, which, by its very nature, is eternal, exists as something inalienable, a necessary αφθαρσια; the ψυχικον, on the contrary, stands in the middle between immortal and mortal. The ψυχικοι obtain immortality, or they become subject to death, according as they give themselves up by their inclinations to the Divine or to ungodliness. The nature of Satan, like that of the ὑλη, is death itself, annihilation, the negation of all existence, which, in the end, when all existence, which has been divided by its means, shall have developed itself to the full extent of all its properties, and shall have fixed itself sufficiently in itself, shall then destroy itself in itself, being overcome by the power of the positive, after it (the negative, annihilating power,) has drawn to itself all its kindred ungodliness. The existence of the first is the pure development of life from within,—an activity which is not directed outwards, and which has no obstacles to overcome; and a tranquillity which is a life and action.

2. The existence of the ὑλη is of itself, and by its own nature, the stillness of death; but after a spark of life has fallen into it, and communicated to it a certain something analogous to life, it becomes in its representative, Satan, a wild kind of self-contradicting impulse.

3. To the Demiurgos, and to those that are his, namely, the Psychical, there is peculiarly assigned an activity directed outwardly; an impelling activity: they desire to do much, as it usually happens with such busy people, without rightly understanding what they do,†—without becoming themselves properly conscious of the ideas which direct them.‡

The doctrine of the redemption took also a very important place in the Valentinian system, and peculiarly forms its centre point; but it was by him, even more than by Basilides, removed from the regions of practical things into those of speculation and metaphysics. As, according to his system, a process of the development of life pervades all regions of existence, and as the disharmony, which, as far as its seed is concerned, first arose in the Pleroma itself, beginning thence, has spread itself farther,* so the *whole course of the world can only then first attain its proper object,* when *harmony* shall be again restored, *in all grades of existence*, as well as in the Pleroma; that which happens in the Pleroma must be imaged in all other grades of existence. And thus, therefore, as the work of redemption takes place in different stages of existence and the same law is here fulfilled in different forms, and in different conditions, it is the same agent of the revelation of the hidden God, the same agent, through whom the life that streamed forth from God becomes united with him again, who, continuing his work, till the completion of the whole, is imaged (or reflected) in different hypostases, wherever he is perfecting his work in different stages of existence. So it is the same idea which is represented in a Monogenes, a Logos, a Christus, and a Soter. The Soter is the Redeemer for the whole of the world that lies beyond the Pleroma, and therefore, also the plastic Being for that world; for in this system, to form and to redeem hang closely together, as is already evident from the twofold operations of the Horos. By means of this *formative process*, the higher nature is first made free from the matter that adheres to it; and out of an unorganic, formless being, is unfolded into a definite, organized being, gifted with individual qualities.† It is by means of redemption that the higher property first attains to its mature and perfect development, and to clear consciousness. Redemption is the completion of the formative process. All the Divine life of the Pleroma concentrates itself, and is

---

found in the writings of Heracleon, quoted by Origen, tom. xiii. Joh. c. 16, 25, 30, 51, 59; tom. xx. c. 20.

* The foundation of the whole of the new creation, lying beyond the Pleroma, which new creation can proceed from division alone.

† [Literally, "into a definite, individual, and organized being."—H. J. R.]

---

* The ουσια πολυσχιδης, which endeavours to assimilate every thing to itself.

† Φυσις πολυεργος, πολυπραγμων.

‡ The documents on which this rests will be

reflected in the Soter, and through him extends its operations for the individualizing of the Divine life, in order that the spiritual natures, which are akin to the Pleroma, may be sown abroad in the world, and ripen into perfect existence. The Christus of the Pleroma is the working principle, the Soter beyond the Pleroma* is the receiving, the forming, and the perfecting principle.†

The Soter first proves his redeeming and forming power on that still imperfect soul of the world, which came from the Pleroma, as this soul must, at some time or other, spread itself abroad over all the spiritual natures that are akin to it, and which sprouted forth from it, as the universal mother of spiritual life in the lower world. (See above.) The Soter is the proper fashioner and governor of the world, as he is the Redeemer; for the formation of the world is the first beginning of the process of development, which can only be brought to completion by means of redemption. The Soter, as the inward active principle, puts into the soul-of-the-world,‡ destined to make up a syzygy§ with him, the formative ideas, and she communicates them to the Demiurgos, who imagines that he is acting independently; and he, unconsciously to himself, under this cultivation becomes animated and influenced by the power of these ideas. Whilst Valentinus‖ represented the Demiurgos and the world fashioned and animated by him as one whole, he paints this whole as an image of the glory of God, sketched by the Soter, as by a painter. But, to say the truth, as every image, from its very nature, is an imperfect representation of the original prototype, and can be rightly understood only by him who has the power of beholding the original,—thus also the Demiurgos, with his creation, is only an imperfect image of the glory of God; and he alone who has received in his inward soul the revelation of the invisible Divine Being, can rightly understand the world as the image, and the Demiurgos as the prophet, of the Supreme God. The inward revelation (which is the portion of the πνευματικοι) is an authentication of the outward, an authentication of the Demiurgos as the representative of God. Valentinus himself expresses this thus:*
"as much as the picture is less than the living countenance, so much the world is less than the living God. And what is the cause of the picture? The greatness of the countenance, which afforded the original to the painter, in order to become honoured by the manifestation of his name; for no form has been invented as an independent thing. But as the name of the thing itself supplies that which is wanting in the paintings, so also the *invisible* God† acts for the authentication of the image which is made."

It is a fundamental notion of the Valentinian and of all Gnostic systems, that *man* is destined to represent and to maintain the connection between the higher world and the empire of the Demiurgos, that is, to reveal the Supreme God in this world. Human nature, and the revelation of God, are here kindred notions; and hence the *first man*‡ [Urmensch] was one of the Valentinian Æons; and, according to other Valentinian systems, it was said, "When God wished to reveal himself, this was called man."§ The Demiurgos created man, to image and represent himself; he breathed into him a soul akin to

---

* In the τοπος μεσοτητος.
† Thus Heracleon says of the Soter, in relation to Christians, that the former receives the Divine seed out of the Pleroma from the latter, as a yet undeveloped seed; and that he communicates to it the formation into a definite and separate being—την πρωτην μορφωσιν την κατα γνεσιν, εις μορφην, και φωτισμον, και πυρ γραφην αγαγων και αναδειξας. Origen, Joh. t. ii. c. 15. To *bring to light, to form*, and to *individualize*, are identical ideas among the Gnostics. The indefinite, the unorganic, corresponds in spiritual beings to the ὑλη. Thus in the Valentinian fragment in Irenæus i. c. 8. § 4, the μορφων, φωτιζων, φανερων, is opposed to the προβαλλων σπερματικως την ὑλην ουσιαν. Christus sows the seed, the Soter harvests it. Origen, Joh. i. 13. p. 48.
‡ Κατω σοφια, Achamoth.
§ [It will be remembered that in this system all the Æons were evolved by pairs, or syzygies.—H. J. R.]
‖ After Plato, who considers the Spirit that fashions the world, and the world animated by him, as one whole, one Θεος γεννητος, εν ζωον; and after the example of Philo, who represents the Λογος, and the body of the world animated by him, as *one whole*.

---

* Clem. Strom. lib. iv. 509. [Sylb. p. 218. Potter, p. 603. Klotz, vol. ii. p. 326-7.]
[The quotation from Valentinus is probably corrupt, and requires the alteration of ἐπληρωσαν into ἐπληρωσεν, which the common interpreters, as well as Neander, have made. The only difficulty lies in the latter part, which I here quote: τις ουν αιτια της εικονος; μεγαλωσυνη του προσωπου παρεσχημενου τω ζωγραφω τον τυπον, ινα τιμηθη δι ονοματος αυτου· ου γαρ αυθεντικως ευρεθη μορφη, αλλα το ονομα επληρωσαν το ὑστερησαν εν πλασει.—H. J. R.]
† God's invisible Being.
‡ The Adam Kadmon of the Cabbala.
§ See Iren. lib. i. c. 12. § 4.

his own being. But, even here, he was acting as the instrument of a higher Being. Man was to represent that first man. Without the Demiurgos being conscious of it, the Sophia communicated to him the spiritual seed, which he transplanted into the soul of man; and thence it happened that man at once revealed something which was of a more elevated nature than the whole creation, into which he entered; so that the Demiurgos himself, and his angels, were seized with astonishment, for as yet they knew nothing of a higher world. The Demiurgos thought that he himself was an independent ruler; but now, to his astonishment, he saw a higher power enter into his dominions. This astonishment is universally repeated, wherever man, limited as he is, being animated by the ideas of a higher world, expresses them in his works, as in art, and indeed, universally, where the hands of men execute any thing in relation to the name of God. Thus it happens that men fall down and worship their own images, being filled with a reverential astonishment by the sensation* of a higher power, which is unknown to them. We will bring forward the words of the man himself: "And just as the angel was seized with fear at that creature ($\pi\lambda\alpha\sigma\mu\alpha$,) when it spoke of loftier things than such as suited its creation, by means of him who had invisibly communicated to it the seed of the life from above, (namely, the Soter,) and when it spoke with freedom and confidence,—so also, in the race of the men of this world, the works of man become a terror even to those who made them, such as pillars, and statues, and every thing which the hands of all men execute in honour of the name of God."†

But that which human nature was universally to represent, became now really brought to pass only in those spiritual men.‡ Through them was the life-giving, purifying principle of the Divinity to be spread abroad, and penetrate even to the utmost limits of the $\H{\upsilon}\lambda\eta$; these spiritual natures are the salt and the light of the earth, the leaven for all the race of man. The $\psi\upsilon\chi\eta$ is only the *vehiculum* for the $\pi\nu\epsilon\upsilon\mu\alpha\tau\iota\kappa\omicron\nu$, in order that it may be able to enter into the temporal world, in which it is to develope itself to maturity. When this aim shall have been attained, the spirit, which is only destined for the life of intuition,* will leave that vehiculum in the lower sphere; and every spiritual nature, as the female and recipient element in regard to the higher world of spirits, will be elevated in the Pleroma to its syzygy with the angelic nature which corresponds to it. Only the highest and immediate intuitive powers (that is the meaning of Valentinus,) will then come into operation. All the powers and modes of operation of the soul, which are directed to that which is temporal and perishable,—such as its powers of reflection, and the understanding, in which, according to Valentinus, is contained the $\psi\upsilon\chi\eta$, will then utterly cease.†

The attractive power, with which the Divine Being works on every thing, without those who receive the impression understanding it, or being able to explain it to themselves, is a favourite notion with Valentinus. The Demiurgos was attracted by the spiritual natures which were scattered among the Jewish people, without being conscious of the reason of it. He made them, therefore, prophets, priests, and kings. Therefore, it happened that the prophets were enabled especially to hint at the higher order of things, which should be brought among men by the Soter. According to Valentinus, a fourfold principle acted upon the Prophets:—

1. The psychical principle, the human and limited soul, the unassisted soul.
2. The *spiritualization of this* $\psi\upsilon\chi\eta$, which is derived from the Demiurgos working upon it.
3. The unassisted $\pi\nu\epsilon\upsilon\mu\alpha\tau\iota\kappa\omicron\nu$.
4. The pneumatical spiritualization, which is derived from the influence of the Sophia.‡

Thus Valentinus, in reference to these four principles, could distinguish in the writings of the prophets, different promises of a higher and lower character and meaning, and a higher and lower sense, which differed from each other, in the same passage.

1. The mere human sayings.
2. The *single* prophecies of future events, which the Demiurgos, who, although not Omniscient, yet looked into a wider circle of the future, was able to communicate; and the prophecies of a

---

* [Ahnung. Literally, a *presentiment*. It expresses here a feeling indicating a sense that leads us to recognise this higher power.—H. J. R.]
† Clem. Strom. lib. ii. 375. [Sylb. p. 161. Potter, p. 448. Klotz, vol. ii. p. 145.]
‡ The $\phi\upsilon\sigma\epsilon\iota\;\pi\nu\epsilon\upsilon\mu\alpha\tau\iota\kappa\alpha\iota$.

* [Das Leben der Anschauung. See Preface. —H. J. R.]
† Comp. Aristot. de Anima., lib. iii. c. 5.
‡ See Iren. lib. i. c. 16, § 3, 4.

Messiah, which came also from the same source, but were still enveloped in a temporal and Jewish form; the prophecies of a Messiah, such as the Demiurgos would send,—a Psychical Messiah for the Psychical world, the ruler of a kingdom of this world.

3. The ideas which verged upon the Christian economy, and pointed to it, the enlightened Messianic notions, brought forward in more or less purity, according as they proceeded purely from the higher spiritual natures, or the immediate influence of the Sophia. This view might lead to remarkable investigations as to the mixture of the Divine and human in the prophets, and introduce conclusions which would be fruitful towards the interpretation of the prophets themselves. The Valentinian view was opposed to the determination of those, who, in spite of the words of Christ in Matt. xi. 9, &c., and in spite of 1 Pet. i. 12, attributed a perfect and Christian knowledge to the prophets. It may be asked, whether Valentinus recognised the beams of higher truth only among the Jews; whether he allowed the existence of spiritual natures only among the Jews, or whether he acknowledged that they were spread abroad also among the heathen. According to Heracleon,* he held the Jews to be the kingdom of the Demiurgos,—the Heathen the kingdom of Matter, or of Satan,—and the Christians the people of the Supreme God; but this does not prove that he excluded from the heathen all that belongs to the superior race; because, although he expressly assigned Judaism to the Demiurgos, he supposed that it contained some scattered seeds of the higher pneumatical system; and although he assigned Christianity to the Supreme God, he saw also, even among the Christians, a large class of Psychical persons. He, therefore, only speaks of the *prevailing ingredients;* and therefore, notwithstanding the prevailing state of the ὑλη among the heathen, he might recognise scattered seeds of the pneumatical. He was in fact obliged to confess this according to his own principles, according to which the higher spiritual principle of life (the πνυματικον) was to pervade all grades of being even to the very limits of matter, in order to prepare the universal annihilation of the ὑλη. What Valentinus says, in the passage above quoted, of the power of art, which turns itself to the formation of idols, allows us to conclude that he judged the polytheistic system more mildly than the common Jews, to whom the idols were only evil spirits, and that he, supporting himself by Acts xvii. 23, believed that even in this system, although it was sullied by the prevalence of the hylic principle, there might be observed traces of an unknown God, who spread his unrecognised influence over all things. Thus Valentinus, in a still extant fragment of a homily,* actually hints at the traces of truth spread about even in the writings of the heathen, in which the inward being of the spiritual people of God, or of the πνυματικοι, who are spread abroad in the whole world, reveals itself. " Much of that which is written in the books of the heathen, is found written in the Church of God; this common part is the voice out of the heart, the law written in the heart; this is that people of the beloved (*i. e.* this higher consciousness which is found in common, is the mark of the scattered community of the Soter, the πνυματικοι,) which is beloved by him, and loves him in return."

The *Soter,* who from the beginning had conducted *the whole process of the development* of the spiritual seed of life, which had fallen down from out of the Pleroma for the formation of a new world, the *invisible Fashioner* and *Ruler* of this new world,—was now obliged at last, himself, to act upon the course of the world, *without any intermediate agency,* in order to spread forth the act of redemption, which he had originally perfected in the mother of all spiritual life, the soul of the world, or the Sophia,—upon all the spiritual life which had flowed forth from her, and thus to bring the whole work to completion. All being, even down to the very hylic matter that struggles against all being, was capable of ennoblement, *each after its own degree.* The Soter must, therefore, enter into connection with all these stages of being, in order to fashion all, both the lower (the Psychical) as well as the higher (the Pneumatical,) into the degree of the higher life, of which each is capable. Except for this, according to the usual course of nature, the Soter could enter into connection only with the spiritual nature, which is akin to him, and such a nature could enter into this tem-

---

* Origen, in Joh. t. xiii. § 16.

* Clem. Strom. lib. vi. p. 641. [Sylb. p. 272. Potter, p. 792. Klotz, vol. iii. p. 128.]

poral world only in connection with a ψυχη.

Valentinus might here coincide with the doctrine of Basilides, only with this difference, that with the first of them, the human part in the person and in the life of the Redeemer received a somewhat higher character, although not the right and becoming one; the Christ, composed and decomposed by him, according to *his own* notions, was always very different from the *historical* Christ.

The Demiurgos had promised to his own people a Redeemer, a Messiah, who would release them from the dominion of the hylical, introduce the annihilation of every thing which opposed itself to his empire,—rule over every thing in his name,—and rejoice all that obeyed him with all kinds of earthly happiness. He sent down this Messiah, who represented the very image of the Demiurgos, out of his own heaven; but this elevated Being could not enter into any connection with matter; nay, as it was to introduce the annihilation of every thing material, how could it receive any thing whatever from matter? There would then have been joined with the material body a material spirit* of life, akin to it, and the source of every thing evil; and how could he have been the Redeemer, if the principle of evil had been present in his own nature? The Demiurgos also formed a body for the psychical Messiah out of the finer ethereal matter of heaven, out of which he sent him down into this world. This body was so formed, by some wonderful contrivance,† that he appeared visibly, and could subject himself to all sensuous actions and affections, and yet do this in a manner entirely different from the usual kind of bodies.‡ But the miracle of the birth of Jesus consisted in this, that the psychical nature which came down from the heaven of the Demiurgos, together with the ethereal body brought from thence, came into the light of the world through the body of Mary only as through a canal.§ But yet this psychical Messiah would never have been able to complete the work laid upon him by the Demiurgos: there was need of a higher power for the conquest of the empire of the ὑλη; the Demiurgos acted as well here as in every thing as the unconscious instrument of the Soter. This latter had appointed the moment in which he would unite himself with this psychical Messiah as his instrument, in order to fulfil the work which had been prepared and promised by the Demiurgos in a far higher sense than he himself anticipated, and to found a Messianic kingdom of a far higher kind, to the real circumstances of which only the most elevated predictions of the prophets, and those not understood by the Demiurgos himself, had pointed.

The psychical Messiah, who did not perceive the destination which was to fall to his lot through his union with the Soter, in the mean time laid before man the Ideal of ascetic holiness. He was able to exert an extraordinary dominion over matter from the peculiar nature of his body. He let himself down, indeed, to man, so as to eat and drink; but still without being subject to the same affections as other men: he carried on every thing after a divine manner.*

At the baptism in the Jordan, where he was to receive his solemn consecration to his calling as the Messiah, from John the Baptist, the representative of the Demiurgos, the Soter, who had thus conducted every thing through his invisible guidance, united himself with him, descending under the symbol of the dove. On this question, *whether the psychical Messiah from the first bore a spiritual nature within him*, which, descending with the vehiculum of a soul, was to develope itself to maturity in this world, that it might then first become capable of redemption; or whether it was only *at his descent into this world* that the Soter first received from the Sophia a spiritual nature as a vehicle, in order to be able to unite himself with the human nature, and that also the higher pneumatical nature was communicated to the Messiah of the Demiurgos during baptism: on this point there might be a diversity of opinions even in the Valentinian school itself.†

---

* Clem. Strom. Lib. iii. 451.

† The latter view is apparently found in a passage of Heracleon; Origen, t. vi. § 23.; Grabe Spicileg. t. ii. p. 89, where I once (see my Genetische Entwickelung, &c., p. 149,) erroneously supposed that I could recognise the doctrine that the Soter himself became man, and that of his union with the human nature from its first development. He explains John i. 27, in his manner, first justly, according to the sense expressed by the words, "John avows that he is not worthy to render the smallest service to the Redeemer;" and then afterwards he arbitralily introduces a higher sense into the simple words, according to

---

* The ψυχη αλογος.   † Ἐξ οἰκονομιας.
‡ Σωμα ἐκ της ἀφανους ψυχικης οὐσιας.—Theodot. Didascal. Anatol.
§ Ὡς δια σωληνος.

According to the doctrine of Valentinus, as well as that of Basilides, the appearance of the redeeming Spirit in human nature, and its union with the psychical Messiah would be the chief business in the work of redemption. He also agreed with Basilides in this, that the Soter had left the psychical Messiah to himself at his passion, but he ascribed more importance than Basilides to the passion of the Messiah, although a theosophy, which sought peculiar mysteries every where, despised a simple explanation, and in consequence of its multitude of mystical and speculative relations and meanings would not allow the feelings of the heart to show themselves; although this theosophy was too contemplative and superhuman to be able rightly to comprehend the passion of Christ in its human and moral aspect. As the psychical Messiah spread himself upon the cross, and with the cross spread himself over the lower world, this was an image of that first act of redemption by which the Soter (see above,) had extended himself over the Sophia with the σταυρος. Just as in the higher region this effected the freeing of the Sophia from that which is foreign to her, so also it effected in the lower the freeing of the psychical from the material, which is the groundwork of all that is evil, even to the final annihilation of it altogether, after it has become dissolved in itself.* By the words, "Into thy hands, O Father, I commend my *spirit*," he commended the πνευματικον σπερμα which was then leaving him, in order that it might not be detained in the dominion of the Demiurgos, but that it might raise itself up free into the higher region, and that all those spiritual natures, whose representative this spiritual nature united with him was, might also be raised up with it. The psychical Messiah raises himself up to the Demiurgos, who transfers to him in his name the sovereign might and rule, and the pneumatical Messiah raises himself up to the Soter, whither all freed spiritual natures are to follow him.

The most important matter, the chief concern for the pneumatical natures in the work of redemption, is still the redemption, which was imparted to human nature by its union with the Soter at the baptism in the Jordan. This must be repeated in every individual case. Valentinus speaks thus of the sanctifying effects of inward communion with the Redeemer. "But there is one Good, (whose free appearance is the revelation through the Son,) and through *him alone* can the heart become pure after all evil spirits have been banished out of the heart, for many spirits inhabiting it will not allow it to be pure. Each one of these fully performs its own work, while they defile it in manifold ways by unseemly desires. And it appears to me to be with such a heart as with an inn, which is trampled upon and trodden down and often filled with dirt, while men dwell within it without restraint, and take no care whatever about the place, as one in which they have no concern. Thus also the heart, until it attains heavenly grace, remains unclean, as being the abode of many evil spirits. But where the Father, the only one that is good, takes possession of it, then is it sanctified and it shines with light; and thus he who possesses such a heart, is declared to be blessed (μακαριζιται) because he will see God."†

He who is thus united with God is already a member of the heavenly com-

---

his own theosophic ideas: ουκ ηδη ειμι ικανος, ινα δι' εμε καταβηι απο μεγεθους και σαρκα λαβηι, ως υπεδημα, περι ης εγω λογον αποδευναι ου δυναμαι, ουδε διηγησασθαι η επιλυσαι την περι αυτης οικονομιαν. We can hardly here, under the term "the flesh," which the Soter, who came down out of the higher region from the bounds of the Pleroma and the τοπος μεσοτητος, had received, understand the body of the psychical Messiah, formed by some peculiar οικονομια; for he is certainly here speaking of the Soter, who revealed himself to John at the baptism, and at all events, according to the Valentinian doctrine, he did not unite himself with the *body* but with the *psychical Messiah who bore this body*. And then John, who here represented the person of the Demiurgos himself, would never have uttered his astonishment thus at this wonderful body, formed by the latter person himself (the Demiurgos.) But the Valentinians called *every covering, every vehicle* for a higher being, which lets himself down into a lower region, a σαρξ. The Sophia gave a σπερμα πνευματικον, in order that he might let himself down to the earth in this as a vehicle for his appearance, and might thereby enter into union with the ψυχη. The opening words of the Didascal. Anatol. give us the proof of this, for it is said, ο πρεσβυτερων σαρκων τω λογω (as well as to the Soter) η σοφια το πνευματικον σπερμα, τουτο στολισαμενος κατηλθεν ο σωτηρ. It was also of this wonderful apparatus that Heracleon spoke.

* The declaration of Heracleon in Origen, t. vi. § 23, τω σταυρω ανηλωσθαι και εφανισθαι πασαν την κακιαν, must be understood in connection with the whole Valentinian system.

† Strom. lib. ii., p. 409. [Ed. Par. 1629.] [Sylburg, p. 176. Potter, p. 488—9. Klotz, vol. ii. p. 191.]

munity, is already incorporated by the power of the Redeemer into the host of blessed spirits, which is thus expressed in the language of the Valentinian school: "As every pneumatical soul has its other half in the higher world of Spirits (the *angel* which belongs to it) for union with which it is destined, so does it receive through the Soter the power to enter at once into this syzygy in regard to its spiritual life."*

As the psychical and pneumatical beings are different from one another in their nature and their destination, so they remain different also in Christianity. There is a χριστιανισμος ψυχικος and a χριστιανισμος πνυματικος. St. Paul declares to the psychical, that for them he has known nothing and could preach nothing but Christ crucified;† that he could not preach to them that wisdom of the perfect which is hidden even to the Demiurgos and his angels. The Valentinians distinguish also, according to their system, *a twofold signification of redemption* and of baptism, in regard to the psychici and the pneumatici. The psychici must be led to believe by means of miracles and other acts that strike the senses;‡ they are only capable *of a belief upon authority*, and not capable *of a persuasion which proceeds from the inward essence of truth*, nor of the intuitive perception (anschauung) *of truth itself*. To such men Christ speaks in John iv. 48. The spiritual men, on the contrary, need no such outward means of instruction : in virtue of their kindred nature they are attracted by truth itself without any intermediate means.§ When truth reveals itself to them, there follows instantly in them a confident belief, such as could not be effected from without, and could only proceed from the immediate influence of truth upon their kindred spiritual nature.|| Their worship of God founded on their knowledge of the truth is the true "reasonable service of God."

That seed of the spiritual nature is that by which men are attracted by the Redeemer, and led to him, the men of the Spirit; therefore, they who possess that seed are the salt and the soul of the outward Church, those through whom Christianity is farther propagated as the forming principle of human nature.* By these spiritual men the illumination of all this earthly universe, the final annihilation of all that is material and evil, is to be prepared, after matter has been deprived of all the life which it has seized upon for itself. Valentinus thus addresses these pretended spiritual men: "Ye are, from the beginning, immortal, and children of eternal life, and ye have been desirous to divide death among yourselves,† in order that ye may exhaust and expend it, and that death may die in you and through you; for when ye dissolve the world, (prepare the dissolution of the material world,) but ye yourselves will not be dissolved, ye are lords over the creation, and over all that is corruptible."‡ Although at the bottom of these high-sounding words, as far as they were applied to the calling of Christians, as instruments for the revelation and extension of God's kingdom, there is something of truth; yet this truth is here mixed with a pride, which in the case of certain peculiarities, might easily introduce the most mischievous excesses of fanaticism. If the Valentinians had been able to found a Church according to their own notions, the Pneumatici would have been the Christian *Brahmins.*

Now, when the end prepared by these spiritual men should have been attained, then, after the dissolution of the whole material world, the Soter, united into a syzygy with the Sophia, and under him the matured spiritual natures in pairs with the angels, were to enter into the Pleroma, and the last (lowest) stage of the spiritual world§ was to receive the psychici under the Demiurgos; *and they also* were to receive that measure of happiness, which was suited to their peculiar nature. The Demiurgos rejoices himself

---

* Heracleon, ap. Origen, t. 13, § 11, κεμιζεσθαι παρ᾽ αυτου την δυναμιν και την ενωσιν και την αναρρησιν προς το πληρωμα αυτης.

† Didascal. Anatol. Of a twofold mode of preaching of St. Paul. In regard to the *Psychici*, εκηρυξι τον σωτηρα γεννητον και παθητον.

‡ Δι᾽ ιεργων φυσιν εχεντες και δι᾽ αισθησεως· πιθεσθαι και ουχι λογω πιστευειν. Orig. t. xiii § 59.

§ Heracleon in Joann. t. xiii. c. 20, the δικτικη ζωης διαθεσις.

|| Ἡ ιδιακριτος και καταλληλος τη φυσει.

---

* See the proof of this in Heracleon, to be given almost immediately.

† While they were sent down into the midst of the material world.

‡ Strom. lib. iv. p. 509. B. [Ed. Paris, 1629.] 'Απ᾽ αρχης αθανατοι εστε και τεκνα ζωης εστε αιωνιας. Και τον θανατον εθελετε μερισασθαι εις εαυτους, ινα δαπανησητε αυτον και αναλωσητε και αποθανη ο θανατος εν υμιν και δι᾽ υμων. Ὁταν γαρ τον μεν κοσμον λυητε, υμεις δε μη καταλυησθε, κυριευετε της κτισεως και της φθορας απασης. [Sylb. p. 218. Potter, p. 603. Klotz, vol. ii. p. 326.]

§ The τοπος μεσοτητος.

in the appearance of the Soter, through which a higher world, to which he had hitherto been a stranger, is revealed to him, and through which also he, being freed from his harassing service, is enabled to enter into rest, and receive an echo of the glory of the Pleroma. He is the friend of the Bridegroom (the Soter) who stands there and belongs to him, and delights himself in the voice of the bridegroom, and delights himself in the fulfilment of the marriage.* John the Baptist spoke those words, John iii. 29, as the representative of the Demiurgos.

§ *Distinguished Men of the School of Valentinus.*

AMONG the men of the Valentinian school, the Alexandrian Heracleon is distinguished by more learning and profoundness than the others. He composed a commentary on the Gospel of St. John, from which Origen† has preserved some fragments of importance, perhaps also a commentary on that of St. Luke, from which (if such be the case,) Clement of Alexandria‡ has handed down to us a fragment,—the explanation of Luke xii. 8. 'It is easy to understand that the deep and inward spirit of St. John's writings would be attractive to the Gnostics. Heracleon brought to the explanation of this Gospel a deep religious feeling directed to interior things, together with an understanding which was clear, whenever he was not led into error by theosophical speculations; but that which *was wanting in him* was a feeling for the simplicity of St. John, and a knowledge or a recognition of the principles of grammatical and logical interpretation in general, without which free room is given to every caprice, even in the interpretation of the Scriptural writers, inasmuch as they, as men, although inspired men, obeyed the laws which regulate the modes of speech and thought among men. Although as far as we can see, Heracleon intended honestly to deduce his theology out of St. John, yet he was altogether taken possession of by his own system, and so thoroughly entangled in it in all his modes of thought and conception, that he could not stir a step free from it,

and involuntarily introduced its views and ideas into the Holy Scriptures, which he considered as the source of divine truth. As a proof of what is here said, we will take a closer view of Heracleon's explanation of the glorious *conversation of our Saviour with the woman of Samaria.* He could not stand by the simple historical narrative, nor content himself with the profound, psychological consideration of this Samaritan woman in her relation to the Saviour. Immediately in this Samaritan woman, who was attracted by the words and the appearance of Christ, an image is presented to his mind *of all* spiritual natures, which are attracted by that which is divine; and, therefore, in this narrative the whole relation of the πνυματικοι to the Soter, and to the higher spiritual world, must be represented. And therefore, the words of the Samaritan woman must bear a double sense; one, a sense of which she herself was conscious, and the other that higher sense, which she uttered as the representative of the whole class of πνυματικοι, without being conscious of it; and therefore, the words of the Saviour in reference to these things must also bear a twofold sense, a higher and a lower, a notion which involves the unnatural supposition of a double conversation going on at the same time. And yet he had seized upon the fundamental idea of the words of the Redeemer in a very understanding spirit, if he could only have prevented himself from being drawn away from the main matter by seeking too much in subordinate particulars. He explains justly the words of Christ, (John iv. 10, 13, 14,) which are to be understood spiritually:* " The water which the Saviour gives, is from his spirit and his power. . . . . . His grace and his gift are something which can never be taken away, nor corrupted, nor consume away in him who partakes of it. . . . . . They who receive *that* which is abundantly given to them from above, themselves also let that which is given to them bubble over for the eternal life of others." But then he draws the false conclusion, that because Christ meant the water which he wished to give, to be taken in a symbolical sense, consequently also the water of the well of Jacob must be understood in a symbolical sense. It was to be a symbol of Judaism, which satisfies not the

---

* The union of the Soter with the Sophia, and of the angels with the spiritual natures in the Pleroma.

† In his *Tomi* upon John, in which he frequently refers to the explanations of Heracleon.

‡ Strom. iv. 503. [Sylburg, p. 215. Potter, p. 595-6. Klotz, vol. ii. p. 316-8.]

* [This passage is quoted, Grab. Spicileg. vol. ii. p. 94-5.—H. J. R.]

desires of the spiritual nature, and of its perishable earthly glory. When the Samaritan woman says, "Give me this water, that I may not thirst, that I may not come hither to draw;" then the burdensomeness of Judaism was to be betokened by this, the difficulty of finding in it (Judaism) the nourishment of the inward life, and its unsatisfactoriness.* When the Redeemer desired the woman to call her husband, he meant her other half in the world of spirits, the angel which belonged to her, in order that she, coming with him to the Saviour, might receive power from him to bind herself with this her other half, and thus unite with him.† The ground for this arbitrary interpretation was this: "He could not speak of her earthly husband, *because he was well aware that she had no lawful husband*. . . . According to the *spiritual* meaning‡ the Samaritan woman did not know her husband; she knew nothing of the angel, that belonged to her: according to the literal meaning,§ she was ashamed to say that she was living in an unlawful connection." Heracleon further concluded, that as the water is the symbol of the divine life bestowed by the Redeemer, so is the pitcher a symbol of the *capacity in the disposition of the Samaritan woman for this Divine life*. *She left the pitcher behind with him*; that is to say, as she had such a vessel with the Saviour, as was fitted to receive the living water, she returned into the world, in order to announce the coming of Christ to the psychical.‖

Heracleon properly opposed the habit of prizing martyrdom as an *opus operatum*. "The multitude," he says,¶ "hold confession before the civil power to be the only thing: but this is wrong, for even the hypocrite might make this confession. *This* is a particular confession; it is not the *common* confession, which ought to be made by all Christians, of which he is here speaking; it is the confession through works and conduct, which answer to a belief in him.* This common confession is followed by that peculiar one, if it be needful, and if reason enjoins it. . . . . . Those persons who confess him with their mouth, may deny him through their works. Those only can truly confess him, who live in the confession of him, among whom he himself confesses, because he has received them into himself, and they have received him into themselves.† Therefore can he never deny himself."‡

We next make mention of PTOLEMÆUS, who to judge from the work of Irenæus, (which was specially levelled against the party of *this man*,) must have laboured much for the propagation of Valentinian principles. One is led to inquire whether it be true, as Tertullian asserts,§ that Ptolemæus was distinguished from Valentinus, because he imagined the Æons rather under the form of Hypostases, while Valentinus conceived them to be powers in-dwelling in the being of God; or at least one inquires, whether this difference was of so much importance; because, in fact, the representation of the Æons by the Gnostics, far from being mere abstract notions of attributes, always must have bordered on hypostasizing.

A very important piece of Ptolemæus, which has been preserved—his letter to one Flora, whom he endeavoured to gain over to the Valentinian principles‖—shows that he was extremely skilful in presenting his views to others in a manner likely to recommend them. As he was apparently writing to a Christian lady of the Catholic Church, he had particularly to remove *the objection*, which she would make on the contradiction *between his doctrines and those of the Church*, and

---

* Το ἐπιμιχθὲν, και δυστρόπιστον και ἀτροφον ἐκείνου του ὕδατος.
† Το πλήρωμα αὐτης. See above.
‡ Κατα το νοούμενον.
§ Κατα το ἁπλοῦν.
‖ The thought of Heracleon is here a just one, that only he who is in union with the Saviour by his feelings can preach him properly to others,—although this just thought is introduced into this place by an arbitrary interpretation of that which is historical. We must here do Heracleon the justice to acknowledge, that Origen, here as well as in many other places, attacks him unjustly, as if he contradicted himself; "for how could the Samaritan," says he, "preach to others, when she had left behind her, with the Redeemer, from whom she departed, her organ for the reception of the Divine life?" But Heracleon was here quite consistent in his application of the allegory; he did not think of *any local leaving behind*.
¶ In the fragment of his Commentary on St. Luke, quoted above.

---

* Here again, what Heracleon says is in itself quite just; and yet his explanation, which has no reference whatever to the context, is quite false.
† Ἐνειλημμένος αὐτους και ἐχόμενος ὑπο τουτων.
‡ Which would necessarily happen, if those who are in connection with him were to deny him.
§ Nominibus et numeris Æonum distinctis in personales substantias, quas Valentinus in ipsa summa divinitatis, ut sensus et affectus et motus, incluserat. Adv. Valentinian. c. 4.
‖ Epiphan. Hæres. xxxiii. §. 3.

against the supposition that the *Old Testament and the creation of the world, did not proceed from the Supreme God.* In regard to the first, he appeals to an apostolical tradition, which had come down to him through a series of hands, as well as to *the words of our Saviour,* according to which men must determine every thing. By tradition he probably means an *Esoteric* tradition, which he, *being self-deceived,* doubtless deduced from some pretended disciple of the apostles; and as to the words of our Saviour, he could easily bring them into accordance with his own system by the *Gnostic exegesis.* In regard to the second point, we may well conceive that he has represented his principles under the mildest possible form, in order to obtain acceptance for them with one who was uninitiated; but still we find in his conclusions nothing which contradicts the Valentinian principles. He combats two opposite errors, the error of those who held that the creation of the world, and the Old Testament, were the work of an evil Being, and the error of those who attributed them to the Supreme God; in *his* opinion, the one party was in error, because it knew *only* the Demiurgos, and not *the Universal Father,* whom Christ, who alone knew him, had been the first to reveal: the other, because it knew nothing of an intermediate Being, like the Demiurgos. Ptolemæus, also, would probably say,—the first view is that of men, who remain Jews even in Christianity; the other that of men, who, without any intermediate state of transition from the service of Matter and Satan, in heathenism, had attained at once to the recognition and knowledge of the Supreme God; and who believed, because they had made this sudden spring in their religion and knowledge, that a similar sudden transition took place in nature. "How can a law," he justly inquires, "which forbids all evil, proceed from an evil Being, who wars against all morality?" And he adds, "They who do not recognise the providence of the Creator in the world, must be blind not only in the eyes of the soul, but even in those of the body."

He throws the Mosaic religious code into a threefold division:—

1. That which proceeds from the Demiurgos;

2. That which Moses settled after the dictates of his own unassisted reason;*

3. The oldest additions to the Mosaic law.*

The Saviour clearly distinguishes the law of Moses from the law of God (*i. e.* of the Demiurgos,) in Matt. xix. 6, &c. He, however, exculpates Moses again, and seeks to show, that he gave way to the weakness of the people only *when forced,* in order to avoid a greater evil. That which proceeded from the Demiurgos he divided again into a threefold division;

1. The purely moral enactments, disturbed by nothing extraneous, which are properly called "The Law," in reference to which, our Saviour says that he is not come to destroy the Law, but to fulfil it; for as it contained nothing alien to the nature of the Saviour, it required only fulfilment; as, for instance, the commandments, *Thou shalt do no murder,—Thou shalt not commit adultery,—*were fulfilled in the commands *neither to be angry, nor to lust.*

2. The law, disturbed by the intermixture of evil, as that part, which permits of revenge, Levit. xxiv. 20; xx. 9: "He who recompenses evil for evil, does no less evil, because he repeats the same conduct, but in a different order."

The Gnostic has here only one measure for all cases; he could not discover the distinction of the politico-juridical from the purely moral, nor the necessary connection between the two, from the very nature of the economy of the Old Testament. And yet he recognises here, as well as in Moses, an element of instruction. "This command," says he, "was, and remains still, in other respects a *just one,* given on account of the weakness of those who receive the Law, though it transgresses *the pure Law;* but it is foreign to the nature and goodness of the Father of all, perhaps not consonant to the nature even of the Demiurgos,† but probably only forced upon him; for while *he who forbade one murder,* commanded a second, he suffered himself to be surprised *by necessity,* without being aware of it." He means to say, that the Demiurgos was wanting, not in the will, but in the power, to overcome evil; and this part of the Law is entirely abolished by the Saviour,

---

* This distinction of different agents (factors) who worked together in the composition of the Holy Scriptures, is quite conformable to the Valentinian notion of Inspiration.

* According to the theory of the Clementine, viz. that when the Law was written down from the oral tradition of it, many foreign additions were mingled with the oldest part of it.

† I have translated after an emendation of the text, l. c. c. 3, which I consider necessary: ἴσως οὐδὲ τουτο, or τῇ τουτου καταλληλον.

as contrary to the nature of the Supreme God.

3. The typical ceremonial Law, which (see above) contains the type of the higher spiritual things, the Law of Sacrifices, of Circumcision, of the Sabbath, of the Passover, and of Fasts. "All this, which was merely type and symbol, was changed after the truth had appeared. The sensuous and outward observance is removed, but it is transferred to the spiritual: the names remain the same, but the things are changed. For the Saviour has commanded us also to offer sacrifices; but not sacrifices by means of irrational animals, nor such incense, but through spiritual praise and thanksgiving, and through charity, and doing good to our neighbour. He wills also, that we should be circumcised; not, however, by the circumcision of the foreskin of the body, but the spiritual circumcision of the heart. He wills also, that we should observe the Sabbath, because he wishes us to rest from doing evil. Also, that we should fast; but not with a bodily fast, but a spiritual, in which abstinence from all evil consists. Our people, however, do observe the external fast, because it may be of some service even to the soul, if reasonably used, and neither used in imitation of any one, nor out of habit, nor on some particular day, as if some one day were appointed for that purpose,—but where it is used also with remembrance of the *real* fast, that those who are unable to keep that fast, may be reminded of it by outward fasting." And yet what true insight into the spirit of the system of religion proposed in the New Testament; what thoughtfulness and mildness of judgment does he show here!

Marcus and Bardesanes* are distinguished persons among those who are called the disciples of Valentinus; we say, "*who are called the disciples,*" because it would probably be more correct to state that both of them drew from the same sources in Syria, the native land of Gnosticism, which Valentinus had used. Marcus apparently came from Palestine in the latter half of the second century. His coming from Palestine appears probable, from the aramaic liturgical formulæ, of which he made use. While in an Heracleon and a Ptolemæus the Alexandrian *style of knowledge and learning* formed rather the characteristic of their theosophy, so on the contrary, in Marcus the *poetic* and *symbolic* was the prevailing character. He brought forward his doctrines in a *poem*, in which he introduced the Æons speaking in liturgical formulæ, and in imposing symbols of worship. (We shall hereafter introduce specimens of these latter.) After the Jewish cabalistic method, he hunted after mysteries in the number and the position of letters. The idea of a λογος του οντος, of a word as the revelation of the hidden Divine Being in creation, was spun out by him with the greatest subtilty; he made the whole creation a progressive expression of the inexpressible.* As the divine seeds of life,† which lie enclosed in the Æons, continually unfold themselves wider and individualize themselves, this represents, that these *names* of the unnameable being divide themselves into their separate sounds. An echo of the Pleroma falls down into the ὑλη, and becomes the formative principle of a new inferior creation.‡

---

* We can only mention Secundus in a cursory manner; for the only thing worth remarking about him is his modification of the ideas of Valentinus, by which he made a distinction in the first *ogdoad* between a τετρας δεξια and a τετρας αριστερα, naming the first, *light*, and the second, *darkness*: this is remarkable, because it shows that, like most mystics, in the pride of his speculation he placed *the original foundation of evil* in God, while he elevated God above the opposition of good and evil, but supposed that the seed of the division took its rise when the development of life began to proceed from God. Irenæus, l. i. c. 11. § 2. A similar view is found with those magi among the Parses, who taught, after Scharistani, that "Yezdan cogitasse secum; nisi fuerint mihi controversiæ, quomodo erit! Hancque cogitationem pravam, naturæ lucis minus analogam, produxisse tenebras, dictas Ahriman." (Hyde, Hist. Relig. Vet. Pers. p. 295.)

---

* Το ἀρρητον ῥητον γενηθηναι.
† The στερματα πνευματικα.
‡ In general, it is a peculiarly *Gnostic* idea, to conceive that the hidden Divinity *expressed himself aloud* till it was re-echoed, and *died away*, and then again that the *echo* fashioned itself into *a clear note [or tone, τον] and into a clear word*, for the revelation of the Divinity; and this idea they could apply under a variety of different relations. Thus Heracleon says. The Saviour is the *Word*, as the revelation of the Divinity, all the body of prophecy, which predicted him, without being justly aware of the idea of the Messiah, in its spiritual sense was only one note [ton,] which preceded the revealing word: John the Baptist, standing in the middle between the economy of the Old and of the New Testament, is the *voice* [or *tone, stimme,*] which is akin to the word, as the word expresses thoughts, with a consciousness of their meaning. The *voice* [stimme, voice, note, or tune,] becomes a *word*, when John becomes the disciple of Christ, and the note [or sound, ton] becomes a *voice* [stimme] when the prophets of the

The second of these, Bardesanes, who is still less to be reckoned as a proper disciple of Valentinus, lived at Edessa in Mesopotamia, as we learn from his name, "the son of Daisan," derived from a river of this name in the town of Edessa: he made himself known by his extensive learning; many among the older writings give notices of changes in the system of Bardesanes. According to the account of Eusebius, he was at first devoted to the system of Valentinus; but when he had seen, after accurate inquiry, how untenable much of it was, he went over to the orthodox Church; and yet at the same time retained much of his old doctrines, so that he became the founder of a peculiar sect. According to Epiphanius he went over from the orthodox Church to the Valentinians. But Ephraim Syrus, the learned Syrian writer, in the fourth century, who lived in the land of Bardesanes, and wrote in his language, and who had read his writings, gives us absolutely no notice whatever of these changes in the doctrinal notions of Bardesanes, and it is easy enough to explain how those false reports arose. Bardesanes, when he spoke publicly in the Church, like the rest of the Gnostics (see above,) made the *prevailing* doctrinal notions his starting point: he let himself down after his own fashion to the capacities of the *psychici*. On many single points he really coincided with those notions more than other Gnostics, and he might also, from sincere conviction, unite against many other Gnostic sects, at that time prevailing in Syria, as against those who denied the connection between the Old and the New Testament, or those who derived the visible world from an *evil* being, or those who held the doctrine of fate to the prejudice of moral freedom; just as the Gnostic Ptolemæus (see above) notwithstanding his Gnosticism, had also written against such people.

It was in entire accordance with the Valentinian system, that Bardesanes acknowledged something in the nature of man, incomprehensible to itself, and elevated above the whole world, in which the temporal consciousness of man develops itself; the human soul being a seed shed abroad from out of the Pleroma; its essence and its powers, which are derived from higher regions, remain, therefore, hidden even from itself, until it shall have arrived at a full consciousness and use of them in the Pleroma.* *This*, however, according to *the Gnostic system*, could only be true about the *spiritual natures*; but according to that system he must have ascribed to the *psychici* also, *a moral freedom, elevated above the power of the influences of nature, or the power of the ὑλη*. He, therefore, although like many of those inclined to Gnosticism, he busied himself with astrology, contended against the doctrine of such an influence of the stars (an εἱμαρμενη) as should be supposed to settle the life and affairs of man *by necessity*. Eusebius in his great literary treasure-house, the προπαρασκευη ευαγγελικη, has preserved a large fragment of this remarkable work; he here introduces among other things the Christians dispersed over so many countries, as an example of the absurdity of supposing that the stars irresistibly influence the character of a people. "*Where they are,*" he says of the Christians, "they are neither overcome by abominable laws and customs, nor does their nativity, deduced from their prevailing stars, compel them to practise the wickedness which is forbidden by their Lord. But they are subject to sickness, to poverty, to pain, and to that which is accounted shame by men. For as our freeman does not suffer himself to be compelled to slavery, and if he is compelled resists those who compel him, so on the other hand, the man who appears to us a slave,‡ does not easily escape from subjection. For, if every thing was in our own power, we should be το παν (the universe,) as, if we were not able to do any thing, we should be the *mere instruments of others*, and not of ourselves. But when God helps, every thing is possible, and no obstacle can exist, because nothing can resist his will.

Demiurgos, together with the Demiurgos himself, arrive at a consciousness of the higher world-system, which the Messiah reveals, and serve that system knowingly and willingly. Origen, t. vi. Joh. § 12. Ὁ λογος μεν ὁ Σωτηρ ἐστιν, φωνη δε ἡ ἐν τῃ ἐρημῳ πασα προφητικη ταξις, την φωνην οἰκειοτεραν οὐσαν τῳ λογῳ λογον γινεσθαι. τῳ ἠχῳ φησιν ἐσεσθαι την εἰς φωνην μεταβολην, μαθητου μεν χαριτι διδους τῃ μεταβαλλουτι εἰς λογον φωνη ἡ (it ought rather to be την,) δωλου δε τῃ ἀπο ἠχου εἰς φωνην.

* See Ephraem. Syr. Opp. Sys. Lat. t. ii. p. 553—5.

† [" Unser Erscheinungsmensch als ein dienstbarer," &c. The original is thus: 'ὡσπερ γαρ ὁ ἐλευθερος ἡμων ὑβριζοντος δουλουιν οὐκ ανηκιζεται, κἄν ἀναγκισθη, νιφισταται τις αναγκιζουσιν, οὐτως οὐδε ὁ φαινομενος ἡμων δουλος ὑβροπος της ὑποταγης ἐκφευγει ῥᾳδιως δυναται.—H. J. R.]

And even if any thing does appear to oppose him, it then happens so because he is the *Good, and suffers every nature to retain its peculiarities and its freewill.*[*] In accordance with his system he searched for traces of truth among all nations, and he remarked in the East Indies a class of sages (the Brahmins, Saniahs) who lived a rigid ascetic life, and amidst idolaters preserved themselves free from idolatry, and worshipped only the one God.

2. *The Gnostic sects, which denied the connection between the Old and New Testaments, and between the visible and the invisible world.*

(a.) *The Ophites.*

As Cerinthus formed the most natural point of transition from the *Judaizing* sects to the *Gnostics*,—so the *Ophites* make the most natural point of transition from the Valentinians to this second class of Gnostics; for it is here shown how the same ideas, by a slightly different turn, may lead to entirely different propositions.

In the system of *this sect*, as well as in that of the Valentinians, the notion of a soul of the world prevailed, of a weak reflection of light from the Pleroma, which falling down into matter, animated the dead mass, and yet was itself affected by matter also; this soul of the world, the source of all spiritual life, which attracts again to itself all which has once flowed from it, this Pantheistic doctrine, of which the seed had already been sown in the Valentinian system, in the Ophitic scheme, only comes forward in greater prominence, as the essential doctrines of Christianity are driven further into the back ground; and even in this respect again, different modifications appear to have found place in different branches of the Ophitic sects. The *same fundamental principle might, at the same time,* be conceived and applied in different modes, just according as the *Christian*, the *purely oriental and theosophic*, or *the Jewish* element happened to predominate in each case.

The *Ophitic* system represented the origin of the Demiurgos, who is here called *Jaldabaoth*, exactly in the same way as the Valentinian; and even in the doctrine of his relation to the higher order of the world, the point of transition (i. e. from one system to another,) may be easily recognised. The Valentinian Demiurgos is a limited Being, who imagines, in his finite faculties, that he acts independently. The higher order of the world is a thing altogether strange to him; he serves it without being conscious of it. In the phenomena which proceeded from it, he was at first entirely at a loss, he was surprised; but this is not the fault of a wicked disposition in him, only of his ignorance. At length he is attracted by the Divine nature, and out of a condition of unconsciousness, attains at length to a state of consciousness, and he now serves the higher order of the world with delight. According to the Ophitic scheme, on the contrary, he is a being not merely finite, but entirely at enmity with the higher order of the world, and obstinate in his hatred of it. Whatever of higher light he derived, in virtue of his descent from the Sophia, he only misused, that he might set himself up against the higher world, and make himself an independent Lord. Thence came the desire of the Sophia to detach him from the spiritual being which had accrued to him, and to draw this latter again to herself, in order that Jaldabaoth, with his whole creation, deprived of all reasonable being, might be destroyed. On the contrary, according to the Valentinian scheme, the Demiurgos forms, for all eternity, a subordinate grade of rational and moral existence; subordinate, indeed, but required for the harmonious development of the whole. And yet, here again, *kindred ideas* are found in the two systems, in the circumstance that the Demiurgos is obliged, without knowing it or wishing it, to serve the Sophia, and to bring to pass the fulfilment of her intentions, and in the end, even *his own fall and annihilation*. This, however, is here no distinction for the Demiurgos, as in the Valentinian system; but in this very circumstance he is placed exactly on the same footing with the Absolute Evil (the evil principle itself.) It flows not from the excellence of his nature, but from the omnipotence of the higher system of the world. Even the Evil Spirit, the *serpent-*

---

[*] [The passage which Neander has here selected is so limited that it does not give an adequate view of the meaning of Bardesanes. The argument of Bardesanes appears to be of this kind: Some things are αὐτεξούσια, and these things are changed sometimes in nations, others are not. The things that are in our own power are not bound down in stern laws of necessity by climate. Such things may be instanced, as circumcision and keeping of the Sabbath; these the Jews celebrate every where.—H. J. R.]

spirit, ὀφιομορφος whose existence arose from the circumstance that Jaldabaoth, full of hatred and envy against man, looked down into the ὑλη, and formed a reflection and image of himself there, even this being was obliged, against his will, to become only an instrument for the accomplishment of her designs. The doctrine of the origin and of the destination of man, in this system, has, however, much in common with the Valentinian, but at the same time, also, much which belongs to another branch of the Gnostic systems.

In order to establish himself as an independent Creator and Lord, and to hold in subjection the six angels* begotten by him, and to distract them, so that they should not look up to and observe the higher Light of the world, Jaldabaoth required his six angels to create man, as their common form, that such a work might set the stamp upon their independent Divine power.† They now create man, who is, however, as their likeness, a monstrous mass of matter, but without a soul; he crawls upon the earth, and is unable to hold himself upright. They bring, therefore, this helpless being, man, to their father, that he may bestow upon him a soul. Jaldabaoth communicated to him a living spirit;‡ and by that means the spiritual seed proceeded, without his being aware of it, from out of his being into the nature of man, whereby he himself became deprived of this higher principle of life: the Sophia had so decreed it. In man (i. e. in those men who have received any portion of the spiritual seed,) the light, the soul, the reason of the whole creation, concentres itself. Jaldabaoth is now seized with surprise and anger, because he sees a being, created by himself, and dwelling within the limits of his dominion, on the point of raising himself above him and his kingdom. Thence arose his endeavour, not to allow him to come to a consciousness of his higher nature, and of the higher world to which he is allied in virtue of that nature, and to keep him in a state of dull unconsciousness, and thereby of slavish servitude. It was from the jealousy of Jaldabaoth, who was thus limited, that there proceeded that command to the first man; but the soul of the world made use of the *serpent-spirit* (of the ὀφιομορφος) as an instrument in order to frustrate the design of Jaldabaoth, while through it she enticed the first man to disobedience. According to another view, the *serpent* was itself a symbol, or a veiled appearance of the soul of the world;* and those Ophites who held this doctrine are the persons, who, properly, bear the name of *Ophites*, because they worshipped the serpent as a holy symbol, to which a kindred notion of the Egyptian religion might have led them, because in that the serpent is considered as the symbol of Kneph, or the ἀγαθοδαιμων, which was similar to the σοφια of the Ophites. At all events it was the soul of the world, by which, either mediately or immediately, the eyes of the first man were opened.

The fall by sin (which gives us a characteristic trait in the Ophitic system,) was the point of transition from a condition of unconscious restriction to a condition of conscious knowledge. Man, become a being of knowledge, now renounces his allegiance to Jaldabaoth, who, being irritated at his disobedience, pushes him out of the ethereal region, where he had hitherto existed in an ethereal body, down into the dark earth, and banishes him into a dark body. Man finds himself now in such a condition, that on the one hand the seven star-spirits attempt to keep him in imprisonment, and to overwhelm the higher principle of consciousness within him,—while, on the other, the *evil* spirits of a purely material nature, endeavour to seduce him to sin and to idolatry, in order that he may become liable to the punishments of the severe Jaldabaoth. But yet the Sophia constantly strengthens anew the men who were of kindred nature with herself, by new communications of that higher spiritual nature; and she was able, during all the destructions and storms, to preserve a race of people belonging to herself from the time of Seth, whom all Gnostics look upon

---

* It must be observed, that according to the Ophitic system, Jaldabaoth and his six angels are the spirits of the seven stars,—the sun, the moon, Mars, Venus, Jupiter, Mercury, and Saturn: the same from which, in the books of the Zabians, and in many systems of Jewish Theosophists, a variety of delusions and seductions of mankind have proceeded.

† Thus they explain the words of Genesis i. 26.

‡ This they thought they found in Genesis ii. 7.

* The serpent, an image of the Ζωογονος σοφια; the form of the intestines winding itself represents the image of a serpent, a symbol of that wisdom of nature, that soul of the world, which winds itself concealed through all the grades of life found in nature. Theodoret. hæret. fab. vol. i. 14. One sees how far more the pantheistic principle here shines through these notions.

as the representative of the πνυματικοι, the men of a contemplative character, in which race she preserves the seed of the spiritual nature.

The doctrines of the Ophites corresponded with those of Basilides and the Valentinians, as to the relation of the *psychical Christ*, or Jesus, to the *Christ of the world* of Æons, who united himself to the former at his baptism. This only is peculiar to them (the Ophites,) that while the higher Christ descended through the seven heavens of the seven angels, or traversed the seven stars, in order to arrive at the earth, he appeared in each heaven, in a form akin to that heaven, as an angel allied to it, and that he concealed from them his higher nature, and attracting to himself all which they still possessed of the spiritual seed, he thus weakened their power. But now, when Jaldabaoth, the God of the Jews, saw his expectations frustrated by his Messiah, and when this Messiah did not further his kingdom as he had wished and expected him to do, but announced the unknown father as the instrument of the higher Christ, and destroyed the law of Jaldabaoth, or rather Judaism, Jaldabaoth then brought about his crucifixion. Jesus remained eighteen months on earth after his resurrection, obtained through the inspiration of the Sophia a clear knowledge of the higher truth, and then communicated it only to a few of his disciples, whom he knew competent to receive such mysteries. Jesus is now raised by the heavenly Christ into heaven, and sits at the right hand of Jaldabaoth, without the latter being conscious of it, in order that he may attract to himself, and receive into himself, all the spiritual substance, which is set free and purified by the operation of redemption among mankind, as soon as that substance has been detached from its covering of flesh. The more Jesus, by this drawing to himself all that is akin to him, is enriched in his own spiritual nature, so much the more is Jaldabaoth denuded of all higher qualities. The object of all this is to set free all the spiritual life which is held captive in nature, and to reconduct it to its original source,—to the soul of the world from which all proceeded: Jesus is the channel through which this happens. The *stars* also must at last be deprived of all being gifted with reason which is found in them.

In this family of Gnostics there were some who maintained even a more consistent pantheism, and supposed that the *same soul* was extended throughout the whole of nature, *animate* and *inanimate* and that, in consequence, all the life which was scattered abroad and held in imprisonment by the bonds of matter in the limited state of individual existence, would at last be attracted by the original source, the soul of the world, the Sophia, from which it had flowed forth, and thus flow back again into it through this channel. Such persons would say, when we use the objects of nature to our sustenance, we draw to ourselves seed which are scattered over them, and we raise them with us to the original source of all things.* Therefore, in an *apocryphal* gospel of this sect, the soul of the world, or the Supreme Being himself, spoke to the initiated thus: " Thou art I, and I am thou; and where thou art, there am I, and I am spread over every thing. Where thou wilt thou canst collect me, and where thou collectest me, there thou collectest thyself." (Chap. iii.)

Pantheism, and the intermixture of the natural and the Divine which flowed from it, by their very nature could not be very exacting in a moral point of view, although in *those men* who had embraced Pantheism, their *previously existing* moral sentiments might communicate even to the system itself a moral spirit which was foreign to its own nature. Pantheism, and a wild enthusiastic spirit of defiance towards Jaldabaoth, and his pretended restrictive statutes, appear in fact to have misled a part of these Ophites into the most unnatural excesses.†

---

* Epiphan. Hæres. 26. c. 9.

† As the accounts of Epiphanius in this matter agree with those of Clement of Alexandria, a person more worthy of credit, and of Porphyry, about similar Gnostic sects, and as they bear an entirely characteristic stamp upon them, we are by no means justified in calling their *correctness* into question. Nor can the fact alleged here be considered a thing to astonish us at all; similar excesses, arising from a pantheistic mysticism, have been often found, not only in the east, but in the west also, as the history of the sects of the middle ages and of modern times will prove. The latest examples may be found in De Potter's Via de Ricci. v. i.

The instances are too well known to readers of any general information to require specification. No references will, therefore, be given. It is enough to state the fact as illustrating a mental and spiritual phenomenon, but it is unfit to dwell upon.

[Other instances might be found in modern days where what was originally, perhaps, only a highly wrought speculative doctrine, became subject to this dreadful perversion. They could easily be cited, but it is needless, and perhaps,

It is of great importance towards the history of the Gnostic sects to inquire, although the inquiry be difficult of solution, whether these Ophites sprouted forth from a religious sect, which originally had no connection at all with Christianity, and whether, on that account, as a part of this sect had already appropriated to itself much which was Christian, a party existed also of those Ophites, who were quite out of the pale of Christianity, and who rather set themselves in hostility to it? The *latter* appears to be attested by an account given by Origen, who says, that the Ophites were *no Christians*, and that they suffered no one who did not curse Christ to enter into their assemblies. He names a certain Euphrates, who may have lived before the birth of Christ, as the founder of their sect.* The *Ophitic pantheism* may very probably have been borrowed from an older Oriental system of religion, and have been set in opposition to Christianity only by some, while it may have been clothed in a *Christian* garb by the others. The remarkable likeness between the *Ophitic* system, those of the *Sabians*, and the *Manicheans* may indicate an older and a common source in an antichristian Gnosis. But, on the other hand, it cannot be denied, that the Ophitic formulæ of adjuration, which Origen quotes immediately after this declaration, plainly contain allusions to Christian notions. And it may still be the case, that although the Ophitic sect appeared from the very first as a Christian sect, yet the contrast to the nature of Christianity which lay in its peculiar constitution also constantly became outwardly more prominent; and that, as the contrast between the Demiurgos and the Supreme God was so strongly brought forward by them, so also, in consequence of the distinction between the *psychical* and the *pneumatical* Christ, there arose at last in some portion of the Ophites, a hostile opposition to the former† (the *psychical;*) so that, to curse the finite Messiah of the psychici, became in the end a token to show that men were disciples of the higher Christ. Something similar is found in the sect of the *Sabians*, who referred *much* which they took out of the history of Christ *to a heavenly genius, the angel of life*, Mando di Chaje, whom they worshipped as the proper Christ, from whom *the true baptism* proceeded, while they referred *the rest* to the Antichrist Jesus, (who had counterfeited the baptism of John,) who was sent by the star-spirits for the seduction of mankind.

(b.) *Pseudo-Basilidians.*

As we see in the Ophitic system how entirely different a direction the principles allied to the Valentinian system may receive by a slightly different modification and application, so we find a similar circumstance in the relations borne by a *variety of the Basilidian scheme*, the doctrines of which are often confused with those of *the genuine Basilidians*. The calm and moderate spirit of the Basilidian system* was here entirely extinguished, and the direct opposition to the Demiurgos, and the Antinomianism, which was connected with it, degenerated here into a wild dreaminess that made light of all that is most holy. According to their theory, the redeeming Spirit† could enter into no connection with the detested dominions of the Demiurgos, and he took upon himself only the semblance of a corporeal form. When the Jews were minded to crucify him, he, as a highly gifted Spirit, knowing how to clothe himself in every kind of corporeal appearance, and to cast every sort of illusion before the eyes of the gross-minded multitude, caused Simon of Cyrene, (Mark xv.,) to appear to the Jews in *his likeness*; he himself took the form of this Simon, and raised himself up unencumbered into the invisible world, making a mockery of the deluded Jews. To these men the doctrine of the cross was foolishness; and in the conceit of their theosophic pride, they mocked those who confessed it as the confessors of a mere illusory phantom. "Such men," they would say, "are no Jews, neither are they Chris-

---

improper, as it might lead to inquiry on a subject, which could end only in disgust. It is enough to state the fact as a mental phenomenon, and to leave any specification till the assertion is called in question.—H. J. R.]

* Origen c. Cels. lib. vi. c. 28, &c. The obscure and uncritical Philaster, who sets the Ophites at the head of the antichristian sects, cannot be valid as an authority.

† I am indebted for this observation to the profound critique on my work about the Gnostics, written by Dr. Gieseler.

* Were it not that Clement of Alexandria spoke of practical errors in pretended followers of Basilides, similar to those found in this sect, we might be led to suspect that those whom Irenæus calls Basilidians had nothing whatever to do with Basilides.

† The νῦς. See p. 257, on the system of Basilides.

tians." They despised the martyrs as men who gave up their life merely to confess in the name of a phantom. "Those who are initiated into the true mysteries know well, that only one out of thousands can understand them: as your νους was able to make himself invisible to all men, so could they* also, like this your νους, hide themselves in all kinds of phantoms, and pretend to take a part in every thing, in order to deceive the gross multitude, and to withdraw from their persecutions."†

(c.) *Sethites and Cainites.*

THE example of the *Sethites* and *Cainites*, who most probably are derived from the same source as the Ophites, teaches us how the same Gnostic principles, by being differently applied, may produce an opposite kind of Gnosis. The *first* of these two sects maintained, that from the beginning *two* human pairs were created, the one by the angels of darkness, from which the race of χοικοι or υλικοι arose, the other, by the angels of the Demiurgos, from which the race of ψυχικοι was derived; that Cain sprung from the first, Abel from the second; and, the two opposite natures contending together, that the weaker psychical nature was overborne; but that then *Sophia* allowed Seth to be born in his stead, in whom (viz. Seth,) she had implanted the higher spiritual seed, by which he was rendered capable of overcoming the hylic principle. From Seth the πνευματικοι derived their origin; but, the opposing powers now seeking constantly to defile the propagation of this spiritual race by the intermixture of ungodly natures, *Sophia*, on this account, produced the deluge, in order again to purify the degenerated race; but her adversaries contrived to suffer a *Ham* to insinuate himself among those who were saved out of the mass of mankind that was destroyed, and by him their dominion was again to be set up and extended. Thence came new mixtures and disorders, and again *Sophia* had to endeavour to produce new purifications: Seth appeared at last in the person of the Messiah.

The *Cainites*, on the contrary, were abominable Antinomians; they went to such a length in their hatred to the Demiurgos and to the Old Testament, that they made all those whom they found represented in the latter (the Old Testament) in the worst colours, their Coryphæi, as being sons of *Sophia* and enemies of the Demiurgos; and hence they claimed Cain for their party. It was these persons who, while they considered the rest of the apostles as narrow-minded men, ascribed the higher Gnosis to Judas Iscariot, who effected the death of Jesus, because he knew, in virtue of his superior illumination, that the destruction of the dominion of the Demiurgos would by this means be brought about.

(d.) *Saturninus.*

WE recognise a peculiar branch of the Gnostic systems in the doctrines of Saturninus, who lived at Antioch in the reign of Hadrian; but we have, it must be confessed, in both the principal sources of information,† too imperfect data, to be able to recognise this system in its whole connection. (We pass over without mention whatever he has in common with the Gnostics, whom we have already described, as to the emanation-doctrines, and as to those of dualism.)

In the lowest grade of the emanation-world, on the very borders between the domain of light and the region of darkness, or of (Hyle) υλη, stood the seven lowest angels, those star-spirits; they unite together in order to win from the region of darkness a land on which they may carry on an independent kingdom. Thus arose our world, into different parts of which these star-spirits apportioned themselves, the God of the Jews being *at their head*: they carry on a constant war against the reign of darkness and Satan its prince, who will not suffer their dominion to be extended at the expense of *his*, and who constantly attempts to destroy that which they construct. Only a faint gleam from the higher regions of light shone down upon them here. This gleam of light filled them with a desire of it, and they wished to possess themselves of it, but were too weak to do so: it constantly recedes

---

* This art of becoming invisible is among the Cabbalistic arts also. A very remarkable instance of this fancy is to be found in Maimonides' history of his own life; and there are generally many interesting echoes of Gnosticism to be found in the latter Jewish sects, which *Beer* has delineated in his instructive history of the Jewish sects. (Brünn, 1822.)

† Irenæus i. 24.

† Epiphanius and Irenæus.

again, just as they desire to lay hold of it. They unite, therefore, in order to drive these higher beams of light into their dominion by means of a form cast after the image of that form of light which played before them. But the form of the angel is unable to raise himself into heaven; he cannot stand upright;* he is a lump of matter without a soul. The supreme Father, from the kingdom of light, at last takes compassion on man, being thus helpless, although made in *his* likeness; he communicates a spark of his own divine nature to him, and man, now for the first time, becomes a being endued with a soul, and can lift himself up to heaven. *In the human natures*, into which it is transplanted, this divine seed of life is to develope itself till it arrives at independence, and after a certain time to return to its original source. Those men who, bearing this Divine seed within them, are destined to reveal the Supreme God on earth, are constantly opposed to those who bear within them only the hylic principle, as being the instruments of the kingdom of darkness. The Supreme God, therefore,—in order to destroy both the kingdom of the star-spirits, of the God of the Jews, which endeavoured to render itself independent, and that of darkness also, and in order to set free those men who were akin to him (the Supreme God,) by means of the Divine seed of life, from the imprisonment of the star-spirits, and to procure them a victory over the kingdom of darkness,—the Supreme God sent his Æon νους down; this Æon being unable to enter into union in any way with the kingdom of the stars, or with the material world, could hence only show himself in the phantom (or semblance) of a corporeal form. The doctrines of Saturninus led to a strict system of asceticism, and to the precept of celibacy, which was possibly, however, observed only in its strictness by those who were *peculiarly initiated* into the sect, and not by its ordinary members.

(e.) *Tatian and the Encratites.*

TATIAN, of Assyria, lived in Rome as a rhetorician, and was there converted to Christianity by Justin Martyr, who had much in common with him, in virtue of the similar mental education he had undergone, as having formerly been a Platonist. As long as Justin lived he adhered to the doctrines of the Church.

And even farther, after the death of Justin, he composed an apologetic writing,* conceived in the same tone of thought, in which, however, there was much which might afterwards afford an opening for Gnosticism. Tatian in this writing, as his master Justin had done, received, after Philo, the Platonic doctrine about matter, in its whole extent, into his system, little calculated as that doctrine was to suit his system, as he at the same time maintained the notion of a creation out of nothing. This Platonic theory also prevailed upon him to maintain the notion of an undivine spirit of life, united with and akin to matter, a reason-counteracting soul; and hence he deduced evil spirits, whom he represents as πνευματα υλικα, little as this theory was in accordance with the Christian doctrine of the nature of the evil spirit, and of the origin of evil. Even in this writing he already maintained a proposition which was elsewhere transplanted by many of the first Christian Fathers from the Jewish theology; viz. that the souls of men, like every thing else, are formed out of matter, and are akin to it,† and therefore, by their nature, mortal; that the first man, living in communion with God, had within himself a *principle of divine life*, of a more elevated nature than this soul, sprung from matter, and that this principle was properly the image of God,‡ whereby he was immortal. By losing this through sin, he fell under the power of matter, and was subject to mortality.

It is easy to see how these opinions, which, according to Tatian's system, were not very consistent with each other, might serve as a means of introduction to the Gnostic ideas of the ὑλη, and of the difference between the ψυχικον, and the πνευματικον; and a system of asceticism, which strove after a complete detachment from the things of sense,§ might be the result.‖ According to the account of Irenæus¶ he formed for himself a system of Æons, like that of the Valentinians;

---

* See the history of the Ophites, page 47.

* His Λογος προς Ἑλληνας.
† Λ πνευλα υλικον.
‡ Θευ εικον και ομοιωστι.
§ [Entsinnlichung.—H. J. R.]
‖ According to Irenæus, i. 28, he maintained *at first* the condemnation of the first man, which would harmonize well enough with the difference we have remarked between the ψυχικ.r and the πνευματικον in the nature of the first man, which latter [i. e. the πνευματικον] he lost by sin.
¶ Comp. Clem. Strom. iii. 465. C. [Sylb. p. 100. Pott. p. 553. Klotz. vol. ii, p. 259.]

but this is not a sufficient ground to conclude with certainty that *his* system was connected with the Valentinian. According to Clement of Alexandria* he belonged to the class of anti-Jewish Gnostics; he referred the contrast made by St. Paul between the old and the new man to the relation between the Old and the New Testaments; but this also he might express according to the Valentinian Gnosis, which sets by no means an absolute opposition between the two systems of religion. A remark of Tatian, which has been preserved, appears to indicate, that he by no means so entirely detached the Demiurgos, the God of the Old Testament, from connection with the higher world.† The words of Genesis, "Let there be light," he considered (an instance, by the way, of his arbitrary mode of Scriptural interpretation) not as the words of a commandment given by the Creator, but as the words of prayer. The Demiurgos, sitting in dark chaos, prays that light may shine down from above. His wild, ascetic turn, however, may have arisen from the following circumstance, namely, that he made a more direct opposition between the creation of the Demiurgos and the higher world, and hence, also, between the Old and the New Testaments, than could find place according to the principles of the Valentinian school; for that practical opposition to the creation of the Demiurgos was usually founded in a theoretical one. Tatian wrote a book on Christian *perfection after the example of our Saviour*,‡ in which he sets forth Christ as the *ideal* of a single and abstinent life. If in this he kept simply to our canonical Gospels, and used no apocryphal narratives,§ in which the picture of Christ had already been drawn after a theosophico-ascetic model, much must have met him here in such direct opposition, that it might have removed him from this mode of thinking. But we see by an example how Tatian was able, by means of his illogical mode of interpretation, to explain into an accordance with his opinions the passages of Scripture the most unfavourable to him, since he could find in the passage in 1 Cor. vii. 5, that St. Paul sets marriage and incontinency on the same footing, and calls them both a service of Satan.* As the disposition for such a theosophic asceticism was then, having arisen in the east, widely diffused, it cannot surprise us to find that there were different sects of such *continentes*,† who had no immediate connection with Tatian.

To these belonged Julius Cassianus, who considered Adam as the symbol of souls sunk down out of a heavenly condition into the world of bodies, and he, therefore, made it a chief point that man should detach himself from matter by a strict asceticism, and on that very account also would not allow any appearance of Christ in the world of bodies; he was therefore, one of the *Docetæ*. He may, probably, have been an *Alexandrian Jew;* his peculiar opinions, his *doctrines* of the materialization‡ of souls and about *matter*, and his docetism, which last theory Philo had already applied to the Theophaniæ (appearances of God) of the Old Testament,§ fitted on remarkably well to notions which had long been current among the Alexandrian Jews, and in his

---

* Stromat. lib. iii. 460. D. [Sylb. p. 197-8. Potter, p. 548. Klotz, vol. ii. p. 259.]

† Thedot. Didascal. Anatol. fol. 806. Origenes de Oratione, c. 24.

‡ Περι του κατα τον σωτηρα καταρτισμου.

§ We should know more of this matter, if the ευαγγελιον δια τεσσαρων had been preserved. This writing appeared to the ancients to be a short harmony of the four Gospels, Euseb. iv. 29; but it is a question whether Tatian did not use, for that work, many apocryphal Gospels at least; as, according to the notice of Epiphanius, p. 26, which is, however, very indefinite—this collection appears to have had some similarity to the ευαγγελιον καθ' Ἑβραιους. Theodoret found more than two hundred copies of this writing in use in his Syrian diocese, and he found a necessity for sending them out of use, because, probably, he found much that was heretical in them.—Theodoret. Hæret. Fab. i. 20. Tatian.

* St. Paul gives permission in that passage only apparently; he withdraws again instantly from that which he permits, by saying, that those who follow his permission serve two masters. By their mutual abstinence united with prayer they would serve God; by the opposite conduct they would serve immodesty, lust, and Satan.—Strom. iii. p. 460. (See note to p. 109.) According to Eusebius iv. 29, he was accused of having made many changes in St. Paul's expressions; but from the words of Eusebius, τινας αυτον μεταφρασαι φωνας ὡς ἐπιδιορθουμενον αὐτον την της φρασεως συνταξιν, we cannot see plainly whether they were changes in favour of his own doctrinal and ethical principles, or changes from Hebraistic expressions into purer Greek; and then one is led to inquire whether Tatian really allowed himself to use such licence as a critic (which may have been the case,) or whether he had only different readings.

† Ἐγκρατιται ἀποτακτικοι.

‡ Einkörperung; Lit. *Embodying, Incorporation.*

§ See Philo on Exod. xxiv. 13. Opp. Ed. Mang. t. ii. p. 679, 656. de Abrahamo, 366. Ed. Francof.

ἐξηγητικα* he endeavoured apparently to introduce these notions into the Old Testament by an allegorizing mode of interpretation, an example of which is to be found in his explanation of Gen. iii. 21, by applying it to the material bodies in which fallen souls are clothed.

Such also were the persons who, after a certain Severus, called themselves Severiani, of whom we know nothing more than that they rejected the epistles of St. Paul and the acts of the Apostles. The first of these circumstances might lead us to *suppose* that they were derived from the Jewish Christians: but this cannot be considered as a proof, because it is also possible that, instead of taking refuge in forced and arbitrary interpretations, in order to bring the authority of those writings into harmony with their own principles, they found it an easier plan to throw away those writings entirely and at once.†

(f.) *Eclectic Antinomian Gnostics; Carpocrates and Epiphanes, Prodicians, Antitacti, Nicolaitans, Simonians.*

As on the one hand, we observe a tendency of Gnosis to *a strict asceticism*, which opposes itself to Judaism as to a sensuous and carnal religion,—so we remark, on the other, that it has also a tendency to a wicked antinomianism, which, confusing Christian freedom and unbridled license, set Christianity in opposition not only to the killing letter of a law, whose commands are outwardly, but to the very inward nature of the law itself, and which therefore, contended against Judaism, and with Judaism also against all moral law, as a thing too limiting for the inward life, and as proceeding from the limited and limiting Demiurgos. This was a misunderstanding against which St. Paul had given warning, when he developed the doctrine of Christian freedom.‡ We recognise in this a pantheistic mysticism, which opposed itself under various forms to the popular religions of the East, which had now mingled itself with the doctrines of the Greek philosophers of Alexandria, in consequence of the then intermixture of Oriental and western modes of thought, and which imagined that in Christianity, as a common religion for all mankind, which destroyed the Jewish exclusiveness, and the old popular religions, it could find a point on which it might engraft itself. *Such an antinomian* GNOSIS is shown in the system of Carpocrates and his son Epiphanes. The first probably lived in the reign of the emperor Hadrian, at Alexandria, where, at that time, there was a religious eclecticism which had struck the emperor himself.* He laid out a system of religion, which was propagated and extended by his son Epiphanes, a young man, who, by the perverse turn of mind given to him by his father, had abused great talents, but who died in the seventeenth year of his age. As Clement of Alexandria says, Carpocrates had busied himself much with the Platonic philosophy, and had instructed his son in it. The Platonic notions of the pre-existence of souls of higher knowledge, as being the remembrance brought from a former existence in heaven, are prominent parts in this system; and the originators of this system seem to have appropriated to themselves much out of the Phædrus of Plato. They made their Gnosis to consist in the recognition of one supreme first existence,† from which all being proceeds, and to which all being strives to return. The finite spirits, which had rule over the individual places of the earth, endeavoured to counteract this universal endeavour after unity; and from their influence, their laws, and their institutions, proceeded every thing which restrains, every thing which destroys and checks, the original and fundamental connection,‡ which is found in nature, considered as the revelation of that Supreme Unity. These spirits endeavour to retain unden their subjection those souls, which, having flowed from out of the Supreme Unity are akin to it, but have sunk down into the material would, and are imprisoned in the body so as to compel them, after death, to enter into new bodies, and to render them unable to raise themselves up in freedom to their original source. From these limiting spirits of the world proceed all popular religions. But those souls, which by the remembrance they retain of their former higher condition, elevate themselves to the contemplation of that Supreme Unity, attain the true freedom and tran-

---

* Clem. Strom. lib. i. 320. [Sylb. p. 138. Pot. ter, p. 378. Klotz, vol. ii. p. 71.]
† Theodoret. hæret. fab. i. 21
‡ Galat. v. 13. et alibi.

* See his Letter to the consul Servianus in Flavii Vopisci Vita Saturnini, c. ii. Illi, qui Serapin colunt, Christiani sunt et devoti sunt Serapi, qui se *Christi Episcopos* dicunt.
† Hence comes the phrase γνωσις μοναδικη, which occurs in Clement of Alexandria.
‡ [Gemeinschaft, communion, common nature.]

quillity, which nothing again can limit or destroy, and such souls raise themselves above the popular gods and popular religions. They considered a Pythagoras, a Plato, and an Aristotle, among the heathen, to belong to this class of men, and Jesus among the Jews. To him they ascribed only a peculiarly pure and powerful soul, by means of which, through reminiscences brought from his former existence, he raised himself up to the loftiest contemplation, freed himself from the limiting laws of the Jewish God, and destroyed the religion which had been established by that God, although he himself was brought up in it. By his union with the μονας he obtained Divine power, in virtue of which he was able to triumph over the spirits of the world, and the laws which they had imposed on nature, to perform miracles, and to endure sufferings in undisturbed tranquillity. By this divine power he was afterwards enabled in freedom to raise himself up again to the Supreme Unity, beyond the power of the spirits of the world. Thus this sect put *no difference* between Christ and other sages of all nations; they taught that every other soul also which could elevate itself to the same height of contemplation, was to be put on the same level with Christ. This sect hardly deserved the name of a *Christian* sect, since they only appropriated to themselves some propositions, taken at their own will and pleasure, out of Christianity, and then connected them with other ideas totally foreign to them. They preverted, after their own Pantheistic mysticism, the assertions made by St Paul of the nothingness of the merit of works, and about justification, not by works, but by faith; for under the name of faith they understood nothing but that mystical brooding over the absorption of the spirit into the original Unity. It needs only faith and love, they said; all outward things are indifferent; he who introduces a moral meaning into outward things, makes himself dependent upon them, and remains subject to the dominion of the spirits of the world, from whom all religious, moral, and political ordinances are derived, he cannot raise himself up after his death, out of the mere circle of Metempsychosis. But he who gives himself up to all kinds of pleasure, without being affected by it, and so despises the laws of those spirits of the world, he raises himself up to *union* with the ONE *First Being*, with whom, being already united here below, he has made himself free from all that can limit his nature.* Epiphanes wrote a book on righteousness, wherein he carries out the principle, that universal nature reveals a struggle after unity and communion; and that the laws of men, which are against this law of nature, but which are unable to conquer the desires planted by the Creator himself in the heart of man, first produced sin. Thus did he pervert what St. Paul had said of the insufficiency of the law to make man holy, and of its object, viz. to call forth the consciousness of guilt, in order that, with profligate pride, he might despise the ten commandments. These sects used to traffic much in magical arts, which they deduced from the power of their union with the First ONE, who is victorious over all the world-spirits; they worshipped an image of Christ, which was said to have come from Pilate, together with the images of heathen philosophers, who, like Christ, had raised themselves above the popular religion; and they worshipped it with heathen ceremonies, which latter certainly were not in accordance with the system of Carpocrates and Epiphanes, but proceeded from the superstition of their followers. At Same, the chief town of the island of Cephalonia, in the Ionian sea, from which the maternal ancestors of Epiphanes were sprung, this young man is supposed to have made so great an impression on the multitude, that they erected a temple, a museum, and altars to him, and offered him *divine worship*. As Clement of Alexandria,† a writer by no means of great credulity, relates this circumstance, which appears by no means incredible, if we take into account the circumstances of those times, we have no reason to doubt the fact. But, perhaps, it was only some members of this sect, which might have found peculiar success on the island; who offered this honour to him, as one of the greatest sages.‡

---

* Iren. i. 25.

† Strom. iii. 428. [Sylb. p. 183-4. Potter, p. 511. Klotz, vol. ii. p. 214-15.]

‡ The spirit of these antinomian, eclectic Gnostics, who arbitrarily jumbled together all religions, and all systems of philosophy, in which they could find a point whereon to fix their own system, as they might do in separate tenets detached from that with which they are connected, is shown in a marked manner in *two inscriptions* which were found very lately in the territory of Cyrene, and which prove the propagation of this sect to have lasted till the sixth century. They were published and explained by Gesenius in his Christmas thesis, 1825, [in dem Weihnachtsprogramm.]

To these unbridled *Antinomians* belongs the sect of the Antitacti (whose fundamental principle it was to set themselves in opposition to the Demiurgos, or the God of the Jews, who had sown evil, imperfection, and weeds, among the works of the Father of good,*) and the Prodicians, the followers of a certain Prodicus. These last maintained that they, as sons of the Supreme God, and as the royal race, were bound to no law, because for the king there was no written law; and hence they were lords of the Sabbath, lords over all ordinances. They apparently placed the worship of God only in the inward contemplation of the Divine nature; they rejected prayer, and probably all external worship, as fit only for puny spirits, who were still under the dominion of the Demiurgos; and they appealed to apocryphal writings that went under the name of *Zoroaster*.†

The first of them, in which the sect conceals itself under general expressions, which may, however, be taken in an innocent sense, ascribes the following words to Simon of Cyrene, whom the pseudo-Basilidians, who had the same sentiments, made a subject of their fictions: φωθ (Hermes Trismegistus, under whose name there exist spurious writings containing much Gnosticism,) Κρονος, Ζωροαστρης, Πυθαγορας, Επικουρος, Μασδακης. (Masdek, the founder of a Persian sect in the time of the Emperor Justinian, who appears, like Prodicus, to have drawn from apocryphal writings that went under Zoroaster's name. See Gesenius, l. c. p. 17.) Ἰωαννης, Χριστος τε και οἱ ἡμετεροι Καιρανακοι καθηγηται, (with which last Clement l. c. p. 722, also classes Prodicus,) συμφωνως ἐντελλουσιν ἡμιν μηδεν οἰκειοπ̔ισθαι, τοις δε νομοις αρηγειν, (*they understood* by these words, according to *their sense* of them, the νομος ἀγραφος, which is derived from the Supreme, is implanted in nature, and strives after communion and unity, with which (i. e. the νομος ἀγραφος) the separating and limiting ordinances of the Demiurgos, the spirits of the world and of men, are at variance,) και την παρανομιαν καταπολεμειν. τουτο γαρ ἡ της δικαιοσυνης πηγη (δικαιοσυνη here has the meaning of the divine natural justice, founded on that νομος θειος; on which Epiphanes wrote a treatise,) τουτο το μακαριον· ἐν κοινῃ ζην.

The other inscription, in which the sect comes forward without disguise, is in the following terms: ἡ πασων οὐσιων και γυναικων κοινοτης πηγη της θεας ἐστι δικαιοσυνης, εἰρηνη τε τελεια τοις του τυφλου, ὀχλου ἐκλεκτοις ὀρχθεις ἀνδρασιν, οὓς Ζαρθης τε και Πυθαγορας, των ἱερεφαντων μιστοι, κοινῃ συμβιωτων συνιντο. We cannot, however, exactly maintain more decidedly, that these inscriptions proceed from the sect of Carpocratians, because so many similar sects, as the Prodicians, the pseudo-Basilidians, the Nicolaitans, &c., had the same principles.

* Τὸ ἀντιτασσεσθαι.

† Clem. Strom. l. 304. [Sylb. p. 131. Potter, p. 357. Klotz, vol. ii. p. 50;] iii. 438. [See Sylb. p. 189, et seq. Potter, p. 526, et seq. Klotz, vol. ii. p. 230.] vii. 722. [Sylb. p. 306-7. Potter, p. 854-5; Klotz, vol. ii. p. 236.]

To this family of Gnostics belong also the Nicolaitans, if the existence of any such sect can be proved. Irenæus, indeed, names such a sect as existing in his time, deducing them from Nicolaus the deacon mentioned in the Acts, and he believed that he found their portraiture in the second chapter of the Revelations.* But it may be doubted whether Irenæus has really penetrated the meaning of the Revelations in this case, and whether the name of Nicolaitans is the proper name of a sect, and still farther, whether it is the name of a Gnostic sect. The passage relates to such persons as seduced the Christians to partake in the heathen feasts at a sacrifice, and the excesses consequent upon them, as the Jews had formerly suffered themselves to be seduced by the Moabites. (Num. xxv.) The name of Nicolaitans might also be a merely *symbolical* name, as such an usage of it would suit very well with the whole character of the Revelations: "destroyer of the people," "seducer of the people," like Balaam, and thus Nicolaitans might mean Balaamites in this sense.† Now it was a favourite idea with Irenæus, that the apostle St. John had actually contended with many different sorts of Gnostics; and he was in the habit of searching for remarks which were meant to oppose the Gnostics, in the writings of St. John. As he found several of those errors, which are blamed in the Revelations, among the Gnostics of his own day, he concluded that the practical errors contended against by the Apostle had also had their foundation in a theoretical Gnosticism, and the name induced him to deduce them from the well known Nicolaus. But, in fact, we find in Irenæus only such *indefinite expressions* in regard to this sect, that it by no means follows necessarily that he wrote from any decided view of them. If we had only the account given by Irenæus, we must acknowledge it as possible that the story of this sect may have arisen solely out of a misunderstanding of the Revelations. Although it might then surprise us that Irenæus, without any ex-

---

* Irenæus i. 26. This refers to their practical errors: qui indiscrete (ἀδιαφόρως) vivunt.—In loc. cit. 11, he speaks of their speculative errors, but he does not altogether separate them from other Gnostics, in order to bring forward what is peculiar to them.

† Balaam, that is, νικολαος; according to the etymology which deduces this name from בָּלַע and עָם.

ternal evidence to induce him, should have made a man, distinguished by having a public office conferred on him by the apostles, the founder of a heretical sect. But such a mistake could never be laid to the charge of that learned Alexandrian Clement, an unprejudiced man, and one accustomed to historical criticism; and he appeals to facts which could not have been invented. There were people who had the corrupt principles which we have mentioned before, viz. that man must conquer his desires by giving himself up to them and not allowing himself to be affected by them, and that he must abuse his flesh and annihilate it by its own instrumentality, in order to show his contempt for it: their motto was words to this effect, which they ascribed to the deacon Nicolaus.* The same Clement afterwards, in another passage, quotes another trait out of the life of this Nicolaus, which this sect used in order to justify their own excesses.† The apostles, it would seem, had reproached him with his jealousy about his wife, and in order to show how little this reproof would attach to him he brought her forward and said, "Let him that will, marry her." But Clement was far from holding Nicolaus to be the founder of this sect, although the sect itself claimed him. He clears the character of that man of the Apostolic Church, and quotes the tradition, that this Nicolaus lived in unspotted wedlock to the end of his days, and left children, whose conduct was irreproachable, behind him. We see, therefore, that Irenæus did not err in *supposing the existence of such a sect, but only in not examining more carefully its pretences.* It was the fashion for such sects, as we have often before remarked, to engraft themselves to some great man or other of antiquity, in their choice of whom they were often guided by accidental circumstances. Thus the Nicolaitans made Nicolaus, the deacon, their founder, without any fault of his. Clement thought that they had only corrupted his words and actions in a perverted manner, and he endeavours to explain both one and the other in a more favourable mode; but one is led to inquire whether Clement has viewed it in a sufficiently critical manner. All which is here ascribed to Nicolaus bears a very apocryphal stamp upon it; and perhaps, that sect had a life of that Nicolaus, in which all this was found, put together by themselves or by others from fictions and unauthentic traditions. If this sect be not the same which was in existence in the apostolic times, a point which cannot be decided with certainty,* the name of the Nicolaitans in the Apocalypse may have induced the later sect to name itself after Nicolaus. But as they probably belonged to the party of anti-Judaizers, and therefore, acknowledge only St. Paul as an apostle, they would also be induced by what they read in the Apocalypse to maintain the antiquity of their sect, as one which the Judaizing St. John had opposed; and the name induced them naturally to deduce it (i. e. the sect) from that Nicolaus. We have before found instances in which the Gnostics chose for their founders persons who appear in an unfavourable light either in the Old or the New Testament.

The Simonians are also to be mentioned here, an eclectic sect, which it is difficult to bring into any *one* definite class, because they appear to have attached themselves, sometimes to heathenism, sometimes to Judaism, or to the religious opinions of the Samaritans; and appear to have been sometimes strict ascetics, sometimes wild despisers of all moral laws (the Entychites.) Simon Magus was their Christ, or at least a form assumed by the redeeming spirit which had appeared also in Christ, whether it was that in their first origin they had really proceeded from the party founded by that Goeta (magician,) mentioned in the Acts, or whether the sect which arose later, merely to please their own fancies, had made Simon Magus, whom the Christians abominated, their Coryphæus, and had forged under his name pretended books relating to the higher wisdom. What some learned men have supposed, viz. that another Simon, distinct from that old Simon Magus, founded their sect, and that he was confused with that older Simon Magus, is too arbitrary a supposition, and is by no means

---

* Το δυν παραχρησασθαι τη σαρκι. Strom. ii. p. 411.
† Strom. iii. p. 436.

* Even supposing that the name Nicolaitans in the Apocalypse should be really the proper name of a party founded by a person named Nicolaus, and that the mere existence of the name there had given occasion for allusions to Balaam, it would still not be a necessary deduction from these premises that this party which was then in existence was a *Gnostic* sect.

required for the elucidation of the historical phenomenon presented to us.*

(g.) *Marcion and his School.*

MARCION forms the most natural close to the series of the Gnostics, because he belongs to the Gnostics only *on one side*, and, on another, rather forms a contrast to them: he stands on the boundary between the Gnostic turn of mind, where speculation was the prevailing characteristic, and a character of mind thoroughly opposed to speculative Gnosticism. Christian feeling is far more appealed to by him than by other Gnostics, because his whole being was far more deeply rooted in Christianity, because Christian feeling was the keynote of his whole inward life, and his whole religious and theological character, while among the rest of the Gnostics this (although sometimes the prevailing turn of mind,) formed only *one* of the dispositions belonging to them, and was intermixed with much of a different character. It is instructive to mark how an endeavour, which proceeded from the very depths of Christianity, could receive an unchristian turn by means of a gross partiality; it is a warning and a startling circumstance to see a man, whose errors themselves were connected with a spirit of love, only that it was a mistaken spirit, and a man, to whom the Christ who filled his heart was one and all, misunderstood and called a heretic by most of the Christians of his own day, because they were unable to understand *his* mode of conception, and indeed, chiefly by those who might have dwelt in the most intimate communion with him, in virtue of that which they bore within their hearts, if any other mode of communication had existed besides those of words and definite ideas, (begriff:) any other mode than that which is only a dim reflection of the inward life,—a source of so many misunderstandings and mutual mistakes among men, which would be removed if one man could read the inward life and conscience of another! What Marcion had in common with the Gnostics, and particularly in common with the Gnostics of this class, was partly the distinction which he made between the God of nature and of the Old Testament, and the God of the Gospel, and the distinction between the Divine and the human generally, as well as many speculative elements, which he connected with his system of religion. And yet he had evidently arrived at that which he had in common with them by an entirely different road. It was in Christ that he first found his God; and that glory of God which had revealed itself to him in Christ, he was never able to find again in nature and in history. The speculative elements, which he borrowed from other Gnostics, were to him only necessary aids to fill up the gaps which his system, being founded on

---

* This Simon Magus, to whom properly no place belongs among the founders of the *Christian* sects, has obtained an undeserved importance in the old Church, by being made the father of the Gnostic sects. As the representative of the whole theosophico-goetic character, in opposition to the simple faith in revelation, he has become in the same manner a *mythical* personage, and given rise to many fables; as, for instance, that of his disputation with St. Peter, and his unhappy attempt at the art of flying; and the *Clementine* is the place where the fable is most ingeniously conducted. But it was an extraordinary circumstance that Justin Martyr, in his second apology before the Roman emperor, should appeal to the fact, that there was a statue at Rome to this Simon Magus, on an island in the Tiber, (ἐν τῳ Τιβερι ποταμῳ μεταξυ των δυο γεφυρων) with the inscription, Simoni Deo Sancto. Although such Goetæ at that time found much acceptance even with the highest classes, yet one can hardly believe that it could have amounted to the erection of such a statue and to a decree of the senate, by which Simon Magus was received into the number of the Dii Romani. We should be obliged to question the correctness of Justin's assertion, even if we were not able to explain the cause of his error. But this seems now to be ascertained, as in the year 1574, at the place designated by Justin Martyr, a stone was dug up, which seemed to have been the pedestal of a statue, and it bore the inscription, "Semoni Sanco Deo Fidio Sacrum." Now certainly this statue was not erected by the Roman senate or emperor, but by one Sextus Pompeius; but Justin, full of the histories then current about Simon Magus, overlooked this, and confused the Semo Sancus (a Sabine Roman deity, which might have remained unknown to Justin, well acquainted with the Greek, but not with the Roman mythology,) with Simo Sanctus, especially as in the surname of that deity Sanctus was sometimes written instead of Sancus. Tertullian, indeed, as better acquainted with the Roman antiquities, might have been able to form a better judgment on the matter, but in such cases he was too prejudiced, and too little inclined to the critical art, to investigate any farther an account which was to his own taste, and came also from a man of reputation. The more critical *Alexandrians* do not mention the circumstance, and Origen, lib. i. contr. Cels. c. 57, by saying that the name of Simon Magus was known beyond Palestine only to the Christians, who knew him from the Acts of the Apostles, seems himself to stamp the story of a statue erected to him at Rome as a fiction. The Samaritan Goetæ and founders of sects, *Dositheus* and *Menander*, (who is made out to be a disciple of Simon Magus,) are even less deserving still of any particular mention in a history of Christian sects.

an entirely different and a *wholly practical* plan, would necessarily have. It was evidently not his intention, like that of other Gnostics, that Christianity should be completed by means of the speculative conclusions of other doctrinal systems, but he wished originally only to restore again to its purity Christianity, which had, in his opinion, been adulterated by admixtures foreign to its nature. The partial point of view, from which he set out with this disposition, was the occasion of most of his errors.

He did not make a secret doctrine the source of the knowledge of this genuine Christianity; but he would not suffer himself to be bound by *a general Church tradition*, because, in his opinion, foreign matter had already mixed itself in such a tradition with pure Apostolic Christianity. As a genuine Protestant (if we may transfer to an ancient day this appellation which arose, indeed, later, but denoted a genuine primitive Christian turn of mind,) he wished to consider the word of Christ and of his genuine disciples [i. e. original apostles, Tr.] the only valid source of a knowledge of the true Gospel. He certainly, instead of recognising the many-sidedness of Christianity from the variety of the instruments selected for its propagation, allowed himself to make an arbitrary division between them, founded on a one-sided view. His endeavour to find the genuine documents of pure original Christianity, led him into historical and critical investigations, which were far removed from the *contemplative* disposition of the other Gnostics. But he gives us here a warning example, how such inquiries, as soon as they are swayed by the preconceived doctrinal opinions, in which the thoughts are fettered, must lead to unhappy results, and how easily an arbitrary hypercriticism is formed in opposition to an uncritical credulity; how easily, in short, man, in struggling against *one* class of doctrinal prejudices, falls into another.

The other Gnostics united a mystical allegorizing interpretation of Scripture with their theosophic idealism. The single hearted Marcion was a zealous enemy of this artificial mode of interpretation. He was, on the contrary, a warm adherent of the *literal interpretation* which was in vogue among the opponents of the Gnostics; and it was shown in his case, how even this mode of interpretation, if it is not combined with other hermeneutic principles, and if it is carried to the extreme, must lead to arbitrary results.

The opposition between $\pi\iota\sigma\tau\iota\varsigma$ and $\gamma\nu\omega\sigma\iota\varsigma$, between an exoteric and an esoteric Christianity, belonged to the essential attributes of the other Gnostic systems; but it was impossible that such an opposition could be recognised by Marcion, whose attachment was chiefly to the practical St. Paul. With him $\pi\iota\sigma\tau\iota\varsigma$ was the common source of Divine life for *all* Christians; he knew nothing higher than *the illumination which all Christians* ought to have; that which he recognised as true Christianity was to be known and recognised as such by all who were generally capable of receiving Christianity; and the only difference he could make was that between mature Christians, and those who still needed farther instruction in Christianity (i. e. Catechumens.) This characteristic of Marcion's doctrine, so wholly unlike the usual spirit of Gnosticism, leads us to conclude that it received its development also in a wholly different mode. But, alas, we have no authentic accounts of the life of Marcion, so as to enable us to inquire into that point satisfactorily. Many gaps in that life can only be filled up by conjecture.

He was born in Pontus in the first half of the second century. If the account of Epiphanius is founded in fact, his father was bishop of that Church; but even then, if it be true, it is still most probable that he was elected to that office when Marcion was already a youth or arrived at the age of manhood; for it is most probable, if we may judge from the development of his system, that Marcion lived the early part of his life as a Heathen, and afterwards turned to Christianity from the free impulse of his own heart. Like many others, he felt himself, in the first glow of faith and love, impelled to renounce every thing earthly; he bestowed his goods or a part of them on the Church, and began to live* as a *continens* or $\dot{\alpha}\sigma\kappa\eta\tau\eta\varsigma$† in strict self-denial. His contempt of nature, which was at first only of a *practical* and *ascetic* kind, proceeding from a falsely conceived opposition between the natural

---

* Pecuniam in primo calore fidei Ecclesiæ contulit. Tertull. adv. Marcion. lib. iv. c. 4. When Epiphanius calls Marcion a $\mu o\nu\alpha\zeta\omega\nu$, he is only making a confusion between the circumstances of his own and of earlier times; and by the word $\mu o\nu\alpha\zeta\omega\nu$ we must understand an $\dot{\alpha}\sigma\kappa\eta\tau\eta\varsigma$. Ephraem Syrus, blames Marcion for acquiring a delusive reputation through his asceticism. Opp. Ed. Lat. Sermo 1. p. 438, and seq.

† See above.

and the Divine, might now, under a variety of different influences, lead a man of a soul so impetuous in its apprehensions and so abrupt in its determinations as his, to a theoretically conceived separation between the God of nature and the God of the Gospel. Nature appeared so cold and stiff to his heart, filled and glowing with the image of the God of love and mercy, as he appeared in Christ. He was, doubtless, right in the belief that the contemplation of nature cannot lead to the knowledge of that Father of love and mercy; he was right in his opposition against the *Deist*, who sets the preaching of nature on the same level with that of the Gospel, and who finds in nature alone and by itself a temple of eternal love; but Marcion was always inclined to push matters to the extreme. Even in history, Marcion, full of the glory of the Gospel, thought that he could find no trace of the God who had revealed himself to him there, (i. e. in the Gospel;) he, like many other zealous Christians, would look back into the heathen world only with horror, and it appeared to him nothing *but the kingdom of Satan;* but even in the Old Testament he could not find again his God and his Christ; his fiery and impatient spirit, which was too deficient in calmness and reflection, to be able properly to investigate the relation between the Old and New Testament, was now at once struck with the contrast between the two forms of religion. He had no notion of a gradual (literally pædagogical) development of the Divine revelation, and Judaism appeared to him too carnal to have proceeded from the same source as the spiritual religion of Christianity; and he believed that that same God of love, of mercy, and compassion, whom he knew from the Gospel, was not to be recognised here, (i. e. in the Old Testament.) It is easy to see that (after this notion of the contrast between the Old and the New Testament had once become the prevailing idea in his soul,) if he, standing in this position, considered the Old Testament, he would be able to find many points on which he could rest this opinion. We must add also, that, according to his principles of a thoroughly literal interpretation of the Bible, he believed that all the anthropomorphical and anthropopathical expressions of the Old Testament must be maintained *to the very letter*, without distinguishing the idea from the dress in which it is clothed.

A man of Marcion's character would naturally be induced by opposition only to develope himself more strikingly in his partial views, and to harden himself in them. In reality he had to contend with such an opposition, and this contention had, no doubt, a remarkable influence on the formation of his religious and doctrinal views. There was, in existence, to say the truth, at that time, particularly in Asia Minor, a false turn of mind, which interpreted the Old Testament without sufficient spirituality, which did not sufficiently distinguish between the different positions taken in the two dispensations, and which in many doctrines (as, for example, the doctrine of Christ's kingdom, the idea of a millenarian kingdom,) mixed up a carnal Judaism with Christianity. This disposition he combated with violent zeal, and blamed, not wholly without foundation, those who were its slaves with adulterating the Gospel, and hence there might easily arise in his mind a suspicion of the genuineness of the whole traditional system of the Church, ($\pi\alpha\rho\alpha\delta o\sigma\iota\varsigma$,) and of the Biblical documents which he had received from that tradition; and hence, also, he may have been induced to endeavour, by his own inquiries, to form for himself a Christianity, purified from all that was foreign to its nature. His contention with this too Jewish disposition then drove him also constantly to conceive the contrast between the Old and the New Testament more and more sharply, and in many things to suppose unjustly that Christianity had been adulterated by Judaism. This enmity of his towards the Old Testament, and many of his opinions connected with it, were, probably, the cause of his being excommunicated at Sinope. On this he travelled to Rome, with a view of seeking whether he could not, in the Church of the metropolis of the world, discover friends to his opinions, which, he was fully persuaded, were the principles of genuine Christianity; and the number of anti-Jewish feelings then prevailing in the Roman Church[*] might give him hopes of success. If the account of Epiphanius is to be relied on, Marcion must have inquired of the Roman clergy how they explained the passage in Matt. ix. 17, in order to elicit from their own mouth the avowal that the new wine of Christianity cannot be poured into the old bottles of Judaism without destroying them. But in Rome also his Dualism in the

---

[*] See in the history of the Cultus, p. 67.

doctrine of the revelation of God could meet with nothing but contradiction, because the acknowledgment of the one same God and of the one same Revelation in the Old and in the New Testament was a portion of the Catholic doctrine of the Church. Rejected here also by the Church, he was driven into forming his anti-Church dispositions into a firm determinate system, and founding an independent community. Up to this time his system had been only founded on practical considerations: the conviction that Christianity had appeared in human nature as something wholly new, unexpected, and unforeseen; that it had communicated to human nature a Divine life, to which there had hitherto been nothing akin in man; that the God, who appeared in Christ, had never before revealed himself, either by nature, by reason, or by the Old Testament, and that nothing bore witness to him, nothing was his work but Christianity;—this was the conviction from which Marcion set out. (It may be a question, whether he had at that time carried out his system farther than this.) But these persuasions, proceeding from his inward Christian life, must have led a thinking man to many inquiries which he could not answer. A Gnostic system would be able to fill up these gaps in his doctrinal views: he might there learn to acknowledge a Demiurgos, different from the perfect God, as the God of nature and of the Old Testament; and a contempt for nature, and a hatred towards matter, as the source of evil, would correspond to his ascetic dispositions. The *Syrian* Gnosis, which, as we have remarked, maintained these points very definitely, would naturally suit him exactly. And thus it happened that he joined himself to one Cerdo, a teacher of this Gnosis, who came from Antiochia, and he borrowed from him the principles needed for the completion of his dogmatical system.

The very nature of Marcion's opinions necessarily implied that he would labour for the propagation of his principles with more zeal and activity than other Gnostics; for, while others believed that they could impart their higher knowledge only to a small portion of Christians, to *the spiritual*, Marcion, on the contrary, was persuaded that his was no other than the original Christian doctrine, which ought to belong to all mankind; and he would, therefore, feel himself impelled to communicate to all Christians the light of truth which had been imparted to him. He, therefore, made several voyages; he spent his life in many struggles both with Heathens and with Christians; to be hated and to suffer he considered as the destination of Christians. "My fellows in being hated, my fellow-sufferers," (συμμισουμινοι και συνταλαιπωροι,) was his usual address to his disciples.* Perhaps, he was at Rome, when Polycarp, the aged bishop of Smyrna, visited Anicetus, bishop of Rome.† Marcion, who, in his youth, apparently had lived on terms of friendly intercourse with the former, and saw him again now after a long lapse of years, went up to him and addressed him thus, "Dost thou remember me, Polycarp?" But this old man, otherwise so full of charity, refused to receive none but the enemies of the Gospel into his kindly affections; and such Marcion appeared to him, for he was unable to recognise in him the Christian character, which was in fact the very foundation of his errors. He answered him, therefore, "Yes; I know the first-born of Satan!" Tertullian‡ relates that Marcion at length testified his regret at the schism which had arisen in the Church; that he had prayed to be again received into the communion of the Church, and that this prayer had been granted, on the condition that he should bring back to the Church those who had been seduced away by him, a condition which his too early death prevented him from fulfilling. It must be avowed that we cannot implicitly trust this account, nor are we able to say whether there be any foundation for it in truth; nor even in that case, *what foundation* there is. Since with Marcion every thing proceeded from the heart, it might easily happen that while he sighed after Christian communion and perceived the evil consequences of schisms, he should at last be softened as his age increased, and should seek again to attain peace with the majority of Christians.

It still remains for us to consider somewhat more closely the system formed by an union between the *practical* disposition of Marcion, and the Gnostic principles of Cerdo. In its fundamental principles this system harmonized with the other Gnostic systems of this second class, only with the distinction, that it was always made pre-eminently clear, that *he* conceived every thing more from

---

* Tertullian, c. M. iv. 36. iv. 9.
† See above; ‡ Præscript. c. 30.

a *practical* than from a *speculative* point of view, and that he was not so deeply interested in what was merely speculative. He assumed three fundamental principles:—

1. A ὑλη, which had existed from all eternity.

2. The *perfect*, almighty, holy God; the God who is Eternal Love, the Good, ὁ ἀγαθος, who alone is to be called God in any proper sense; who, in virtue of his holy essence, cannot come into any contact whatever with matter; who forms only through communication of himself a life akin to himself, and does not act on that which is without.

3. The Demiurgos, a subordinate Being, of limited power, standing between good and evil, who is named a God only in an improper sense (as the name of God is transferred also to other beings, Ps. lxii.,)* who is in avowed enmity with matter, and endeavours to bring it into subjection to himself, and to form it, but is never able wholly to subdue its opposition.† The ungodly Being of matter, which resists all fashioning and forming, is the source of all evil; and this ungodly Being, concentrated in that power of blind impulse which is associated with matter, is Satan. The distinction he draws between true moral perfection, which consists in holiness and love, whose essence it is only to impart itself, only to bless, to make happy, to redeem—and bare righteousness, justice, or uprightness, which weighs every one according to merit—rewards and punishes, recompenses good with good, and evil with evil, and which brings forth only outward propriety of conduct,—this was the fundamental practical notion, on which all Marcion's other notions rested. Whilst some formed to themselves assuredly too gross anthropopathical representations of the retributive justice of God, which could not well be reconciled with the idea of a God, who is Love. Marcion, in combating these representations, (as he was generally, from his impetuous and rugged nature, inclined, in controversy, to carry matters to the utmost extremity,) made out an absolute contradiction between justice and holiness, so that it was impossible, in his opinion, that both attributes should exist side by side in the same being. It must be confessed, that while he opposed *justice* to *holiness*, and under the former name collected together all the marks which he believed that he could find in the Old Testament (when interpreted and considered in his own prejudiced views,) as characteristic of the Demiurgos, he made to himself a conception of *justice*, which was by no means consistent or tenable; intimate consistency, with him, always depended more on the *heart* than on *abstract conceptions*.

As far as our present means of information extend, the mode in which Marcion considered the relation of the Demiurgos to the perfect God, in reference to the origin of the latter, appears very indefinite. As we find elsewhere, among the Gnostics, nothing but Dualistic systems, and none in which *three* principles, wholly *independent on each other as to their origin*, were acknowledged, it seems most natural to look on the matter in the following light, viz: that Marcion also deduced the origin of the imperfect Demiurgos, according to a certain line of development, from the perfect God—and certainly it is the notion which comes most readily into the human mind, to deduce that which is imperfect from that which is perfect. There is nothing to contradict this supposition; for, even if we grant that no passage is found in ancient authors, from which it can strictly be proved that Marcion derived the origin of the Demiurgos from the Supreme God,* yet, at any rate, there is no passage, in any writer worthy of credit, on such a point, from which the contrary can be proved. We can only say, that the indefiniteness in the accounts of ancient writers arises from the circumstance that Marcion, interested only in the practical view of these subjects, has not declared himself with sufficient definiteness, in a speculative point of view, on the relation of the Demiurgos to the Supreme God.

The point, then, which Marcion deemed of practical importance, was to maintain the doctrine of *a wholly new creation*, by means of Christianity, and to cut in sunder that thread, by which Christianity might be connected with the world, as it was in its earlier condition. The Demiurgos, therefore, of Marcion, did not act in obedience to more lofty ideas, to which he was subservient, as an instrument,

---

* Clem, Strom. lib. iii. p. 425. Tertull. c. M. lib. i. c. 7—15.

† Ephr. Syr. Orat. 14, p. 468, D.

* And yet one of the Fathers, Rhodon ap. Euseb. v. 13, says that Marcion acknowledged only δυο ἀρχας.

although unconsciously, or even against his own will, but he was an entirely independent, self-existent, Creator of an imperfect world, which corresponded to his own limited nature. On this account Marcion did not assume, with the other Gnostics, that to man, as the image of the Demiurgos, a still higher principle of life was imparted by the Supreme God; but he recognised in the whole nature of man, as a work of the Demiurgos, only such elements as could proceed from such a Creator. The Demiurgos created man, as the highest work of his creation, after his own image, to represent and to reveal it. The body of man he formed out of matter, whence its evil desires; to this body he imparted, out of his being, a soul akin to himself. He gave him a law, in order to prove his obedience, and to reward or to punish him according to his desert. But the limited Demiurgos could never have imparted to man a Divine principle of life, capable of triumphing over evil. Man yielded to the temptations of sensual pleasure, and thereby was subjected, with his whole race, to the dominion of matter, and the evil spirits, which were its offspring. Out of the whole race of degraded man, the Demiurgos chose only one people for his own especial guidance. He revealed himself peculiarly to this people, the Jews, and gave them a religious code, consisting—as it corresponded to his own nature and character—*on the one hand* of a ceremonial religion, which busied itself only in externals, and *on the other* of a positive (literally, commanding,) imperfect morality, without an inward Divine life, without any power to produce a true inward sanctification, without the spirit of love. He rewarded those who faithfully observed this law, with a happy condition after death, adapted to their limited nature, in company with their pious forefathers.*

The Demiurgos was not powerful enough to make his people the ruling nation, and to extend his dominion over the whole earth: but he promised to those who were devoted to him, a Redeemer, a Messiah, through whom he would at last obtain this object in a contention with the hostile powers of the ὐλη, and through whom he would gather together the scattered Jews, exercise a severe judgment over the heathen and **sinners, and lead his people to an undisturbed enjoyment of all earthly happiness, in a kingdom that should rule over the whole earth.** But the perfect God, whose nature is compassion and love, could not allow this severe sentence, upon men who were overcome by their own weakness, to take effect. It is consistent with his character not to look to merit, like the Demiurgos, but out of free love to take care of those who are altogether alien to him, of the lost; and not to begin with proposing a law, on the observance or nonobservance of which the fate of man should depend, but to reveal and impart himself, as the source of all holiness and blessedness, to those who are but willing to receive him. The appearance of Christ was *the self-revelation** of the Supreme God hitherto wholly hidden from this lower creation. Perhaps, before Marcion became a Gnostic, he had, in his own country, embraced that form of the so-called *Patripassianism*† which was current in Asia Minor, which maintained that the same Divine subject was betokened by different names only as spoken of under different relations; as the Father, when spoken of as hidden,—as the Son, or the Logos, when self-revealing; and that it was only this self-revealing God who had united himself with a human body. At all events this view was the most suited to the system and the mind of Marcion. It was a welcome thing to him, to remove the distinction which the Church doctrine acknowledged between Christ and the Supreme Being; he was thoroughly imbued with the conviction, that Christ and Christianity are nothing but a communication of the Supreme God himself to man in his limited condition. (It is well to remark, generally, that among the Patripassians the *practical view* of Christianity was especially the predominant one.) As now Marcion, in the character of a Patripassian, would admit of no perfect human personality in Christ, it was the more easy for *Docetism* to insinuate itself into his views. This Docetism was not only founded in his view of matter, but it was thoroughly suited to the whole nature and spirit of his dogmatic views in every respect. Christianity, according to him, was to appear as a fragmentary thing,

---

* Apud inferos in sinu Abrahami. Tertull. c. M. lib. iii. c. 24. Clem. Strom. lib. v. f. 546. [Sylb. 233. Potter, 645. Klotz, vol. iii. p. 4.]

* Tertullian, c. M. lib. i. c. 11.
† Of which we shall speak more at large in our section relative to the formation of the Church doctrines.

entirely without preparations for it, and not to be attached to any thing else; as Tertullian excellently said, with Marcion every thing is to be *sudden*. His gospel, therefore, began with the journey of Christ to Capernaum in the fifteenth year of the reign of Tiberius; and his sudden appearance as a teacher.*

According also to the theory of Marcion, Jesus *was not the Messiah promised by the Demiurgos* through the prophets, as many of the tokens of the Messiah contained in them are wanting in him; and, on the contrary, that which is peculiar in *his* character, and in *his* operations, is by no means to be found among the Messianic traits delivered to us in the prophets. Marcion endeavoured to go through with the contrast between Christ, as the history of the Gospel represents him, and the Christ of the Old Testament: even in this we see how deeply the image of Christ had stamped itself upon his warm heart; but even that very circumstance rendered him unjust, by leading him to expect that the foretype, which was given to the prophetic view under a veil, which was to be for a time, should fully equal the reality that appeared. It was then to be considered only as an *accommodation*, when Jesus called himself the Messiah, in order to find a point by which the Jews might unite themselves to him; to win their confidence through a form which was familiar to them, and then to insinuate the higher things into this form.† It was natural enough that Christ, who presupposed only a sense of the needfulness of that which had hitherto been wanting to man, a feeling of the need in which man stands of help and redemption, and required only an acceptance, in childlike faith, of the divine source of life which he communicated to man; it was natural, according to these views, that he should find no acceptance with the self-righteous servants of the Demiurgos, self-contented in their own limited nature, and should find a more ready entrance into the hearts of the heathen, who had abandoned themselves to the feeling of their misery. The Demiurgos would of course necessarily attack him, as one that wished to destroy his kingdom, under the pretence of being the Messiah promised by him. He wished to bring about his death through the Jews, who were devoted to him, [i. e. the *Demiurgos*, Tr.] but he could effect nothing against the surpassing power of the Supreme God. The passion of Christ would serve only for the fulfilment of his [i. e. *Marcion's*, Tr.] benevolent designs, in respect to human nature: the heart of Marcion must have been interested in a love, that suffered, and obtained the victory through suffering; in him, whom alone he acknowledged as our apostle, he found a great deal about the sufferings of Christ for human nature,—and yet this did not well consist with his Docetism Marcion appropriated to himself the doctrine which already existed in the tradition of the Church about the descent of Christ into the world below;* but one is inclined to inquire whether he can have taken a doctrine on the mere authority of the tradition of the Church; and it will surely prove to be the case, that he has been willing to overlook that which would not otherwise be satisfactory to him in this authority, for the sake of its value in a dogmatical point of view, because its doctrine suited so well with his whole system. This doctrine is, indeed, distinctly proclaimed in the first epistle of St. Peter; but with the ultra-Pauline Marcion, St. Peter was no genuine apostle. Still, he might think, perhaps, that he found this doctrine in an epistle of St. Paul himself, namely, in Ephes. iv. 9. Other Gnostics gave it a different application, because with them this earth itself was the lower world [unterwelt, under-world] into which Christ descended, in order to set free the captives. Marcion understood the expression, lower world, in the sense given to it by the Church doctrine, namely, the general abode of departed spirits. Only he did not receive the common opinion, that Christ descended, in order to place the saints of the Old Testament in connection with himself. These were, like the Jews on earth, incapable of enjoying the blessings of a redeeming, eternal love, in consequence of their self-righteousness, and the enjoyment of a happiness which satisfied their limited nature. But Marcion, the friend of the heathen, could never have adopted the notion, that so many heathens who had died previously should be given up to the power of the Demiurgos, and be excluded from the benefits of redemption; Christ, therefore, descended below, in order to preach the

---

* Tertull. iv. 17.
† Ut per solenne apud eos et familiare nomen irreperet in Judæorum fidem, c. iii. 15.

* The Descensus Christi ad inferos.

Gospel to the heathen, who were dead, and to bless them.*

It would seem, although it cannot be decided upon with absolute certainty, that Marcion taught that the Messianic prophecies of the Old Testament would still be fulfilled with reference to the believers in the Demiurgos. The Messiah promised by the Demiurgos was to appear, and would execute a severe penal sentence against those who were not freed from his power by faith in the higher Christ, would raise up the dead saints of the Old Testament, and unite all in a millennial reign of earthly happiness. The eternal *heavenly kingdom*, to which Christians belonged, would then form the proper contrast to the transitory *earthly kingdom*. The souls of the Christians would lay aside their gross bodies, as the chicken raises itself out of the egg, as the kernel throws away the shell, or leaves the outer covering in the earth, and raises itself up free into the light of day; as the ripe fruit falls away from the stalk.†

A doctrinal system like that of Marcion, in which the contrast between the Law and the Gospel was thus declared, could be followed only by a holy, moral system; for he made out the difference between the two to consist in this, that the *first* (the law,) could communicate to man no true inward sanctification, no power for victory over evil; but the *second* (the Gospel,) brought man, through faith, into connection with a divine source of life; which connection would necessarily reveal itself through the conquest of evil, and through the sanctification of the life. Even the most zealous opponents of Marcion, who were glad to rake together all the evil they could possibly accuse him of, and who did not recognise the essential difference between the system of Marcion and all other Gnostic systems, could not deny that the Marcionites were entirely distinguished by their conduct from those Gnostic antinomians, who preached up a life of lawlessness after man's own fancies; they could not deny, for instance, that they (the Marcionites,) were on a par with the strictest Christians in their abhorrence of the heathen theatres and public pleasures.‡ While many Gnostics, through their doctrine, that an accommodation to the predominant errors of the times is allowable, or through the principle that outward things are a matter of no consequence, made it a very easy thing to escape the duty of martyrdom; the Marcionites, on the contrary, certainly believed themselves bound to give their witness to Christianity,* which was deeply engrafted in their hearts. But how all that belongs to our nature is sanctified and ennobled by Christianity, was a truth which Marcion could not acknowledge, because he did not recognise the God in Christ as the God of Nature. In this point of view, the teachers of the Church might justly make this reproach against him, that his Dualism, in union with Christianity, which always pursues the view of an ennoblement of nature through a divine principle of life, is practically illogical; as, for example, in the celebration of the Sacraments. The ascetic turn which Marcion had, even when he was a member of the Catholic Church, and in which, as we have before observed, his system had found a natural point to engraft itself upon, was now again still more furthered and strengthened by his more fully formed views of nature, and of the creation of the Demiurgos. He reckoned a mode of life, such as was led in the Catholic Church only by certain classes of ascetics, to be an essential part of Christianity: Christians were, even here below, to lead a heavenly life, entirely freed from all defilement through matter; he who was incapable of leading such a life, must remain in the class of Catechumens, and could not yet be admitted to Baptism.†

Whether Marcion recognised only St. Paul as a genuine apostle, and condemned, after the fashion of ultra-Paulites, all the rest of the apostles, as Judaizing adulterators of Christianity; or whether he only declared *the writings that were published under their names to be spurious documents, counterfeited by Judaizing Christians,* cannot be decided with certainty from the unsatisfactory nature of the existing accounts; but the first is the most probable. This supposition suits best with the character of the abrupt and

---

* See Irenæus, i. c. 27, § 2, c. i. 24.
† Tertullian, iii. 3, 4, & 24; iv. 29; iii. 29. Eph. Syr. Orat. 52, 6, p. 551-2.
‡ Tertull. c. M. i. 28

* See, for example, Euseb. iv. 15; vii. 12. De Martyr. Palæstinæ, c. 10.
† Tertull. c. M. lib. iv. c. 34. Quomodo nuptias dirimis? nec conjungens marem et feminam, nec alibi conjunctos ad sacramentum baptismatis et eucharistiæ admittens, nisi inter se conjuraverint adversus fructum nuptiarum.

violent Marcion, who was more ready to make points of contrast than to look for means of accommodation. It is certain that he acknowledged as the genuine sources of Christian knowledge nothing but the epistles of St. Paul, and an original Gospel, which, by mistaking a passage, he supposed to have been cited by St. Paul. But as he set out from the settled opinion, that these documents were no longer found in their original condition, but had been adulterated by the Judaizers, whose form seems to have haunted him like a spectre, he allowed himself to use criticism *ad libitum*, in order to restore them to their original form. His pretended original Gospel, used (as he fancied,) by St. Paul, had arisen from a mutilation of the Gospel of St. Luke.* Certainly his criticism was by no means logical; for much remained, which nothing but a forced system of exegesis, through ignorance of right hermeneutic principles, could possibly bring into harmony with the system of Marcion.

Marcionite Sects.

While among other Gnostics the caprice and the multifariousness of their speculations and fictions caused the later disciples, in many respects, to depart from the doctrines of their Master; on the contrary, in the system of Marcion, the predominance of a practical turn, and the meagreness of the speculative part in comparison of the other Gnostic systems, were the cause of the changes which his disciples, among whom a practical disposition was not so predominant as with him, made in his doctrines. Many appropriated to themselves the elements of other Gnostic systems, which did not suit that of Marcion, in order to fill up the gaps which they believed they found in in it. Many, like the Marcionite Marcus,† received the doctrines of the Syrian Gnosis, relative to the creation of man;‡ namely, that the Supreme God had communicated to man something of his own Divine Life (the πνυμα,) but that man had lost it by sin,—a view which was repugnant to the whole character of the Marcionitish system; for, according to the ideas of Marcion, until the appearance of Christ, *nothing whatever* that was akin to the Supreme God could have been in existence in this world. While Marcion would not make any further conclusions relative to the ultimate fate of the Demiurgos and of the Psychici; on the contrary, Lucanus the Marcionite determined that all which is Psychical, is perishable, and that nothing but the πνυματικον, which has become participative of the divine nature, is immortal.*

Apelles had for a season withdrawn himself from the predominant practical turn of Marcion, and had indulged in many speculations, entirely foreign to the original Marcionite system; but at length the original practical disposition broke forth again, and became prominent in him in a remarkable manner. Tertullian† gives an unfavorable account of the morals of this man; but a teacher of the Catholic Church, at the beginning of the third century, named Rhodon, whose testimony is unsuspicious as being that of an enemy, defends him against this reproach, for he represents him as a man generally respected on account of his conduct.‡ Probably there was no other origin to these accusations, than the entirely innocent intercourse of Apelles with a female philosopher, named *Philumene*, as people were always ready to lay every thing that is evil to the charge of a person who has once been branded as a heretic. Philumene can only be reproached with having forgotten her calling as a woman, and having, in consequence, fallen into a sort of dreamy enthusiasm, and Apelles, with having encouraged her in this, and looking on her fantastic essays, which proceeded from an unhealthy condition, as *revelations*, which he took the trouble to interpret.§ But the notice which Tertullian gives us is of considerable use, viz: that his long sojourn at Alexandria superinduced a change in his *originally Marcionitish* views; for all which we can deduce from the scattered accounts in Tertullian, Origen, Epiphanius, and in the treatise of Ambrose de Paradiso, indicates the remodeling of his system through the influence of the Alexandrian

---

* An elaborate discussion of Marcion's Canon of the New Testament would be out of place here, but on this subject see more in the learned and acute investigations of my friends Hahn and Olshausen, and in my Genetic Development of the Gnostic systems.
† In the Dialog. de Recta Fide. See the Opp. Origen. T. i.
‡ See p. 47, the account of the Ophites, and Saturninus, p. 51.

* See Tertullian de Resurrect. Carn. c. 2. Orig. c. Cels. lib. iii. c. 27.
† Præscript. Hæret. c. 30
‡ Euseb. v. 13.
§ His book of φανερωσις, which is no longer extant.

Gnosis. And hence it arises, that he set the visible and the invisible order of the world, the Demiurgos and the Supreme God, and the Old and New Testaments, in more connection with each other than the system of Marcion permitted. While he set out from the principle, that the Old Testament comes from different origins,—partly from the inspiration of the Soter, partly from that of the Demiurgos, and partly from that of the evil spirit, who has every where troubled and defiled the Revelations of the Divine,* —he was desirous of culling out in all cases that which is good. I use all the writings of the Old Testament, he says, while I gather together that which is useful.† He appealed to that declaration, so often quoted by the ancients, and which is, perhaps, attributed to our Saviour, in the Ευαγγελιον καθ' Εβραιους, "Be ye trusty money-changers, who are able, universally, to distinguish between the genuine and the counterfeit gold, the true and the false." (Γινεσθε δοκιμοι τραπιζιται.) In age, Apelles, finding no satisfactory conclusion in his speculations upon the incomprehensible, took refuge in the faith which obeys an inward necessity without being able to solve every difficulty to itself, (difficulties which, in his case, met him even in that which he could not choose but to recognise;) he could do no other, he said; he felt himself obliged to *believe* in one eternal God, as the original cause of all existence, but he could not scientifically prove how all existence was necessarily to be traced back to the one original principle. The Church-teacher, Rhodon, to whom he made these communications in confidence, laughed at him as one who pretended to be a teacher, but only *believed* what he taught, and *acknowledged* that he could not prove it; but one is inclined to ask, whether the laugher in this case was wiser than the man whom he laughed at, and whether Rhodon himself, in the strict sense of the word, could prove that which Apelles avowed that he only believed. Apelles appeared to have no more taste for controversy on these subjects. "Every one," he said, "may keep to his own faith; for every one who places his confidence on him that was crucified, will come to the bliss of heaven, provided only he shows his faith by good works."

ADDITIONAL REMARKS.

On the Cultus of the Gnostics.

WE have hitherto considered the Gnostic sects only in reference to their faith and moral systems; it will be instructive, however, just cursorily to compare their different dispositions in regard to their modes of worship, (their *Cultus*.) Even here also we find the differences, which were often repeated in after times. Many Gnostics—as, for example, Ptolemæus—in virtue of their more inward Christianity and their predominantly intellectual character, were able to conceive the relation of all exterior observances of religion to its real essence, more justly than other Church-teachers, who could not separate the *outward* from the *inward*, in religion, with such clearness of conviction and view. There were, besides, some who, like the Jewish religious idealists at Alexandria, out of their theosophic idealism rejected all exterior worship, as only fit for the Psychici, who are still imprisoned in the bonds of their senses, and are unable to raise themselves up to the pure spiritual view [anschauung;] and these persons would allow nothing to be availing but a religion of the inward spiritual view [Geistesanschauung.] raised above all that is outward and sensuous. These persons would say, that man cannot represent the overwhelming and divine mysteries by sensuous and transitory things, and that real redemption consists only in knowledge.† But the same theosophic disposition might also bring with it a symbolic *Cultus*, full of mystic pomp, as we see in the case of the *Marcosians*,‡ from whom Irenæus traces those idealists, who threw aside all outward religious observances. In accordance with the distinction between a psychical and pneumatical Christianity, they made a distinction also of a *twofold baptism*.

---

* In a work which he called Conclusions, (Συλλογισμοι,) he endeavoured to indicate the contradictions to be found in the Old Testament.

† Χρω απο πασης γραφης, αναλεγων τα χρησιμα. Epiphan. Hæres. 44. § 2.

† Iren. 1. c. 24. § 4. Theodoret. Hæret. fab. i. c. 10. If the *Caians*, against whom Tertullian writes in his book *De Baptismo*, were identical with the Gnostic Cainites, with whom they are sometimes confounded, then we must place these latter in the same class, which well suits their whole character; but the grounds on which those Caians determined against the necessity of the external rite of baptism, do not look like the wild dreamy spirit of the Cainites; and besides, there is nothing peculiarly *Gnostic* in them, [namely, the Caians.]

‡ Followers of Mark.

1. The baptism into Jesus, the Messiah of the Psychici, through which the believing Psychici obtained remission of their sins, and the hope of an eternal life in the kingdom of the Demiurgos.

2. The *pneumatical* baptism, a baptism into the heavenly Christ who was united with Jesus, through whom spiritual natures attain to a self-consciousness, and to perfection, and enter into communion with the Pleroma. Their ceremonies, and the formulæ they used in baptism, were probably different, according as a person obtained the *first* or the *second* baptism, and was received into the class of *Psychici* or *Pneumatici*. The latter was apparently accompanied with more pomp than the other. According to the Gnostic idea, (see above,) viz., that the baptized and redeemed pneumatical nature entered into a spiritual marriage (a syzygy) with its other half in the world of spirits, the *angel* which makes one whole with it;— according to this idea they celebrated baptism as a marriage feast, and adorned the chamber where it was to take place as a marriage chamber. One of the formulæ used in the baptism of a Pneumaticus, was this : [You are baptized] " Into the name which is hidden from all the Divinities and Powers (of the Demiurgos,) the name of Truth,* which Jesus of Nazareth hath drawn up into the Light-Zones of Christ, the living Christ through the Holy Spirit, for the angelic redemption,†—that name through which all attains its perfection." The baptized person then said, " I am *confirmed* and redeemed ;‡ I am redeemed in my soul from this world, and from all which proceeds from it, through the name of Jehovah, who has redeemed the soul of Jesus,§ through the living Christ." Then the assembled throng spoke thus : " Peace (or health) to all, over whom this name rests." Then also they imparted to the baptized the consecration to the Christian priesthood, which was used also in the Church, by means of anointing ; but in this case it was performed with costly ointment (balsam,) for the widely extending perfume of this was to be a symbol of the overpowering delight of the *Pleroma*, which the redeemed were destined to enjoy. Among these *Marcosians* we find, at first, the use of extreme unction ; they anointed the dying man with that ointment mixed with water, and used with it formulæ, to the purport that the souls of the departed must be able to raise themselves up free from the Demiurgos and all his powers, to their mother, the *Sophia*.* The Ophites, also, had these same forms of adjuration for the departed. And that mystical table of the same sect, which contains a symbolical representation of their system (their διαγραμμα,) is well known.

As Marcion in his whole character and spirit was essentially different from the rest of the Gnostics, so also did he differ from them in respect to his principles about the ordinances of worship. By his simple and practical turn of mind, he was far removed from that mysticism that delighted in outward pomp; but then he was far removed, also, from that proud contemplative idealism. His endeavour was here also to bring back the original Christian simplicity of the service of God; and he combated many new ordinances, as corruptions of that original simplicity.† And thus, with respect to the practice which was then about in its commencement, of dividing divine service into two parts,‡ the one, which the Catechumens were to stay out, and the other, at the commencement of which they were to be dismissed, he appears to have contended against it, as an innovation foreign to the spirit of Christianity. He said, Just as in any other good thing, let the mature Christians suffer those who are yet under instruction, such as the Cate-

---

* The ἀληθεια, the self-revelation of the Bythos.

† Εἰς λυτρωσιν ἀγγελικην. For the redemption of that, of which this spiritual nature, as well as the angel which belonged to it, must become a partaker, in order that both together might become capable of entering into the Pleroma, which was only possible to them in their mutual union, and not in their state of separation.

‡ Ἐστηριγμαι και λελυτρωμαι. See above, about Horus.

§ I think, that in that formula we must read του Ἰησου, instead of αὐτου.

---

* Iren. I. 21. Exorcism in Baptism also, was well suited to the Gnostic theory of the indwelling of manifold πνευματα ὑλικα [spirits of a gross and sensuous nature, derived from their connection with matter.—H. J. R.,] till the redemption [of the individual.] Exorcism (ἰδως ἐξορκιζομενον) makes its appearance at first, even earlier than in the North African Church, (see above,) in the Didascal. Anatol. p. 800, col. iv. D. But here it may be quoted as being a custom of the Alexandrian Church in general, and not as a custom peculiarly Gnostic.

† Apparently, Tertullian had the *Marcionites* especially in his view, when he says of the heretics, Præscript. c. 41, " *Simplicitatem* volunt esse prostrationem disciplinæ, cujus penes nos curam *lenocinium* vocant."

‡ Afterwards called the Missa Catechumenorum, and the Missa Fidelium

chumens, to take part in prayer also: they must not reserve any thing from them on this account; nor exclude them on it from participation in the prayers of the Church.*

We must, however, limit the praise which has been bestowed upon Marcion, if he was really the original author of the superstitious custom, founded on a misunderstanding of the passage in Scripture, 1 Cor. xv. 29, namely the custom of bestowing baptism on a living person, which was to be availing to a Catechumen who had died without baptism; but it is altogether without foundation, that the introduction of such a mistaken baptism has been laid to the charge of Marcion, to whose simple evangelical spirit such superstition was entirely unsuited. If such a superstition prevailed afterwards among the Marcionites, who had spread themselves among the country people of Syria, in the fifth century, we can only say that it is not fair to charge the founder of the sect with that which is found among men, who are certainly very unlike him.†

II. *Manes‡ and the Manichees.*

THE power of the simple Gospel had by degrees triumphed over Gnosticism, although the remains of Gnostic sects maintained themselves in the East down to later centuries. Gnosticism had produced the effects it was calculated to produce;

---

* Marcion, according to Jerome, Comment. in Ep. ad Galat., appealed to Galat. vi. 6, while with a thorough disregard of the context in that passage, he understands κοινωνειν in an intransitive sense, and translates the verse: "Let the Catechumen partake of all that is good, together with his instructor." Hence, the notion of the Gnostics was also present to the mind of Tertullian, when he reproached the heretics, l. c. in this manner: "Imprimis quis catechumenus, quis fidelis incertum est. Pariter adeunt (ecclesiam,) pariter audiunt, pariter orant."

† Tertullian, De Resurr. Carnis, c. 48, & Adv. Marcion. lib. v. c. 10, by no means speaks as if, in his time, such a baptism, which violates the passage on which it is founded, had been actually in use in any place; only he supposes the possibility that such a custom may have existed in the time of the apostle, who may have alluded to that; and in the latter passage he considers another explanation of 1 Cor. xv. 29, to be more probable. But what Chrysostom remarks upon this passage can only be applied to many ignorant Marcionites of *his* time, and not, by any means, to Marcion himself, and the older Gnostics.

‡ [Neander constantly uses the name Mani, but as I believe Manes is the form usually adopted in English, I have changed it.—H. J. R.]

it had, by the struggle that took place, awakened the powers of the soul, and by the contrast it offered, it had brought the meaning of the chief doctrines of Christianity into a clearer consciousness and acknowledgment. But in the third century a new and remarkable phenomenon, thoroughly akin to Gnosticism, arose out of the intermixture of oriental theosophy with Christianity, namely, Manicheeism. No essential difference is to be found between this system and those of the Gnostics, especially of the second class, except that here the Christian element was far more crushed by the intermixture of strange materials than in most of the Gnostic systems, and Christianity was properly used only as a symbolical covering for ideas foreign to it, so that one might often throw away the Christian terms which are used, and find notions, which, in their application here, appear to resemble a mixture of Parsic, Brahminical, and Buddhist religious doctrines, more than Christianity. And further, the oriental element is not at all mixed, as it is in the Gnostic systems, with Jewish theology and Platonic philosophy. The comparison of the Manichean system with the Basilidian, the Saturninian, and the Ophitic, and with the religious system of the Zabians, hardly allows us to escape recognising one common source for all.

As far as relates to the history of Manes, the founder of this sect, we have two kinds of sources of information, which coincide with each other only in a very few circumstances, and in all besides are entirely different; these are the *Greek* and the *Oriental* sources. The accounts of Cyril of Jerusalem, of Epiphanius, and of the ecclesiastical historians of the fourth and fifth centuries, point our attention to one common source.† This source is the Acts of a disputation said to have been held with Manes by Archelaus, bishop of Cascar.‡ But these Acts are preserved to us in at least a very unsatisfactory form, as they have descended to us, with the exception of some frag-

---

† Eusebius, who wrote before this document was promulgated, was unable to relate any thing of the personal history of Manes.

‡ Kaskar; if the name be not a corruption. It may, perhaps, (although on the evidence of a very uncertain conjecture,) be a corruption for Charran in Mesopotamia (חָרָן.)

ments in Greek, only in the Latin translation from a Greek writing, which perhaps, itself is only an unfaithful translation, from a Syriac original.* These Acts plainly contain a narration, which hangs together ill enough, and bears a tolerably fabulous appearance. Even supposing there is some truth as a foundation for these Acts, which may well be as there is much in the mode of bringing forward the doctrines which bears marks of truth, and is confirmed by a comparison with other representations, yet still the Greek writer appears to have mixed with it much that is false, from ignorance of oriental languages and customs, by intermingling and confusion of different narrations, and by exaggeration and a deficiency in critical qualifications.† We are well aware how difficult it was to a Greek to place himself in the condition of a people totally foreign to his own nation, and to conceive it altogether justly.

In some points, even from the scanty means which we have for the unravelling of this historical enigma, we are enabled to detect traces of the mistakes which have formed the foundation of these accounts. The first origin of the Manichean doctrines is derived from a Saracenic merchant, called Scythianus, who is represented, during long travels in Asia, Egypt, and Greece, to have acquired great riches, and procured himself an intimate acquaintance both with Oriental and Grecian philosophy. This Scythianus is represented to have lived near the apostolic age; but this, even according to this narrative itself, appears to be an anachronism, for Manes himself is not made to live till some generations after that age. Still, in this Scythianus we recognise an historical personage really connected with Manes; we find letters of Manes addressed to a man of this name, who was also probably an oriental Theosophist.* The heir and disciple of this Scythianus appears to have been one Terebinth, who was afterwards called Buddas. The name Buddas† reminds us of the old system of religion, opposed to Brahminism, which took its origin from Eastern India, which is still prevalent in Ceylon, Thibet and the Birman Empire, and has extended its influence even to the tribes of Tartary. The relation of the miraculous birth of Buddas reminds us of the similar accounts given of the birth of the Indian Buddha. The pantheistic portion of Manicheeism may be compared, in many respects, with the pantheistic parts of the old Buddhaism. Manes is represented, in fact, to have travelled to the East Indies and China, and many of the later Manichees appeal to the circumstance that Manes, Buddhas, Zoroaster, Christ, and the Sun (the higher spirit which animated the Sun,) are the same; that is to say, all these founders of a religion are only different Incarnations of the Sun,‡ and therefore, there is, in these different systems, only one religion under different forms.

In the Oriental accounts there is far more internal connection; but these are found in writers very much later than the Greek documents. The Orientals have, however, without doubt, made use of earlier documents, and in their use of them they were not exposed to the same causes of error, as those which led the Greeks astray.§

---

* Jerome, De Vir. Illustr. 72, informs us that these Acts were originally written in Syriac; but among the Orientals, the first Father to whom these Acts were known is Severus, bishop of Asmonina, in Egypt, who wrote about the year A. D. 978. See Renaudot, Hist. Patriarch. Alexandr p. 40. His relation of the matter differs in many respects from the edition of these Acts which has descended to us, and it is far simpler, which seems to indicate that the Acts of which he made use, were not ours, but another document akin to it, and that, perhaps, which furnished the foundation of ours. Heraclian, bishop of Chalcedon, in Photius cod. 95, says that a person named Hegemonius drew up these Greek Acts.

† Beausobre has properly discarded the Western accounts, which he was well persuaded were untenable, and confined himself wholly to the Oriental. There is nothing striking in what Mosheim has advanced against him in this matter.

* See Fabricii Biblioth. Græc. vol. vii. 316.

† It has been justly remarked, that the Greek Τερεβινθος, is perhaps, only a translation of the Chaldee בוטמא by which the Hebrew אלה is rendered in the Targum, and which the Alexandrian translators render by Τερεβινθος. And besides, Terebinth, or Buddas, like Scythianus, may have been an historical person, to whom much that belongs to the Indian Buddha may have been transferred.

‡ The later offsets of the Manichees, when they entered into the Catholic Church, were obliged to condemn the doctrines before maintained by them: την Ζαραδην και Βουδαν και τον Χριστον και την Μανιχαιον ινα και την αυτον ειναι. See Jacob. Tollii Insignia Italic. Traject. 1696. p. 134.

§ The Oriental accounts are to be found in Herbelot, Bibliothèque Orientale, sub v. Mani; in the History of the Sassanidæ, by the Persian historian, Mirkhond, ap. Silvestre de Sacy, Mémoires sur diverses Antiquités de la Perse: Paris, 1793; in Abulpharage, and Pocock, Specimen Histor. Arab.

In order properly to appreciate the phenomenon presented by the appearance of a man like Manes, we must compare together the circumstances and the relations under which he was formed. Manes was born a Persian, but we are led to inquire whether this geographical term is to be used in its strictest limits, or whether we are only to understand by it some one province of the great Persian empire. The latter view is supported by the circumstance that Manes composed his *writings* in the Syriac language, from which we might be led to conclude that he derived his origin from one of those provinces of the Persian empire, where Syriac was the language of the country. But this argument is not entirely demonstrative; for without this supposition it may well be conceived, from the intimate connection between the Persian Christians and the Syrian Church, the Syrian language might already by that time have become the language of theological books among the Persian religious teachers, and that Manes also might, in consequence, have been induced to make use of it, although it was not his mother tongue, more especially as he might thereby hope to further a more general reception of his doctrines in other districts. If these accounts, indeed, are to be relied on, Manes was born in a family of the class of Magi, (the priests of the Persian religion,) was converted to Christianity in the days of manhood, and became the presbyter of a Christian congregation at Ehvaz, or Ahvaz, the chief town of the Persian province Huzitis. At all events, it is most probable that Manes was brought up in the religion of Zoroaster, and afterwards embraced Christianity.

We do not know enough of the progress of his life to be able to decide whether he was at first fairly and thoroughly converted from the religion of his fathers to Christianity, but that afterwards being repulsed by the form in which the latter appeared to him in the doctrines of the Church, he freshened up the fundamental ideas of his earlier religious habits of thought again in his soul, and then believed that the true light could not be given to Christianity till it was united with them; . . . . . . or whether from the very first he had been attracted by the analogy of Christianity to many Persian notions, without remarking the essential difference between similar ideas in Christianity and in the Persian religion according to their peculiar conception and connection in each, so that from the very first he had only formed a peculiar religious system for himself by an amalgamation of the Persian and the Christian. It is easy to explain, in any case, how a man brought up in the Persian religion believed that he could observe a striking connection between the ideas of a kingdom of Ormuzd and Ahriman, and those of a kingdom of Light and Darkness, of God and Satan; between the Persian doctrine which allows man to struggle for the kingdom of Ormuzd against the kingdom of Ahriman, and the Christian doctrine, which would make man struggle in the service of Christ against the kingdom of Satan. In the Persian religion, the centre point of all was the idea of redemption out of the kingdom of Ahriman, and the final triumph of the kingdom of Ormuzd. In Christianity he found the tidings of a triumphant appearance of Ormuzd himself upon the earth, through which the complete triumph of the kingdom of Light, and the complete destruction of the kingdom of Darkness were prepared.

Exactly at the time in which Manes appeared, after the Persians had freed themselves from the Parthian dominion, and re-established their old kingdom under the dynasty of the Sassanidæ, the endeavour was again awakened among them to purify the old religion of Zoroaster from the foreign admixtures which had made their way into it during a foreign rule, and to restore it again to its original purity and glory. But contests had now arisen as to what the pure doctrine of Zoroaster was, especially on those points on which the Zend books contained only hints, (e. g. on the relation of the good and the evil principle to each other.) Councils were held, in order to decide the disputes, at which pretended prophets appeared, who professed to decide every thing according to Divine illumination.* The religion of Zoroaster, thus refreshed with new power, and setting itself up in hostility to all foreign religions, which had hitherto been tolerated, now also entered on a contest with Christianity, which under the Parthian domination had been able to propagate itself without obstruction. Under such circumstances, it was easy for a man of an ardent and bold spirit, like Manes, to

---

* See Hyde, Hist. Relig. vet. Pers. p. 276; Mémoires sur diverses Antiquités de la Perse, par S. de Sacy, p. 42.

indulge the thought of establishing the identity of Christianity, purified, as he would think, from all extraneous matter, with the pure doctrine of Zoroaster, and by this means to be the first to make clear the proper meaning of the Christian doctrine, and at the same time to further the extension of Christianity in the Persian empire; he wished to be looked upon as the Reformer, both of Christianity and Parsism, called and enlightened by God. Christianity appeared to Manes to be far more akin to the doctrine of Zoroaster than to Judaism. He derived the adulteration of the doctrine of Christ from the mixture of Christianity with Judaism, which was entirely foreign to its nature. He was shut out from the communion of the Christian Church, and turned himself now to Christians and believers in the religion of Zoroaster, with the desire that they should recognise him as an inspired (*lit.* enlightened,) reformer of religion. He maintained, like Mahomet in later times, that he was the Paraclete* promised by Christ, and under this name he by no means understood the Holy Ghost, but a human person; an inspired teacher promised by Christ, who should carry on further the religion revealed by Christ in his Spirit (i. e. the Spirit of Christ,) should purify it from the mixture made in it by Ahriman, especially from those corruptions which proceeded from its amalgamation with Judaism, and should make known those truths which mankind in earlier times had not been in a condition to understand. Through him Christianity was to be set free from all connection with Judaism which had proceeded from Ahriman; and that which the evil spirit, in order to adulterate Divine truth, had intermingled with the New Testament, which by no means contained the uncorrupted doctrine of Christ, was to be separated from it. Through him that *perfect* knowledge was to be given, of which St. Paul had spoken as of something reserved against a future season, (1 Cor. xiii. 10.)† Thus Manes might name the promised Paraclete and the apostle of Christ at the same time, as he began the letter in which he wished to develope the fundamental doctrines of his religion (the Epistola Fundamenti, so celebrated among the Manichees), with these words:—Manes, chosen to be an apostle of Jesus Christ, through the choice of God the Father. These are the words of salvation out of the living and eternal source."*

It was in the latter part of the reign of the Persian king Shapur I. (Sapores,) about the year 270, that he first came forward with these pretensions. With an ardent and profound spirit, and with a lively imagination, he united varied knowledge and talents for the pursuits of art and science, which he used for the propagation of his doctrines. He is represented as having been distinguished among his contemporaries and countrymen as a mathematician and astronomer;† the fame of his skill in painting was long remembered in Persia. At first he succeeded in obtaining the favour of that prince; but when his doctrines which, in the opinion of the magi, were heretical, became known, he was obliged to seek safety from persecution, by flight. He now made long journeys to the East Indies, as far as China, and probably used these journeys towards the enriching of his religious eclecticism. He remained for a time in the province of Turkistan, and prepared there a series of beautiful pictures, which contained a symbolical representation of his doctrine,—the book which was named by the Persians Ertenki-Mani. It may, probably, have happened that he withdrew into solitude in order to receive the revelations of God, as he declared that he devised these images (which represented his conceptions) amidst calm reflection in a cavern, and maintained that he received them in his mind‡ from heaven. Whether it be true, as the Orientals relate, that in order to deceive the credulous populace, he gave out that he raised himself in the body up to heaven, and thence brought down those emblems with him,§ we must

---

* Augustin. c. Epistol. Fundamenti, c. 5.

† It must, however, be acknowleged that they possessed no great knowledge in these subjects. It is in the highest degree probable that much in his system, even if we cast away the mythical dress in which it is enveloped, was closely connected with an imperfect knowledge of these sciences.

‡ [In seinem Sinne . . . This may be explained, as meaning impressions *on the sensorium*. I have used the word *mind*, taken in a lax sense.—H. J. R.]

§ He must secretly have caused himself to be supplied with provisions in the cavern, where he remained, according to some, *four* years, according to others, *one* year.

---

* See Mirkhond ap. Sacy, p. 294. Tit. Bost. c. Manich. lib. iii. in Canisii Lection. antiq. ed. Basnage, and Bibl. Patr. Galiand, t. v. p. 326.

† See the Acta cum Felice Manichæo, lib. i. 9. opp. Augustin. t. viii.

DUALISM OF MANES—PARSISM.

at least leave undecided. After the death of Sapor, in the year 272, he returned to Persia, and found a good reception for himself and his pictures at the hands of his successor, Hormuz (Hormisdes.) This prince assigned him as a secure residence, a castle called Deskereth, at Khuzistan, in Susiana. But after this prince had reigned two years not quite complete, Behram succeeded him (Baranes.) This prince showed himself favourable to him at first, but perhaps, only out of dissimulation, in order to give him and his adherents a feeling of security. He caused a disputation to be held between him and the magi, of which the result was that Manes was declared a heretic. As he would not retract, he was* flayed alive in the year 277,† and his skin stuffed and hung up before the gates of the town Djondischapur, in order to intimidate his followers.

The main point of dispute among the Persian theologians which was treated of at the restoration of the original religion by the founders of the dynasty of the Sassanidæ, was one which is most obscurely expressed in the documents of the Zoroastrian creed, (the Zend-avesta,) namely, the inquiry, whether we are to believe in an absolute Dualism, and consider Ormuzd and Ahriman as two self-existing beings from all eternity opposed to each other, or whether *one* original being is to be supposed,‡ from whom Ormuzd and Ahriman received their existence, and that Ahriman is an originally-good being, but a fallen one. The former doctrine was that of the Magusaic sect,§ among the Persians, which Manes joined; for it was his object to represent the opposition of light and darkness as absolute and irreconcilable, although either consciously or unconsciously, a pantheism, which was enveloped in a mystical dress, might be at the bottom of this Dualism, in which the idea of evil was conceived more in a physical than in an ethical light.‖ He imagined, therefore, two principles absolutely opposed to each other, together with their creations of an opposite character also: on the one hand, God, the original good, from whom nothing but good can proceed, from whom every idea of destroying, of punishing, and of corruption is far removed, the original Light, from which pure light flows; . . . . on the other hand, the original evil, which can only destroy and undo, and whose very being is wild confusion that fights against itself,—matter, darkness, from which powers strictly corresponding to itself proceed, a world full of smoke and vapour, and at the same time full of fire, which only burns and cannot give light.* These two kingdoms originally existed entirely separate from each other. The Supreme God, the King of the kingdom of Light, existed as the original source of the world of emanations akin to himself, and those Æons, the channels through which light was propagated from the original source of light, were most closely connected with him; and to these, as representatives of the Supreme God, his very name was transferred, which were thence called Divinities, without prejudice to the honour due only to the first of Beings.† In the epistle in which Manes brought forward the fundamental doctrines of his religion,‡ he thus portrays this Supreme God at the head of his kingdom of Light :§

"Over the kingdom of Light ruled God the Father, eternal in his holy nature, (*geschlechte*, lit. *generation*, or *race*, or *kind*, *species*, *genus*,) glorious in his power, the TRUE, by the very nature of his being, always holy in his own eternal existence, who carries within himself wisdom and the consciousness of his life, with which he comprehends the twelve members of his Light, that is to say, the overflowing riches of his own kingdom. In every one of these members there are hidden thousands of innumerable and immeasurable treasures. But the Father himself, who is splendid in his glory and incomprehensible in his greatness, has connected with him holy and glorious Æons, whose number and greatness cannot be reckoned, with whom this holy

---

* A cruel mode of putting criminals to death, common in the East.
† The chronology is, it must be confessed, very uncertain here.
‡ Zervan Akarene, the time that has neither beginning nor end, answering to the αιων Βυθος.
§ Schahristan. ap. Hyde, p. 205.
‖ See pg. 5, the Introduction to the History of the Gnostic Sects.

* The emblems under which Manes represented the kingdom of evil bear the most striking resemblance to those which we meet with in the religious system of the Sabians. It was said, and not badly, by Alexander of Lycopolis, in his treatise, πρις τας Μανιχαιου δοξας, c. ii., that Manes, under the word ὑλη, understood την εν ἑκαστῳ των οντων ατακτον κινησιν.
† As the Amschaspands Ized, of the Religion of the Parsees.
‡ The Epistola Fundamenti.
§ Augustin, contra Epist. Fundamenti, c. 13.

all-glorious Father lives, for in his lofty kingdom none dwells subject either to want or to weakness. His resplendent kingdoms, however, are founded on the blessed earth of light in such a manner, that they can neither be rendered weak, nor shaken at all."* The powers of darkness fell together in wild confusion, until in their blind career of strife they came so close to the kingdom of light, that at length a gleam out of this kingdom, which had hitherto been entirely unknown to them, streamed upon them. They now left off their contention against one another, and, involuntarily attracted by the shining of the Light, they united together to force their way into the kingdom of Light, and to appropriate to themselves some portion of this light.† It appears here somewhat inconsistent in Manes, who ascribes an impurturbable firmness to the kingdom of Light, to say, "But when the Father of the most blessed Light saw a great devastation arise from the darkness, and threaten his holy Æons, had he not sent a special Divine power‡ to conquer and annihilate the race of darkness at once, in order that after its annihilation peace might be the portion of the dwellers in the light."§ Simplicius and Euodius have reproached him here with a contradiction to himself; but this accusation relates rather to the *mythical or symbolical mode of representation*, than to the train of thought which it envelopes. The fundamental notion of Manes, as of the Gnostics, was this, that the blind power of nature which opposed the Divine Being, being tamed and conquered by mixture with it, would be rendered utterly powerless.

The King of the kingdom of Light caused the Æon, *the Mother of Life,** to emanate from him to protect its borders. The very name of this Genius shows that it represents "*the supreme soul of the world*," that the Divine light giving up the unity of the kingdom of light, was now to divide itself into a multitude, and develope itself in the struggle against the ungodly into separate beings, each with a peculiar existence. The *Mother of Light*, like the ἄνω σοφια of the Valentinian system, may not have been affected as yet by the kingdom of darkness . . . . and herein would also lie the difference between the higher soul of the world, belonging to the kingdom of light, and a *reflection* of it, which had mingled itself with the kingdom of darkness.† This *Mother of Light* produced the First-man (original-man,) in order to set him in opposition to the kingdom of darkness . . . . and here is the idea of the dignity of human nature, which we observed among the Gnostics.‡ The *First man* sets out upon the contest with the five pure elements, fire, light, air, water, and earth.§ We here also recognise the character of Parsism, the veneration of an originally pure nature, which was troubled only by being intermixed with Ahriman; and according to the Parsic doctrines, a life streaming forth from the kingdom of light is acknowledged among the original elements, and they are called forth through its fruitful and enlivening power, as fellow-champions against the destroying influence of Ahriman.

But that *First Man* was conquered in the contest, and became in danger of falling into the kingdom of Ahriman; he prays to the King of the kingdom of

---

* This earth of light Manes did not conceive as any thing distinct from the original Supreme Being, but all was only a different modification of the one Divine Being of Light.

† We recognise the idea which is the foundation of this, namely, that Evil is at enmity with itself, and unites only when it engages in a contest with Good, which is the attractive power with which Good acts upon Evil itself; a thing which certainly is a contradiction to the Dualistic dogma of an Absolute Evil.

‡ Aliquod nimium ac præclarum et virtute potens numen. In the system of Zoroaster also the Amschaspands is represented as an armed champion for the kingdom of light.

§ The Epistola Fundamenti in the Book *de fide contra Manichæos*, c. 11, which, perhaps, proceeded from the pen of Euodius, bishop of Uzala, in Numidia. (This is to be found in the Appendix to the viiith tome of the Benedictine edition of Augustine.)

* μητηρ της ζωης.

† Simplicius in Epictet. p. 187. ed. Salmas. gives an excellent portraiture of the Manichæan doctrine in this respect; οὔτε τὸ πρῶτον ἀγαθὸν κεκινῆσθαι λέγουσιν, οὔτε τὰ ἄλλα ἀγαθὰ τὰ προσεχῶς αὐτῷ συνόντα, τὴν μητέρα τῆς ζωῆς, καὶ τὸν δημιουργὸν (the ζῶν πνεῦμα) καὶ τους ἐκεῖ αἰῶνας.

‡ The πρῶτος ἄνθρωπος of Manes is to be compared with the πρῶν ἄνθρωπος of the Valentinians, the Adam Kadmon, and especially the Cajomorts of the Zend-avesta, about whom there are many points of resemblance. It is most highly probable that Manes received this Parsic idea into his system.

§ According to the notion of Manes, every thing which exists in the kingdom of Light has its counterpart in the kingdom of Darkness. The dark earth stands opposed to the *earth of light*, and the five elements of darkness are opposed to the five pure elements.

Light, who causes the *Living Spirit* to emanate in order to assist him.* This lifts him up again into the kingdom of Light; but the powers of darkness had already succeeded in destroying a portion of the armour of the First Man, and swallowing up a portion of his existence as a being of light; and thus we arrive at the notion of the *Soul of the World* mixed with matter.† Here we find also an affinity with the Gnostic notions, according to which the κατω σοφια was saved out of the kingdom of Hyle by means of the Soter sent to her assistance; but still it was, nevertheless, a seed of the Divine Life, fallen down into the matter, which (i. e. the seed,) must be purified and developed.‡ This must necessarily happen; through the magical power of the Divine Life, of the Light of the Soul, the wild stormy kingdom of darkness is to become involuntarily softened, and at last rendered powerless. The taming of that stormy, blind power of Nature is just the very object of the formation of the world. Manes is said to have attempted to make his doctrine intelligible by the following parable: A good shepherd sees a lion fall upon his flock, he digs a pit, and throws a he-goat into it; the lion runs up eagerly in order to devour the goat; but he falls into the pit and cannot get out of it again. The shepherd, however, succeeds in drawing up the goat again, while he leaves the lion shut up in the pit, and thereby renders him harmless to his flock;§—just as the kingdom of Darkness becomes harmless, and the souls swallowed up by it are at last saved, and brought back again to their kindred habitation. But now after the *Living Spirit* had raised man again to the kingdom of Light, he began preparations for the process of purifying the *soul that is intermingled with the kingdom of Darkness*, and this is the cause of the whole creation of the world, and the object of all the whole course of the world.‖ That portion of the soul which had not been affected by connection with matter, or with the Being of Darkness, he raised up above the earth, so that it should have its place in the sun and in the moon, and thence should spread forth its influence, in order to free the souls which were akin to it, and which were held captive by the kingdom of Darkness, and spread abroad over all nature, through the purifying process of the development of the vegetative and animal life, and thus to attract them to itself again.

Manes also, in a manner similar to the Parsic conception of the universe, beheld the same struggle between Ormuzd and Ahriman, and the same process of purification in the physical as well as in the moral world. In contradiction to the spirit of Christianity, he mixed the physical with the religious and ethic, founded doctrines of belief and morals on speculative cosmogonies, and a natural philosophy, which being deduced more from inward conceptions than from experimental knowledge, must often have been unintelligible. Such a mixture was alike prejudicial to religion, which became flooded by a multitude of things wholly foreign to it and to knowledge, which thus is compelled to lose that soberness of understanding which is necessary to her.* Just as in the Parsic system of religion, in the struggle between Ormuzd and Ahriman in the physical and the spiritual world, the sun and the moon perform an important part in the conduct of the general system of development and purifica-

---

* The ζων πνευμα in the Gnostic Acta Thomæ, which contain much that resembles Manicheeism.
† The ψυχη απαντων.
‡ Titus of Bostra, lib. i. c. Manich. c. 12, thus excellently portrays the Manichœan doctrine: ὁ ἀγαθὸς δυναμιν ἀποστελλει τινα, φυλαξευσαν μεν ἀνθεν τους ὁεους, το δ' αληθες δυλεχα εσμενην εις σκευσιν τη ὑλη σαφρονισμον, ἰδθη τρεπειν τινα ὡσπερ θηριον.
§ Disputat. cum Archelao, c. 25. This parable bears altogether the stamp of genuineness, at least it is in the spirit of Manicheeism.
‖ Just as in the Valentinian scheme, the *Soter* operates after he has first raised the *Sophia*.

* How little Manicheeism understood the interests of religion and the nature of Christianity; how little it understood the one thing needful for man, is shown by the remarkable words in which Felix, the Manichee, endeavoured to prove that Manes was the reformer of religion (the Paraclete,) promised by Christ. "Et quia venit Manichæus et per suam prædicationem docuit nos initium, medium et finem; docuit nos de fabrica mundi, quare facta est et unde facta est, et qui fecerunt; docuit nos quare dies et quare nox; docuit nos de cursu solis et lunæ; quia hoc in Paulo nec in cæterorum apostolorum Scripturis, hoc credimus, quia (*dass, that*) ipse est Paracletus." Augustin. Acta. c. Felice Manichæo, lib. i. c. 9. In Alexander of Lycopolis, in Egypt, the opponent of Manicheeism in the beginning of the fourth century, we find the opposite error to this of a dilution of Christianity, which, mistaking its peculiar and essential features, refers it only to certain general religious and moral truths, torn away from that with which they are connected in Christianity. With him the chief matter of Christianity is the doctrine of an eternal God, as Creator, and good morality for the people. See the beginning of his treatise against the Manichees.

tion, so also was it in the system of Manes. Almost what the Zoroastric system taught of Mithras as the Genius (Ized,) of the Sun, was attributed by Manes to his Christ, the pure soul, whose operations proceeded from out of the sun and the moon. As he derived this soul from the *original man*, he made this the explanation of the Bible-name, *the Son of Man*, (υἱὸς ἀνθρώπου,) and as he distinguished the *pure, free* soul, whose throne is in the sun, from the soul which is akin to it, and extended throughout all nature, but defiled and imprisoned by its mixture with matter; he also made a distinction between a Son of Man elevated above all connection with matter, and subject to no suffering, and a Son of Man crucified, as it were, in matter, and subject to suffering.* Where the seed sown burst forth out of the dark bosom of the earth, and developed itself into plants, blossoms, and fruit, there Manes saw the victorious development of the principle of Light freeing itself by degrees from the fetters of matter; and he saw here that the living soul, as it were, which is kept bound in the limbs of the *Princes of Darkness*, being released from them, soars up aloft in freedom, and mingles in the *pure atmosphere*,† where the souls, which are perfectly purified, ascend the *Ships of Light* (of the sun and of the moon,) which are prepared to conduct them to their native place. But that which bears upon it multifarious stains is by degrees and in small quantities distilled from them‡ by the power of heat, and mingles itself with all trees, plants, and vegetables.

These were samples of his mystical philosophy of nature, which were brought forward sometimes in singular myths, which, although occasionally indecent, were nothing very remarkable to the imagination of Oriental people, and sometimes under the covering of Christian expressions. Thus the Manichees could speak of a suffering Son of Man who hangs on every tree, of a Christ crucified in every soul and in the whole world, and they could explain the symbols of the suffering Son of Man in the Last Supper according to their own sense. Just as well, also, or rather with greater justice —for this intermixture of religion with the knowledge of nature was more heathen than Christian—the Manichees might use heathen myths as a covering for their ideas; and thus the boy, Dionysos, torn to pieces by the Titans, as celebrated in the Bacchic mysteries, is nothing but the soul swallowed up by the powers of darkness, the Divine life divided into pieces by matter.*

The Powers of Darkness were now threatened by the danger, that by means of the operation of the Spirit of the Sun upon the purifying process of Nature, all the Light and Life kept prisoners in their members would be by degrees withdrawn from them, namely, the soul which had been seized upon by them, which struggles after a release, and which is always attracted by the kindred spirit of the Sun, constantly frees itself more and more and flees away, so that at last the kingdom of

---

* The υἱὸς ἀνθρώπου ἐμπαθής and the υἱὸς ἀνθρώπου ἀπαθής.

† The pure holy air, which is exactly in accordance with the Parsic Worship of Nature, and a common term in the Zend-avesta.

‡ [I have some doubt as to the construction of the original sentence. But I conceive the 'ihnen,' '*from them*,' to refer to the purified souls,—that these stains are separated from them.—H. J. R.]

* See Alexand. Lycopol. c. 6. The following are a few peculiarly characteristic Manicheean passages, as proofs of the exposé given above. In the Thesaurus of Manes the following passage occurs: "Viva anima, quæ earundem (adversarum potestatum) membris tenebatur, hac occasione lunata evadit, et suo purissimo aeri miscetur: ubi penitus ablutæ animæ adscendunt ad lucidas naves, quæ sibi ad evectionem atque ad suæ patriæ transfretationem sunt præparatæ. Id vero quod adhuc adversi generis maculas portat, per æstum atque calores particulatim descendit atque arboribus, cæterisque plantationibus ac satis omnibus miscetur." Euodius de Fide, c. 14. From the Letter of Manes to the maiden Menoch, we have this passage: "agnoscendo ex quo genere animarum emanaveris, quod est confusum omnibus corporibus, et saporibus et speciebus variis cohæret." Augustin. opus imperfectum contra Julian, lib. iii. § 172. There is also a passage of Faustus, the Manichee, who lived in the first half of the fifth century, in which the Holy Ghost is represented as the enlivening and sanctifying power of God, working through the air towards the purifying process of Nature; and the doctrine of the birth of Christ from the Virgin (which the Manichees, being Docetæ, cannot agree to in its proper sense,) is represented as a symbol of the birth of that *patibilis Jesus* from the virgin bosom of the earth through the operation of the power of the Holy Ghost: "Spiritus sancti, qui est majestas tertia, aeris hunc omnem ambitum sedem fatemur ac diversorium, cujus ex viribus ac spiritali profusione terram quoque concipientem gignere patibilem Jesum, qui est vita ac salus hominum, omni suspensus ex ligno. Quapropter et nobis circa universam (i. e. all productions of Nature, considered as revelations of the same Divine *principle of life*, suffering under the imprisonment of matter, revelations of the same Jesus Patibilis,) et vobis similiter erga panem et calicem par religio est." August. c. Faust. c. xx.

Darkness, robbed of all its stolen Light, should be wholly abandoned to its own inward hatefulness and to its death. What then was to be done? A Being was to be produced, into which the Soul of Nature, that struggles to free itself, should be driven and fast bound, in which all the scattered Light and Life of Nature, all which the Powers of Darkness kept imprisoned in their members, and which was constantly more and more enticed away from them by the power of the Sun, is concentrated; this is The Man, the image of the Original Man, and therefore, already destined through his form to rule over nature.* The matter stands thus. The Lofty Light-Form of the original Man (which was also apparently peculiar to the Son of Man dwelling in the Sun)† sends down light from the Sun into the kingdom of Darkness, or the Material World; the Powers of Darkness are seized with desire after the Light-Form, but with confusion also. Their Prince now speaks to them: "What think ye that great Light to be which rises up yonder? Behold! how it shakes the pole, how it strikes to earth many of our Powers! Therefore, is it fitting, that ye should rather bestow on me whatsoever ye have of Light in your powers; and then I will make an image of that Great One, which appears full of glory, through which we may rule, and may hereafter free ourselves from our abode in Darkness." Thus human nature is the image, in this dark world, of higher existence, through which the higher (every thing of a higher nature) may be attracted hither and held fast. After they had heard this, and had consulted together for a long time, they thought it best to fulfil his desire, *for they did not believe that this Light could long maintain itself among them,*‡ and therefore, they considered it best to offer it to their Prince, because they did not doubt that by this means they should obtain the predominance. The Powers of Darkness now paired themselves, and begat children, in whom their common natures and powers were again represented, and in whom every thing which they had of the essence of Light and Darkness in them reproduced itself. All these children of theirs the Prince of Darkness devours, and by this means concentrates in himself all the Light-Existence which was spread abroad among the individual Powers of Darkness, and he produced Man, in whom all the powers of the kingdoms of Darkness and of Light, which had here intermingled with each other, assembled together. Hence Man is considered as a microcosm,—a reflection of the whole world of Light and of Darkness, a mirror of all the Powers of the Heaven and of the Earth.*

---

* Compare the parallel doctrines of the Ophites.
† Alexand. Lycopolit. c. 4, εἰκόνα δὲ ἐν ἡλίῳ ἱδρύσθαι ταύτην, ἥτις ἐστὶ τὸ τοῦ ἀνθρώπου εἶδος.
‡ This is the most important matter.

* Manes, Ep. Fundamenti; Augustin. de Natura Boni, c. 46. Construebantur et continebantur omnium imagines, cœlestium ac terrenarum virtutum: ut pleni videlicet orbis, id quod formabatur, similitudinem obtineret. We must not here suppress the fact, that in respect to the main matter of the formation of man *a somewhat different* construction of the Manichean system is possible; which Mosheim, with his peculiar acuteness, has thoroughly worked out, and for which certainly something of weight may be advanced. Unfortunately, the gaps which have been left in the extant fragments of Manes, which are the most secure foundation for any account of his system, are too great to allow us to decide the inquiry by his own words. We have followed that *mode of construction* by which man was supposed to be created later than the rest of Nature, in order to keep fast in Nature the soul whose tendency was to escape. The last quoted words of Manes appear to support this representation. So also does the Disputat. Archelai, § 7, as well as the words of Alexander of Lycopolis, about the form of man shedding down light from the sun. It would then be the same Spirit of the Sun, who, after the first separation of Light from Darkness, operating upon the purifying process of Nature, had put the Powers of Darkness (who feared to be thereby robbed of all their spiritual being which constantly escaped from them) into confusion, and which afterwards appeared in Christ as the Redeemer. To this the passage of Alexand. Lycop. appears to point, c. 4, τὸν δὴ Χριστὸν εἶναι νοῦν, ὃ δὴ καὶ ἀφικόμενον ποτε, (then, when the Powers of Darkness endeavoured, by the formation of man, to retain the soul which threatened to escape from them, and thus to frustrate the work of the Spirit of the Sun,) πλησίον τι τῆς δυνάμεως ταύτης, πρὸς τὸν Θεὸν λελυμένοι καὶ δὴ τὸ τελευταῖον, &c. The fragments also of a Manichee in the preface to the Third Division of Titus of Bostra, may be conveniently explained in the same manner.

But we might also, with Mosheim, set the formation of Man in the system of Manes *before the whole creation of the world.* The Powers of Darkness were disturbed at the appearance of the ζῶν πνεῦμα, which threatened to tear away from them all the souls they had seized upon. Hence they now united themselves in order to form Man, after the image of that original Man, whom they saw shining from afar (this was that 'ille magnus qui gloriosus apparuit,') in order that they might through him enchant and hold fast the souls which the Living Spirit threatened to rob them of. It was, then, after the intention of the Living

That which is here described, is repeated constantly in the course of Nature, when at the birth of a man, the wild powers of Matter, the Powers of Darkness, pairing themselves together, produce a human Nature, in which they mingle together whatsoever they have both of the higher and of the lower Life, and in which they endeavour to fetter the Soul of Nature, which, while it struggles after freedom, is held prisoner by them.*

Also, according to the Manicheean scheme, the Powers of Darkness are involuntarily subservient to a higher law, and by their machinations against the kingdom of Light, prepare destruction for themselves The Light, (*lit.* Light Nature, or particles partaking of the essential attributes of Light) or the Soul, concentrated in man's nature, thereby only arrives the sooner at a consciousness of itself, and at the development of its own peculiar nature. As the common Soul of the World endeavours to subject to itself all existing Matter, i. e. the great Body of the World, so must this Soul, derived as it is from the same origin as that, govern this miniature material world. "The first soul," says Manes,† " which flowed forth from the God of Light, received this form of the body, in order that it might govern the body by its restraints, (*lit.* bridle.") The soul of the First Man,‡ as standing nearer to the Original Source of the kingdom of Light, was, therefore, endued with pre-eminent powers. But yet, in consequence of its double descent, the Nature of the First Man consisted of two opposite parts; the one a soul akin to the kingdom of Light, already in possession of the fulness of its power, and the other a body akin to the kingdom of Darkness, together with a blind matter-born capability of desire, which it derived from the same kingdom.*

Under these circumstances, all depended, with the Powers of Darkness, on their being able to oppress the Light-Nature which had been superinduced on man, and to retain it in a condition of unconsciousness. They invited man to eat of all the trees of Paradise, that is, to enjoy all earthly desires, while they only wished to restrain him from eating of the tree of the knowledge of Good and Evil, that is, from attaining to a consciousness of the opposition between Light and Darkness, or between the Divine and the Ungodly in his own nature, and in the whole world.† But an angel of Light, or rather the Spirit of the Sun himself, persuaded man to transgress the commandment, that is, he led him to that consciousness which the Powers of Darkness wished to withhold from him, and thereby secured him the victory over them. This is the truth, which is the foundation of that narrative of Genesis, only we must change the persons engaged in the transaction, and instead of *God* we must put the *Prince of Darkness*, and instead of the *Serpent* we must put the *Spirit of the Sun*.‡

As now the kingdom of Light had triumphed over the Powers of Darkness, the latter made use of a new means, in order to take prisoner the Light-Nature, which had now attained to self-conscious-

---

Spirit, to free at once the imprisoned souls, had been frustrated by these machinations, that he for the first time thought of the creation of the world, in order to effect *by degrees, what he had been prevented from accomplishing at once.* The words of Alexander of Lycopolis, who, however, did not find himself quite at home in the train of thought belonging to the Manicheean system, appear to support this view, when he accuses the Manicheean system of inconsistency, (Inconsequenz:) c. 23, ἐν ᾑλίῳ δὲ τὴν εἰκόνα (τοῦ ἀνθρώπου) ἱδράσθαι λέγουσιν, ὃς ἐγένετο κατ᾽ αὐτοὺς ἀπὸ τῆς πρὸς τὴν ὕλην ὑστέρον διακρίσεως, for, according to these words, (if Alexander has understood Manes properly, or the Manichee whose works he read, has properly represented the doctrines of his master,) Manes must have imagined the separation of the soul unaffected by Matter, or of the Spirit of the Sun, to have taken place before the rest and after the formation of man.

* The words of Manes, l. c., are these, "sicuti etiam nunc fieri videmus, corporum formatricem naturam mali inde vires sumentem figurare." These words seem important as a hint, which indicates the symbolical meaning of the whole narration.

† In the letter quoted above.

‡ "Quasi de primæ facta flore substantiæ," says Manes, l. c.

* The ψυχὴ ἄλογος.

† See Disputat. Archelai, c. 10.

‡ This would be the explanation of the doctrine of Manes, if the representation given by the Manichee in Titus of Bostra, (at the end of the preface to Section III.,) be the original one; and it may be said that it suits the Manicheean system extremely well, and dovetails in with the account given of it in the Disputation of Archelaus. It may, perhaps, surprise us, that Manes, who was brought up in the Parsic religion, should have made *the serpent*, which among the Parsees is the symbol of Ahriman, into the symbol of the Good Spirit; but according to the view given above this consideration forms no difficulty. As he saw in the religious documents of the Jews so many corruptions derived from the Spirit of Darkness, he saw his corruptions and falsifying influence exerted also in a wilful corruption of this narrative, by changing the places of those engaged in the transaction.

ness, and to detach it from its connection with its original Source. They seduced the First Man, by means of the Eva bestowed upon him as a companion, into giving himself up to fleshly desires, and thereby, becoming untrue to his nature as a Being of Light, to make himself the servant of a foreign domination.* The consequence which flowed thence was, that the Soul, which by its original power ought to raise itself into the kingdom of Light, divided itself by propagation, and became enclosed anew in material bodies, so that the Powers of Darkness could forever repeat what they had done at the production of the First Man.

Every man also has now the same destination as the first, namely, to rule by means of the power of the Spirit over matter. Every one consists of the same two parts, of which the nature of the first man consisted, and therefore, all depends upon this, that man remembering his origin, should know how to separate these two parts properly from each other. He who thinks that he has received his sensuous nature, (sinnlichkeit,) together with its appetites, from God,—he who does not know from the very first origin of human nature, that it (viz. this sinnlichkeit, or his corporeal and sensuous endowments,) proceeds from the kingdom of Darkness, will easily allow himself to be seduced into serving his senses, and thereby lose his higher Light-Nature, and become unfaithful to the kingdom of Light. Therefore, does Manes say in his Letter of Principles, (Epistola Fundamenti,) "If it had been given to man to know clearly the whole condition of Adam's and Eve's origin, they would never have been subjected to decay and death." And hence, also, he writes to the virgin Menoch† thus: "May our God himself enlighten thy soul, and reveal to thee thy righteousness, because thou art the fruit of a godly stem.‡ Thou also hast become Light, by recognising what thou wast before, and from what race of Souls thou art sprung, which being intermingled with all bodies is connected with various forms; for as souls are engendered by souls, so is the form of the body composed of the nature of the body. That also, which is born of the flesh is flesh, and that which is born of the spirit is spirit. But know that the spirit is the soul, soul of soul, flesh of flesh."* He then appealed to the *custom of infant baptism,* which was even then prevalent in *the Parsic Church,* as a proof that Christians themselves, by their mode of proceeding, took for granted such an original defilement of man's nature. "I inquire," he says, in the Letter† we have quoted, " whether all evil is *actual* evil ? Wherefore, then, does any one receive purification by means of water, before he has done any evil, as he cannot possibly have been obnoxious to evil *in his own person?* But inasmuch as he has been the subject of no evil, and yet must be purified, *they* point out *ipso facto,* a descent from an evil race; even they themselves, whose fancy will not allow them to understand what they say, nor what they assume."

The particle of Light *(literally,* the Light-Nature,) which from its removal from the source of that concentrated Existence-of-Light (literally, Light-Being) in the person of Adam, from which all souls emanated, was constantly becoming more and more defiled through its continued connection with matter,—so that it now remained no longer in possession of the original power which it had, when it first flowed forth fresh from the original source of the kingdom of Light. The Law, however, presupposes the original power of the Light-Nature, to be still in existence, in order that it (the Law) may be put in practice. "The Law is holy," says Manes, " but it is holy for *holy souls,* the commandment is upright and good, but for *upright and good souls.*"‡ He says in another passage,§ "If we do good, it is not the work of the flesh, for the works of the flesh are manifest, (Gal. v. 19;) or if we do evil, then it is not the work of the soul, for the fruit of the Spirit is

---

* As we have no accounts of the arrangement of these events in the Manicheean system as to the time of their occurrence, we may also place their relations to each other in a different manner. It may be supposed that Adam first allowed himself to be seduced into sin, but afterwards being brought by the influence of the Sun-Spirit to a consciousness of the opposition between the flesh and the Spirit, and Light and Darkness, that he began a more holy life. See Augustin. de Moribus Manichæorum, lib. ii. 19.

† Augustin. op. imperfect. c. Julian. lib. iii. § 172.

‡ The Revelation consists in man's being brought to a consciousness of his Light-Nature.

---

* According to the Light-Emanation System adopted by Manes, he could not make any difference between the Spirit of God and the spirit of man, between *spirit* and *soul.*

† Augustin. op. c. Julian. imperfect. lib. iii. § 187.

‡ L. c. c. Julian. iii. 186.   § L. c. 177.

peace, joy. And the apostle exclaims, in the epistle to the Romans, "The good which I would, I do not, but the evil which I would not, that I do." Ye perceive, therefore, the voice of the contending soul, which defends its freedom against lust, for it was distressed, because Sin, that is, Satan, had worked all lust in it. The reverence for the Law discovers all its evil, because the Law blames all its practices, which the flesh admires and esteems; for all bitterness in the renunciation of lust is sweet for the soul, which is nourished thereby and thereby attains to strength. At last the Soul of him who withdraws himself from every gratification of lust, is awake, it becomes mature, and increases; but the gratification of lust is usually the means of loss to the soul.* And now, in order at last to free the souls which are akin to him from the power of Darkness, to animate them anew, to give them a perfect victory over it, and to attract them to himself, the same spirit of the Sun, who has hitherto conducted the whole process of purification for Nature and for the spiritual world (which two, according to the principles of Manes here laid down, make up only one whole) must reveal himself in human nature.†

But between Light and Darkness no communion is possible. "The Light shines in Darkness," said Manes, using the words of St. John, after *his own interpretation*, "but the Darkness cannot comprehend it." The Son of the Original Light, the Spirit of the Sun, could not ally himself with any material body; he could only envelope himself in a phantomic form, perceptible by the senses, in order that he might be perceived by man as a creature of sense. "While the Supreme Light," Manes writes,‡ "put himself on a footing with his own people as to his nature, he assumed a body among material bodies, although he himself is everything, and only one whole nature." By an arbitrary mode of interpretation, he appealed for a proof of his Docetism, to the circumstance, that Christ once, (John viii. 59,) when the Jews wished to stone him, escaped through the midst of them without their being able to lay hold on him, and also that Christ at his transfiguration appeared to his disciples in his true Light-Form* He assumed improperly the name Christ or Messias, in accommodating himself to the notions of the Jews.† The Prince of Darkness endeavoured to effect the crucifixion of Jesus, because he did not know him as the being elevated above all suffering; and this crucifixion was, of course, nothing but an apparent one. This appearance represented the crucifixion of the Soul overwhelmed with matter, which the Spirit of the Sun desired to elevate to himself. As the crucifixion of that soul which was spread over all matter only served to facilitate the annihilation of the Kingdom of Darkness, so also still more did that *apparent crucifixion of the Supreme Soul*. Therefore, Manes said, "The adversary, who hoped that he had crucified the Saviour, the Father of the righteous, was crucified himself; that *which happened*, and that which seemed to happen in this case, were two different things."‡ The Manicheean view, which made the doctrine of Christ crucified merely symbolical, is clearly displayed in an apocryphal *writing about the travels of the apostles*.|| While John is in anxiety during the passion of Christ, the latter appears to him and tells him, that all this happens only for the lower multitude in Jerusalem.§ The human person of Christ now disappears, and instead of him there appears a cross of pure light, surrounded by various other forms, which, nevertheless, represented only *one form* and *one image*, (as a symbol of the various forms under which the *one Soul* appears.) From above the cross there proceeded a divine and cheering voice, which said to him, "The Cross of Light will, for your sake, be called, sometimes the Logos, sometimes Christ, some-

---

* On the Incarnations of the Sun in the old Oriental religions, see Kreuzer's Symbolik, (New edition, 2d Part, 53, 207.) It was quite consistent, according to the Manicheean System, for the Manichees to say, (ap. Alexander of Lycopolis, c. 24,) that Christ, as the νους was τα οντα παντα. So also in the Acts of Thomas, p. 10, κυριε, ο εν πασιν ων και διεχχομενος διαπαντων και η κινμενος πασι τοις εργοις σου και δια της παντων ενεργειας φανερουμενος.

† In the Letter to one Adas or Addas. Fabricii Biblioth. Græca, ed. nov. vol. vii. p. 316.

* See the Fragment from the Epistles of Manes, l. c.

† η του Χριστου προσηγορια ονομα εστι κατα χρηστικον. l. c.

‡ From the Epistola Fundamenti, Euod. de fid. c. 28. την δυναμιν την θειαν ενηρμοσθαι ενεσταυρωσθαι τη υλη. Alex. Lycopolit. c. 4. Christus in omni mundo et omni anima crucifixus. Secundin. Ep. ad Augustin. The words of Faustus the Manichee are these: Augustin. c. Faustum, lib. xxxii. Crucis ejus mystica fixio, qua nostræ animæ passionis monstrantur vulnera.

|| περιοδοι αποστολων. Concil. Nic. II. actio v. ed. Mansi, t. xiii. p. 167.

§ τω κατω ὑλη.

times the Door, sometimes the Way, sometimes Jesus, sometimes the Father, sometimes the Spirit, sometimes Life, sometimes the Truth, sometimes Faith, and sometimes Grace."

As Manes joined those among the Parsees who maintained an absolute dualism, he did not propose as the object of the whole course of the world a reconciliation between the good and the evil principle, which would not have suited his theory, but an entire separation of Light from Darkness, and an utter annihilation of the power of the latter. After matter had been deprived of all Light and Life, which did not belong to her, she was to be burnt up into a dead mass.* All souls might become partakers of redemption in virtue of their Light-Nature; but if they voluntarily gave themselves up to the service of evil or of Darkness, by way of punishment, after the general separation of the two kingdoms, they were to be driven into the dead mass of matter, and set to keep watch over it. Manes in his *Epistola Fundamenti* expressed himself thus on this point: those souls which have allowed themselves to be seduced from their original Light-Nature through love of the World, and have become enemies of the Holy Light, that is, which have armed themselves openly for the destruction of the Holy Element, which serve the fiery Spirit, and have oppressed by hostile persecution the Holy Church† and the elect to be found in it,‡ that is, the observers of the commandments of heaven—these souls will be detained far from the blessedness and the glory of the Holy Earth. And because they have suffered themselves to be conquered by evil, they will remain in company with this family of evil, so that *that Earth* of peace and those regions of immortality are closed against them. That will happen to them for this reason, that, because they gave themselves up to evil works, they became estranged from the Life and Freedom of the Holy Light. Thus, they cannot be received into that kingdom of peace, but are chained down into that terrible mass (of matter left to itself, or Darkness,) for which a guard is necessary. These Souls will thus remain entangled among those things, which they have loved, for they did not separate themselves from them, while they had the opportunity.*

In regard to the Manicheean view of the *sources of knowledge* of religion, the revelations of the *Paraclete or Manes*, were the highest, the only *infallible* sources, by which all others must be judged. They set out from the principle that the doctrines of Manes include the absolute truths, which are evident to our reason; whatever does not accord with them, is contrary to reason, and false, wherever it may be found. But they now accepted also the writings of the New Testament in part; but, while they judged of them according to the paramount principle stated above, they allowed themselves a very arbitrary line of criticism in respect to their dogmatical and ethical use.† Partly, they maintained that the original documents of religion had been adulterated by various interpolations of the Prince of Darkness,‡ (the tares amidst the good wheat;) partly, Jesus and the apostles were supposed to accommodate themselves to the opinions prevalent among the Jews, in order, gradually, to render men capable of receiving truth in its purity; and partly, the apostles themselves were supposed on their first entrance upon the office of teachers, to have been under the influence of many Jewish errors. Thence they gathered that it was only by the instruction of the Paraclete, that men could learn to separate the true from the false in the New Testament. Faustus, the Manichee, thus brings forward the principles of Manicheeism in this respect:§ "We only receive that part of the New Testament, which was spoken to the honour of the Son of Glory, either by himself or by the apostles, and even then, only that which was spoken when they were already *perfect* or *believers*. We will take no account of the rest, neither what was spoken by the apostles in simplicity and ignorance, while they were as yet unacquainted with the truth, nor of that which was attributed to them with evil intentions by their enemies, nor of that which was imprudently maintained by their writers,∥ and

---

* Tit. Bostr. l. c. 30. Alex. Lycopol. c. 5.
† That is, the Manicheean sect.
‡ A persecution of the *Brahmins* of the Manichees, or the Electi, which was a special crime; all this was in full accordance with the oriental ideas of the priesthood.

* De Fide. c. 4.
† Titus of Bostra says this of them in the very beginning of his third book.
‡ See above, the similar principles used in the Clementine in regard to the Old Testament.
§ Ap. Augustin, lib. 32.
∥ Namely the Evangelists, who were not apostles.

handed down to their successors. I think, however, that HE was born of a woman in sin, was circumcised as a Jew, that he sacrificed as an Heathen, that he was baptized in an inferior manner, and was carried about the wilderness by the Devil, and exposed to the most painful trials." The same Manichees who were content that their reason should be fettered by all the decisions of Manes as divine revelations, were zealous for the rights of reason, and wished to be looked upon as the *only reasonable* men, when they employed themselves in separating what is conformable to reason in the New Testament from that which contradicts it. Faustus, the Manichee, speaks to one, who believes without critical discrimination in *all* which is contained in the New Testament, *" Thou, that believest all blindly; thou, that dost banish reason, the gift of nature, out of mankind; thou, that makest it a scruple to thyself to judge between truth and falsehood! and thou, that art not less afraid to separate good from its contrary, than children are afraid of ghosts!"**

The Manichees had a *composition of their religious society*, entirely peculiar to themselves, in which the character of Oriental Mysticism may be recognised. Manes separated himself wholly, as it follows from what is said above, from the greater number of the Gnostic founders of sects, as these latter wished to change nothing in the existing Christian Church, but only to introduce a secret doctrine of the πνυματικοι to run parallel with the Church belief of the ψυχικοι. Manes, on the contrary, wished to be looked upon as a Reformer of the whole Church, sent from God, and endued with divine authority; he wished to give a new form to the Church, which he thought entirely dislocated by the intermixture of Judaism and Christianity;† there was to be only *one true Christian Church*, which was to be moulded after the doctrines and principles of Manes. In this, only two orders were to exist, according to the distinction between an *exoteric* and an *esoteric* doctrine, which was a fundamental feature of the Oriental systems of religion. The *auditores* were to form the great mass of the exoterics; the writings of Manes were read to these, and the doctrines laid before them in their symbolical and mystical clothing, but they received no explanation as to their interior and hidden meaning.* We can easily imagine how the expectation of the *auditores* was put to the stretch, when they heard these enigmatical and mysterious high-sounding things laid before them, and, as it often happens, hoped that they should find lofty wisdom in what was enigmatical and unintelligible! The *esoterics* were the *Electi*, or *Perfecti*,† the *Caste of Priests*,—the *Brahmins* of the Manichees.‡ They were to lead, in celibacy, a strictly ascetic and wholly contemplative life; they were to refrain from all strong liquors, and from all animal food; they were to be distinguished by a holy innocence, which injures no living creature, and a religious veneration for the Divine Life which is spread abroad throughout all nature; and, hence, they were not only neither to kill nor wound any animal, but not even to pull any vegetable, nor to pluck any fruit or flower. They were to be provided with all that was needful for their subsistence by the *auditores*, by whom they were to be honoured as beings of a superior kind. From this caste of priests the leaders of the whole religious society were chosen. As Manes wished to be looked upon as the Paraclete, promised by Christ, he chose twelve apostles also after the example of Christ. And this arrangement was to be constantly maintained, that twelve such persons, under the name of *Magistri*, should lead the whole sect. Above these twelve stood a thirteenth, who, as the head of the whole sect, represented Manes. Under these stood seventy-two bishops, who were to answer to the seventy or seventy-two§ disciples of Jesus, and then below these, presbyters and deacons, and lastly, roving missionaries of the faith.‖

There is considerable obscurity about the question, what the Manichees held as to the *celebration of the sacraments*. This arises from the circumstance, that naturally enough, no authentic account could be known of that which took place in the assemblies of the *Electi*, which were held

---

* Augustin. c. Faust. lib. xviii. and also lib. xi.
† Hence he called other Christians, not Christians, but Galileans. Fabric. Bibl. Gr. vol. vii. p. 316.

* It certainly follows from this, that the writings of Manes must contain a certain interior meaning, understood only by the *electi*.
† τελωαι, according to Theodoret, an appellation which re-appeared again among the Gnostic Manichæan sects of the middle ages.
‡ Faustus, as quoted by Augustine, calls them the " Sacerdotale Genus."
§ According to the well known *varia lectio*.
‖ Augustin. de Hæres c. 46.

very secretly; and as the *auditores* might be supposed to answer to the catechumens, and the *Electi* to the *Fideles* of the general Church, it may at once be imagined that the sacrament could only be celebrated among the *Electi*. The belief, that we are justified, in consequence of the inference, which has been quoted, as made by Manes from the prevailing custom of infant baptism, in supposing that infant baptism prevailed among the Manichees, is unsound, as Mosheim has already shown; in that passage, Manes intended to controvert his adversaries out of their own conduct in respect to principles, which that conduct necessarily presupposed, without intending to convey any approbation of that conduct. And besides, the use of baptism might appear to the Manichees, according to their own theory of the pure and holy Elements, as a suitable ceremony for initiation into the interior of the sect, or for reception into the number of the *electi*. And yet it may also be thought that they were not favourable to this symbol, as being a Jewish one, which came from John the Baptist; perhaps, from the very beginning no other kind of initiation was practised among them, than that which we find afterwards among the offsets of the Manichees in the middle ages; and perhaps, the use of baptism had only proceeded in certain parts of the sect from an adherence to the prevailing custom of the Church.* The *celebration of the sacrament of the Lord's Supper* might be perfectly well interpreted according to the mystical natural philosophy* of the Manichees. Augustine, as one of the *auditores* among the Manichees, had heard that the *electi* celebrated the Lord's Supper; but he knew nothing of the mode in which it was done.† It is only certain, that the *electi* could drink no wine, but whether they used water like the Encratites, the so-called ὑδροπαραστάται, or what other measures they took, we have no means of determining. The *sign of recognition* among the Manichees was the giving of the right hand to each other when they met, as a symbol of their common redemption from the kingdom of Darkness through the freeing power of the Spirit of the Sun; while that was repeated in them, which had taken place in their Heavenly Father the Original Man, when he was in danger of sinking down into the kingdom of Darkness, and was again lifted up through the right hand of the Living Spirit.‡

In regard to the *festivals of the Manichees*, we may observe that they celebrated Sunday, not as commemorating the resurrection of Christ, which did not suit their Docetism, but as the day consecrated to the Sun,|| who was in fact their Christ. In contradiction to the prevailing usage of the Church, they fasted on this day. The festivals in honour of Christ, of course, did not suit the Docetism of the Manichees. While, indeed, according to the account of Augustine, they sometimes celebrated the festival of *Easter* in accordance with the prevailing usage of the Church, yet the lukewarmness with which this celebration took place, may

---

* From the words of Felix the Manichee, lib. i. c. 19, ut quid baptizati sumus? we cannot prove that the Manichees considered baptism as a necessary initiatory ceremony, for here also the Manichee is rather using an argumentum *ad hominem*, and he may have received baptism *before* his conversion to Manicheeism. From the passages in the Commonitorium, quo modo sit agendum cum Manichæis (to be found in the Appendix to the 8th. vol. of the Benedictine edition of St Augustine,) where a distinction is made between those Manichees, who had been received, at their conversion to the Catholic Church among the *Catechumens*, and those who were received, as *being already baptized*, into the number of the *Pœnitentes*, it is also entirely impossible to draw the conclusion, that baptism was in use among the Manichees; and still less does it follow, because such a distinction is made between baptized and unbaptized among the *electi* themselves, who transgressed, that baptism was voluntarily received only by a *certain part* of the *electi*; for here also the author may be speaking only of such persons as had received baptism in the Catholic Church before their conversion to the Manicheean sect. The passage in Augustin. de Moribus Ecclesiæ Catholicæ, c. 35, where he makes the Manichees offer it as a reproach to Catholic Christians, that even fideles et jam baptizati lived in marriage and in the various relations of family life, and possessed and administered earthly property, by no means proves that among the *electi* there was a class of persons, who, having voluntarily submitted to baptism, were the only persons who, through an inviolable engagement were bound to a strict ascetic life; for the FIDELES and the BAPTIZATI, two exactly equivalent expressions, here have a general correspondence with the *electi* of the Manichees. Mosheim's distinction, therefore, between baptized and unbaptized *electi*, however natural it may appear when abstractedly considered, seems altogether arbitrary.

* In accordance with the notion that the fruits of nature represented the Son of Man crucified in nature.

† Augustin. contra Fortunatum, lib. i, in the addendum.

‡ Disputat. Archelai, c. 7.

|| Besides many other passages, see Augustin. c. Faustum, lib. xviii. c. 5, " Vos in die, quem dicunt solis, solem colitis."

be explained from the circumstance that they could not be touched by any of those feelings, which gave so much holiness to this festival in the eyes of other Christians. On this account they celebrated the more solemnly the martyrdom of their founder, Manes, which took place in the month of March. It was called Βῆμα, (suggestus, Cathedra,) the festival of the Chair of the Teacher, the festival dedicated to the memory of the teacher illuminated by God. A teacher's chair gaily ornamented and enveloped in costly cloths, was placed in the room where their assemblies were held, and five steps, apparently as a symbol of the five pure Elements, led the way to this chair. All the Manichees testified their reverence for this chair, by falling down before it to the earth, after the Oriental fashion.*

As far as the *moral character* of the Manicheean sect is concerned, since it is necessary on this point accurately to distinguish between the different periods in the history of a sect, we have too scanty notices of the *first adherents* to it, to allow us to pronounce any definite opinion on the point. Thus much only may be asserted, that Manes intended to maintain a severity of morals in his doctrine; but it must be acknowledged, that the mystical language in which it was conveyed, which was occasionally indecent, might introduce among uneducated and unrefined men the intermixture of a sensuous extravagance, likely to prove dangerous to purity of morals.

Almost immediately that the Manichees began to spread in the Roman empire, a violent *persecution broke out against them.* They were peculiarly obnoxious to the Roman government as a sect, which drew its origin from the Persian empire, then at war with the Roman, and which was connected with the religion of the Parsees.

---

* Augustin. contra Epist. Fundamenti, c. 8, c. Faustum, lib. xviii. c. 5

The Emperor Diocletian (A. D. 296,) issued a law against this sect, by which the leaders of it were condemned to be burnt, and their other associates, if they were of an ordinary rank of life, were to be beheaded and suffer a forfeiture of their estates.*

---

* In regard to the train of thought and the language, in which the edict is composed, it contains all the internal marks of genuineness. It is difficult to conjecture by whom and with what intention such an edict could have been invented *in this form*. A Christian, who might have been inclined to palm such an edict upon the world, in order to drive the emperors to a persecution of the Manicheean sect, would not exactly have chosen Diocletian, and still less have attributed such language to him. Although the later Christians, in their notions of a dominant religion, transmitted traditionally to them through the Fathers, had much that was analogous to the thoughts of the Heathen, yet a Christian would never have expressed himself *altogether in this fashion*.

Why should not the Manicheean sect *already* have been able *by that time* to extend itself towards Proconsular Africa; for the Gnostics had been preparing the way there, the Manichees certainly were *at an early period* spread abroad in these districts, and the chronological data relative to the first history of this sect are so uncertain? It is said in the law, "si qui sane etiam honorati aut cujuslibet dignitatis vel majoris personæ ad hanc sectam se transtulerunt," but it does not necessarily follow from this, that the emperor had any certain account of the propagation of this sect among the *first* classes, and it would not be surprising in the then attachment of persons of distinction, (who are always glad enough, besides, to have something that implies distinction in religion,) to Theurgical studies, and to endeavours after sublime determination relative to the World of Spirits, if a mysterious religion of this kind, with such lofty pretensions, found a ready acceptance with them. Besides the *argumentum e silentio*, in historical criticism, is very uncertain; if no particular circumstances conspire to give it greater weight, and the fact that the ancient Fathers of the Church did not quote a decree of Diocletian against the Manichees, easily admits of a satisfactory explanation. And yet this decree is quoted as early as Hilarius, who wrote a commentary on the epistles of St. Paul, in the comment on 2 Tim. iii. 7.

THE ALEXANDRIANS

In order properly to understand the development of the peculiar theological spirit of this school, we must fully enter into its relations with regard to the three different parties, in connection with which, and in opposition to which, it was formed, and the different spiritual dispositions of which, it hoped to be able to reconcile and to unite together by means of a higher principle, which would smoothe down the contradictions between them.

These relations were,

1. Their relation to the *Greeks*, who sought after wisdom, who despised Christianity as a blind, reason-hating belief, and who were only strengthened in their contempt of it, by the sensuous conceptions of the uninformed and abruptly repulsive Christians by which they were met.

2. Their relation to the Gnostics, then very common in Alexandria, who at the same time spoke with contempt of the blind belief of the sensuous multitude, and by the promise of a higher exoteric religious creed, attracted to themselves the Heathens who were inquiring after wisdom, and the Christians who were unsatisfied with the common instruction in religion.

3. Their relation to that first class of pastors of the Church, whose views were of a *Practical-realistic nature*, and particularly those among them who were very *zealous*, to whom from the speculative pride and presumption of the Gnostics, all speculation and philosophizing, and every attempt at any thing like a Gnosis, were objects of suspicion, and were always fearful of the intermixture of foreign philosophical elements with Christianity.

By means of a Gnosis,* proceeding from faith, and engrafting itself on that faith in harmony with it, the Alexandrians expected to avoid the one-sided and false views of these three dispositions, and to appropriate to themselves whatever there was of truth in each of them, nay, even to be able to reconcile them to each other.

In their theory of the relation of γνωσις to πιστις they differed from the Gnostics in this respect, that they recognised πιστις as the foundation of the higher life for *all* Christians, as the common bond, by which all, however they might differ from each other in intellectual culture, might be united into one Divine community. They even also opposed the unity of the Catholic Church, founded on this faith, to the discrepancies of the Gnostic schools (διατριβαι,) the one with the other, and they did not assume different sources of knowledge for πιστις and γνωσις, but the same, for both; namely, the tradition of the main doctrines of Christianity, existing in all Churches, and Holy Scripture; they ascribed to Gnosis only the work, of bringing into full consciousness, that which was first acquired by faith and received into the inward life, of developing it according to its full extent and its internal connection, of grounding it upon knowledge, and presenting it to others with knowledge, of proving that this is the genuine doctrine, which came from Christ, of giving a reason for it, and of defending it against the reproaches of its adversaries among the heathen philosophers and heretics. They used here for their motto the *passage of Isaiah*, which appears already to have been used as a motto in more ancient days, and which afterwards was the motto to designate the relation between faith and knowledge from the days of Augustine to those of the scholastic theology formed upon Augustine—the passage found in Isaiah vii. 9. This passage, indeed, if taken only in the Alexandrian version, and without reference to the context, may bear this meaning :* ἰαν μη πιστευσητε. οὐδε μη συνητι, if ye believe not, neither will you attain to knowledge—which words they first took in this sense : whosoever does not believe in the Gospel, cannot attain to an insight into the spirit of the nature of the Old Testament; and *then* in the sense which is akin to it: without faith in Christianity man cannot penetrate into the deeper knowledge of the nature of the Christian doctrines.‡ Thus Clement says,

---

* γνωσις ἀληθινη opposed to the ψευδωνυμος.

* Just as in later times, many passages of the translation of the Bible by Luther have become current, as proofs, for some proposition which had reference to Christian faith, or Christian life, although this application of them was not in conformity with the meaning of the original. [How often *e. g.* have the words, "Search the Scriptures," been cited as a *command*, by persons who did not dream that the original would bear a very different sense, 'Ye search the Scriptures;' and that some distinguished critics have maintained that the latter sense is the more appropriate. See Bp. Jebb's Sermon on this text.—H. J. R.]

‡ Stromat. lib. ii. 362 A ; lib. i. 273 A ; lib. iv.

"Faith is as necessary for the spiritual life of the Gnostic, as breath is for the animal life."* They endeavoured to make good the substantial nature, the dignity and power of Faith against the heathen and heretics. Clement combats the notion, that Faith is a mere arbitrary opinion. Faith with him is a free apprehension of the Divine, preceding all demonstration,† a practical assent, in virtue of the feeling of truth implanted in the nature of man, and in virtue of the natural disposition to a belief in the truth that reveals itself to man; unbelief is, therefore, in his opinion, a *deficiency* on the part of man ;‡ and he says in another passage, "He who believes on the Son, has eternal life. Since then, the believers have life, what higher thing remains for them, than the possession of eternal life? But nothing is deficient in Faith, which is perfect and self-sufficient in itself."§ Clement here sets forth as the characteristic of Faith, that it brings with it the pledge of the future, that it takes beforehand the future as a present possession.‖ How a deeper knowledge of that which is believed proceeds, by means of the enlightenment of the reason, from a Faith, which passes into the interior life, while that which is believed is enacted in life (lit. *becomes lived,*) is beautifully explained by Origen in the passage quoted above,¶ where he says, after quoting a narrative from the Gospel, "He who believes and understands what is written in Isaiah vii. 9, will have received understanding, from his faith, according to the measure of his faith; and when he has received this, let him say what he has a right to say after the foundation of his faith, in the spirit of his faith, in the spirit of these words : *I believe, and therefore, I speak*, Ps. cxvi. 10; Rom. x. 10.** Let such an one believe not merely in Jesus, and on that which is written in this place, but let him recognise the sense that is included in it; for he who remains in the truth of faith, and lives in the word by works corresponding to the word, learns the truth, as Jesus promised, and is made free by the truth." What Clement also says about the new powers of perception for Divine things proceeding from this inward life of faith, is beautiful : " See, says the Logos, (Isaiah xliii. 9,) I will make a new thing, which no eye hath seen, and no ear hath heard, and hath not entered into the heart of any man, 1 Cor. ii. 9. Which may be beheld, received, and comprehended with a new eye, with a new ear, with a new heart, by faith and understanding, in as much as the disciples of the Lord speak, understand, and act spiritually."*

This is exactly the peculiar Christian feature in this Alexandrian theory, that they do not conceive Gnosis to be a matter of mere speculation, but as something proceeding from a new inward living power, produced by faith, and shown in conduct, as a *habitus practicus animi* ; and thus Clement says :† " As the doctrines, so must the conduct also be, for the tree is known by the fruits, not by the blossoms and leaves, and Gnosis comes also from the fruits and the conduct, not from the doctrine and the blossoms; for we say that Gnosis is not only doctrine, but a Divine knowledge, that light, which arises in the soul out of obedience to the commandment, which makes all things clear, and teaches man to know what there is in creation and himself, and how he can stand in communion with God, for what the eye is to the body, that Gnosis is in the soul." No knowledge of Divine things can exist, without a life in them, which comes from faith ; *here knowledge and life become one.*"‡

---

528 B; and Origenes in Matt. Ed. Huet. p. 424.] [The passages of Clemens are in Pott. p. 432. 320, 625 ; in Sylb. 156, 117, 226.]
* Stromat. lib. ii 373.
† Περληψις εὐγνωμενος προκαταληψεως.—Stromat. lib. ii. 371. [Pott. 444. Sylb. 159.]
‡ Stromat. lib. ii. 384.   [Pott. 459. Sylb. 165.]
§ Pædagog. lib. i. c. 6.
‖ ἐκεῖνο δε το (τῳ) πιστευσαι ἠδη προειληφοτες ἐσομενον, μετα την ἀναστασιν ἀπολαμβανομεν γενομενον.
¶ Compare also Stromat. vii. 731. [Pott. 864. Sylb. 310.] Faith is a good indwelling in the soul (ἐνδιαθετον τι [τι] ἀγαθον,) while it acknowledges God, and values Him, without an effort, and therefore, must man, proceeding from this faith, and increasing in it by the grace of God attain as far as possible the kingdom of him (God).
** These words also are not used properly, according to the Alexandrian version, and in conformity with the context; but the sense which Origen attaches to them, and the theory built upon them, are clear; all deeper development of the sense of Holy Scripture, or of the doctrines of the faith, must proceed from a life in faith.

* Clem. Stromat. lib. ii. 365 B. [Pott. 436. Sylb. 156.]
† Stromat. lib. iii. 444. [Pott. 531. Sylb. 191.]
‡ Clem. Stromat. lib. iv. 490: ὡς μηκετι ἐπιστημην ἐχειν και γνωσιν κεκτησθαι (τον γνωστικον) ἐπιστημην δε εἰναι και γνωσιν. [Pott. 581. Sylb. 210.]

He might certainly have obtained this idea from what the Neo-Platonic philosophy which is older than Plotinus, taught, concerning the identity of *subject* and *object* in the case of the highest con-

This is, therefore, in the Alexandrian theory, the *subjective* condition and the *subjective* nature of Gnosis; as far as regards the *objective* sources of knowledge, from which the 'Gnostikos' was to endeavour constantly to learn with greater clearness and depth the truths received through faith by him into his inward life: these were, according to Clement—*the Holy Scriptures*. Although many who were deficient in the education requisite for the purpose of investigating Scripture for themselves, only held fast the essential fundamental truths, which had been communicated to them at their first instruction, in accordance with tradition; the Gnostikos was to distinguish himself from the common race of believers, by proving these truths by a comparison of Scripture with itself, and supplying all that was needful to them, by knowing how to combat from the same Scriptures the errors which opposed them, and thus a faith grounded on much Biblical knowledge, was in his case to take the place of a belief on the authority of the Church. Clement uses the following language:* "Faith is, then, the shortly-expressed knowledge of that which is essential, but *Gnosis* is the strong and firm demonstration of the things received by faith, grounded on faith by means of the teaching of our Lord, by which faith is raised to an enlightened belief not to be shaken."† And, in opposing the proofs grounded on the undeceiving touchstone of Scripture to the reproach of the Heathens and Jews, that it is impossible, from the many sects among the Christians to know where truth may be found; the same writer says, "We do not confide on men, who only proclaim their own judgment, to whom we might, in like manner, oppose our own judgment. But since it is not enough, merely to express our own opinion, but we must support what we say, we do not wait for the witness of men, but we support what we say, by the word of the Lord, which is the most worthy of confidence of all modes of proof, or rather which is the only one, by the knowledge of which, those who have only just tasted the Scriptures, are *Believers*—those who have gone farther and are more accurately acquainted with the truth, are ' *Gnostics!*'*

Hence Clement calls the *Gnosis*, which proceeds from a comparison of different passages of Scripture with one another, and developes the consequences which flow from the recognised doctrines of faith, a faith according to knowledge (*literally*, a knowing faith.)† With him, therefore, the *Gnostic* is one, who has grown gray in the study of the Holy Scriptures, and whose life is nothing else than works and words, which correspond to the Divine truths received traditionally.‡ But it is only to the *Gnostic* that the Holy Scripture brings such a knowledge of Divine things, because it is he only, who brings to it a believing sense (or capacity)—a sense capable of receiving that which is Divine. Where a man wants this sense, Scripture appears unfruitful.§ This inward sense is, nevertheless, not sufficient to deduce out of the Scriptures the truths contained in them, to develope their whole extent, and to unite them into a systematized whole, so as to defend them against Heathens and Heretics, and to apply them to all which had hitherto been objects of human knowledge. For this there was needed a previous learned preparation, and such could not have been created anew at once by Christianity; but Christianity was obliged to engraft itself here on the class of learning and cultivation of mind here in vogue, just as it had grown up into existence and was ready for it, in order that Christianity, as the leaven for all mankind,‖ might by degrees penetrate it,

---

dition of intuitive perception; but he might have drawn *the thing* itself from his inward Christian experience and conceptions, without our assuming any other hypothesis to explain the circumstance, and he need not be supposed to have borrowed any thing from the Neo-Platonic philosophy, except the *form* in which he represented his notions. And besides, since the influence of spiritual phenomena, which lay hold deeply of the life of their age, extends far wider than is immediately perceptible, and cannot be mechanically reckoned, who can determine how far Christianity had already influenced the spiritual atmosphere, in which certain ideas became current?

* Stromat. vii. 732. [Pott. 865-6. Sylb. 311.]
† Ἡ μὲν οὖν πίστις σύντομός ἐστιν, ὡς ἔτος εἰπεῖν, τῶν κατεπειγόντων γνῶσις, ἡ γνῶσις δὲ ἀπόδειξις τῶν διὰ πίστεως παρειλημμένων ἰσχυρὰ καὶ βέβαιος, διὰ τῆς κυριακῆς διδασκαλίας ἐποικοδομουμένη τῇ πίστει, εἰς τὸ ἀμετάπτωτον καὶ μετ' ἐπιστήμης καταληπτὸν πυραγγιμώσσα.

* Stromat. vii. 757. [Pott. 891. Sylb. 322.]
† ἐπιστημονικὴν πίστις. Stromat. ii. 381. [Pott. 454. Sylb. 164.]
‡ Stromat. vii. 762-3. [Pott. 896. Sylb. 323.]
§ Stromat. vii. 756. τοῖς γνωστικοῖς κεκινηκασιν αἱ γραφαί.
‖ Clement has beautifully alluded to this parable of the leaven. "The power of the word, given to us, which does much with small means, which attracts every one, who receives it unto him, to itself in a secret and invisible manner,

and give its own peculiar turn to this cultivation of mind.

The Alexandrian Gnosis by this, now attracted to itself a multitude of reproaches from the other party, which compelled it thoroughly to justify its method of proceeding. This contest, which has often been repeated in history, is an interesting one. It was objected to the Alexandrian party, that the prophets and apostles had no philosophical education and attainments. Clement answered, "The apostles and prophets spoke certainly as disciples of the Spirit, what it inspired them to say; but we cannot reckon on a guidance of the Holy Spirit that stands in the place of all human means of information, in order to unravel the hidden sense of their words. The training of the mind by learning, must make us capable of developing the whole intention of the sense communicated to them by the inspiration of the Holy Spirit. He who wishes to become enlightened in his thought by the power of God, must already be accustomed to philosophize on spiritual matters; he must already have attained for himself the proper frame of thought, which may be then illuminated by a higher Spirit. He needs a dialectic education of the mind, in order to be able sufficiently to distinguish the ambiguous and synonymous terms of Holy Scripture."* Against those who maintain that man ought to content himself with faith, and who cast away all the knowledge, which men wish to use in the service of faith, he says—" As if, without even using any care towards the culture of the vine, they expected at once to obtain the grapes. The Lord is represented to us under the image of a vine, from whom we must harvest fruit with the reasonable carefulness and the skill of the husbandman. He must cut, dig, bind up, and do every thing of that kind, he needs the hook, the axe, and other tools of husbandry for the care of the Vine, in order that it may preserve fruit that we may enjoy."† He had to defend the Alexandrian Gnosis against the reproach, that Divine revelation is not allowed to be the self-sufficing source of truth; that it is made to need completion and support from foreign sources; and that those who are not well informed and highly educated, are excluded from a knowledge of it. He says in reply*—" If we are to make a distinction *of those*, who are always ready to complain, we should call philosophy something, which co-operates towards the knowledge of truth: an endeavour after truth—a preparatory training of the Gnostic, and we do not make the co-operating principle the original cause, nor the chief. Not as if that last could not exist without philosophy, for certainly *all of us*, without a general and encyclopædical instruction,† and without the Hellenic philosophy, but many also, even without being able to read and write, being laid hold of by the Divine philosophy, which comes from the barbarians, have received by the power of God through faith, the doctrine concerning the being and attributes of God, (*literally*, the doctrine about God.) The doctrine also of our Saviour is perfect in itself and self-sufficing, as the power and wisdom of God; but the Hellenic philosophy which is added to it, does not make the truth more powerful, it only renders ineffectual the sophistical attacks against it; and as it wards off delusive machinations against the truth, it is called the proper ward and fence of the vineyard.‡ The truth of the faith is as it were the bread necessary for life; the form under which it is represented to us, is to be compared with that which is eaten with the bread, and is like the dessert."

While, on the whole, Clement is distinguished by the mildness and moderation with which he opposed the adversaries of the Alexandrian Gnosis, he himself was well aware how much their anxiety was awakened by the adulterations of simple Christianity among so many sects, who mixed with the Gospel, elements the most uncongenial to its nature; and he well knew, also, how natural it is for men to confound the abuse and the right use of the same thing with each other. The zeal, however, of his adversaries,

---

and conducts his whole nature to an unity (literally, a oneness.") ἡ ἰσχὺς τῶν λογῶν, ἡ δοθεῖσα ἡμῖν, συντόμως οὖσα καὶ δυνατὰ πάντα τὸν δεξάμενον καὶ ἐντὸς ἑαυτοῦ κτησάμενον αὐτὴν, ἐπικευμμένως τε καὶ ἀφανῶς πρὸς ἑαυτὴν ἕλκει καὶ τὸ πᾶν αὐτοῦ σύστημα ὡς ἐν ἑνὶ τινι συνάγει. Stromat. lib. v. p. 587. [Pott. 694. Sylb. 249.]

* Stromat. i. 292. [Pott. 342. Sylb. 126. N. B. This passage is not exactly translated from Clement, but paraphrased and a little altered.—H. J. R.]

† L. c. p. 291.

* Stromat. i. 318. [Pott. 376. Sylb. 138.]

† ἄνευ τῆς ἐγκυκλίου παιδείας.

‡ What the ancients said generally of Dialectics in relation to philosophy, that they were its fence, was applied by the Alexandrians to the relation of philosophy itself to the Christian Gnosis

which was certainly often a blind zeal, and the persuasion that this too sensuous, and one-sided disposition stood much in the way of the Spirit of Christianity, which endeavoured to ennoble all human things, and that many were thereby deterred from Christianity, led him to speak somewhat too sharply against their opponents, and did not suffer him to do becoming justice to their pious zeal, as when he says,* "It is not unknown to me, what many ignorant and clamorous persons† constantly say, that our faith must confine itself to the most necessary and essential points, and must let go all foreign and superfluous matters, whereby we are detained with things that do not contribute towards our object." And in another passage‡ where he says: "The multitude in their anxiety lest they should be carried away by the Hellenic philosophy,§ dread it, as children dread masks. But if their faith is of such a kind (for I cannot call that knowledge) as to be overturned by plausible discourses, then it may just as well be overturned, in regard to these people, for they themselves confess, that they have not the truth; for the truth cannot be overturned, false opinions may." Now this is dealing out a hard and unjust sentence, if we refer it to persons; for all worth was not to be denied to the faith of these persons, although they did not feel confidence in their own ability, to enter into a contest with a spirit of understanding prejudiced against the faith, and although they were afraid of being constantly disquieted in the enjoyment of that, which was to them their dearest possession. But if we look at it objectively it is a great and an instructive truth for all ages, which the free spirit of Clement here proclaimed; that Christianity need fear nothing from any opposition, but that the truth, when placed in opposition to that which is false, only shines forth the brighter. In conformity with that declaration, which is ascribed to our Saviour in the Apocryphal Gospels γινεσθε δοκιμοι τραπεζιται (be ye skilful money-changers,) the Gnostics, according to Clement, ought to be able universally to distinguish mere appearances from the truth, as he would false money from genuine; and hence, to fear no might of false appearances. He needed an acquaintance with the Grecian philosophy, just to be able to point out to the philosophically educated heathens, its errors and unsatisfactoriness, to battle with them on their own ground, and thence to lead them to the knowledge of the truth. Clement says*—"Thus much I say to those who are desirous of finding fault, that even if philosophy be useless, yet the study of it is useful, because it is useful fully to prove that it (philosophy) is useless. For we cannot condemn the Heathens by a mere prejudice against their doctrines, unless we go into the development of particulars with them, until we compel them to accede to our sentence: for a refutation combined with a knowledge of the matter before us, is the most likely mode of obtaining their confidence." And in another passage he says†—"For we must give to the Greeks who ask for that wisdom, which is in esteem among them, such things as they are accustomed to, in order that they may be brought to a belief in the truth by the most easy way, through their own proper method. 'For I became,' says the apostle, 'all things to all men, that I might win all.'"

The most eager antagonists of this free spirit, in order wholly to condemn the occupying ourselves with the Grecian philosophy, appealed to the Jewish tale related in the Apocryphal Book of Enoch, that all the higher branches of knowledge had come to the Heathens in an unlawful manner, through the communications of fallen spirits, and they looked upon all heathen philosophers without distinction, as instruments of the evil Spirit. They either considered the whole antichristian world only in stern opposition to Christianity; they confounded that which is heathen with that original and divine system, without which the heathenism that only adulterated and troubled this original system, could never even have existed at all; they would not so much as hear of any point through which Christianity could be engrafted on a nature and qualities in man, which are akin to the Divinity, and which beam through it constantly

---

* Stromat. i. 278. [Pott. 326. Sylb. 120.]
† ὁμαθως ψοφωδεις.
‡ vi. 655. [Pott. 780. Sylb. 278.]
§ In Stromat. vi. 659, Clement, in a manner full of spirit, says: "Most Christians handle the doctrines after a clownish manner, like the companions of Ulysses, who got out of the way, not of the Sirens, but of their music and song, by shutting their ears out of ignorance; because they knew, that if they have once given their ear to the Hellenistic knowledge, there is no chance of their turning again from them." [See p. 337.]

* I. 278. [i. e. Ed. Paris. In Sylburg, ed. p. 120. In Potter, vol. i. p. 327. Klotz, vol. ii. p. 15.]
† V. 554. [Pott. 656. Sylb. 237.]

even in its worst corruption; and yet without such a point, Christianity could never have propagated itself upon the heathen soil;—or else, like the impetuous, fiery Tertullian—the friend of nature, and of all the original revelations of life, the enemy of art, and of all perversion (of such revelation)—they saw in philosophy only the hand of Satan, that adulterates and mutilates the original nature of man. Clement endeavoured to refute this party also on their own principles. "Even if this view were just," he says, "yet could Satan deceive men only when he clothed himself as an angel of light: he must attract man by the appearance of truth, and by the intermixture of truth and falsehood; and man must always seek the truth, and acknowledge it, let it come from whom it may. And even this communication can only take place in accordance with God's will, and therefore, must have been contemplated in the plan of education proposed for humanity by God."*

But this view, however, which was so exceedingly contradictory to the natural development and progress of human nature, was thoroughly repugnant to his own sentiments; and he expresses himself very strongly against it, when he speaks in conformity with his own views. "Is it not then absurd," he says, "while we attribute disorder and sin to Satan, to make him the giver of a good thing, i. e. philosophy? for he appears, under this point of view, to have been more benevolent towards good men among the Greeks than Divine Providence."†

Clement was inclined rather to seek in the progress of the Greek philosophy the work of God in his care for the improvement of man, and a preparation for Christianity adapted to the peculiarities of the Greek character; as it is impossible to deny that the philosophical development of the human mind, which proceeded from the Greeks, tended both negatively and positively to render the soil capable of the reception of the Gospel. The idea of the Divine education of man as a great whole, was Clement's favourite idea, and he conceived the object of this great scheme to be Christianity; and to this he attributed the dealings of God, not only with the Jewish people, but also those with the heathen world, although not in the same manner. The Alexandrians combated that confined view [lit. particularism] which would limit the government of God, in whom we live, and move, and are, only to the narrow limits of the Jewish people. Thus Clement says, "Every good impulse comes from God; he uses those men who are fit to lead and to instruct other men,* as instruments for [the improvement of] the greater mass of mankind. Such men were the better class of Greek philosophers. Philosophy, which forms man to virtue, cannot be a work of evil; it can only be a work of God, whose work every impulse to good is. And all, which is given by God must be given and received with advantage. Philosophy is not found in the hands of the wicked, but it was given to the best among the Greeks; and it is, therefore, evident whence it was given,—it must have been given by *Providence*, which gives to every man that which is adapted to his peculiar condition. It is clear also that the law was given to the Jews, and philosophy to the Greeks, till the appearance of our Lord; and hence proceeds the universal call to a peculiar people of Righteousness, in virtue of the doctrine which we receive by faith, as the one God of both, the Greeks and the barbarians, or rather of the whole race of man, brought all together through the one Lord.† "Before the appearance of our Lord, philosophy among the Greeks was *necessary for righteousness*, but now it is *useful* for the furtherance of holiness, as a kind of preparation for the demonstration of the faith; for thy foot will not stumble, if thou trace up every good thing, whether it belongs to the heathen or to us—to Providence; for God is the cause of every good thing, but partly in an especial manner, as (he is the cause) of the Old and the New Testament, and partly in a more remote (or derivative) manner, as he is of philosophy. But, perhaps, even this was also given in an especial manner to the Greeks at that time, before the Lord called the heathen also, for it educated the heathen as the law did the Jews for Christianity, and thus philosophy was a degree of preparation for him, who was to be

---

* This is the substance of passages found in vi. 647. [Pott. 773. Sylb. 274.] and i. 310. [Pott. 367. Sylb. 134.]

† L. c. vi. 693. [Potter, vol. ii. p. 822. Sylburg, 294. Ed. Klotz, vol. iii. p. 198.]

* The ηγεμονικα and παιδευτικα

† vi. 393, 4, [Potter, vol. ii. p. 822, 823. Ed. Sylb. p. 294. Ed. Par. 693, 694. Ed. Klotz. § 158, 159, vol. iii. p. 197, 198. The passage is abridged. I have followed the German.—H. J. R.]

brought to perfection by Christ."* When Clement speaks here of a righteousness to be attained by philosophy, he does not mean to say that philosophy can impart to man the disposition requisite to the fulfilment of his moral destination, and the attainment of the happiness of heaven; he makes a distinction between a doctrine justifying man, which with him can be only the Gospel, and such a one as can merely prepare him for that.† He makes a distinction between a certain degree of awakenment in the moral and religious conscience, as well as of excitement to moral endeavours, and of moral preparation; and between the universal perfect righteousness, which is the object of the whole nature of man,‡ and is opposed to that cultivation of man's nature which is only partially adapted for a certain condition of human development: he himself says of the Greek philosophy,§ that it is too weak to practise the commandments of God, and that it makes men capable of receiving the most majestic doctrines only by ennobling their morals, and by furthering their belief in the superintendence of Providence.|| "As God," says Clement, "willed the salvation of the Jews, by giving them prophets, so also he separated the most pre-eminent among the Greeks from the mass of ordinary men, by making them come forward as their own prophets, in their own language, inasmuch as they were capable of receiving the blessing of God..... As now the preaching of the Gospel has come at a convenient season,¶ so also were the law and the prophets bestowed upon the Jews, and philosophy upon the Greeks at the proper time, in order to accustom their ears to the Gospel message."*

Clement had observed, from intercourse with many who had received a philosophical education, and perhaps, had learned also from his own experience, that previous philosophical culture might become a means of facilitating conversion, (*lit.* a transition point,) to Christianity, as he appeals for proof of what has been alleged to the circumstance, that those who received the faith, whether prepared for it by the Greek philosophy, or by the Jewish law, were both led to the *one* race of the redeemed people.† As the Pharisees, who had mixed the law of God with human traditions, by Christianity attained to a right knowledge of the law; so the philosophers, who had defiled the revelation of Divine truth to the soul of man by the partial and imperfect views to which human nature is liable (*lit.* by human *one-sidedness*) attained to true philosophy by means of Christianity.‡ Clement, in order to represent the ennoblement of philosophy afforded by Christianity, uses the simile of a graft which had been used by the apostle in a kindred sense, and was very expressive and well adapted to denote the ennoblement of human nature by Christianity. The wild olive tree§ is not deficient in sap, but in the power of properly concocting the juices which circulate through it. Now, when the germ of the garden olive is engrafted upon the wild stem, the former obtains more sap, which it appropriates to itself, and the latter the power to assimilate (or digest) it. Thus also the philosopher, who is compared to the wild olive tree, has much which is undigested, because he is full of the versatile spirit of inquiry, and longs after the noble nourishment of truth; and if he now receives Divine power through faith, then

---

* Strom. i. 282. [i. e. ed. Paris, vol. i. p. 331. Ed. Pott. p. 121, 122. Ed. Sylburg. vol. ii. p. 20. Ed. Klotz.]

† Διδασκαλια η τι δικαιουντα, η τι ως τουτο χειραγωγουσα και συλλαμβανουτα, vi. 844.

[The context is here important. Clement says, that as every relation (πατρια) ultimately ascends to God the Creator, so also to the Lord must be referred, η των καλων διδασκαλια, η τε, &c. Potter's edit. vol. ii. p. 770. Sylburg. p. 274. Klotz, vol. iii. p. 134.—H. J. R.]

‡ η καθολου δικαιοσυνη, Strom. i. 319. [Potter. vol. i. p. 377. Sylb p. 137. Klotz, vol. ii. p. 70.]

§ i. 309. [Pott. i. p. 366. Sylb. p. 133, Klotz, vol. ii. p. 57.]

|| Αμηγεπη σωφρονιζουσα το ήθος και (al. και το ήθος) προτυπουσα και προτυρουσα εις παραδοχην της αληθους την προσιναν δεξιωσα. [Ita ap. Neand. δεξιζουντα, Potter, Klotz, &c., which seems the right reading.—H. J. R.]

¶ κατα καιρον, i. e. after human nature had been prepared for it by the previous dealings of God.

* τας οκοας εθιζουσα προς το κηρυγμα. Strom. vi. 636. (Potter, vol. ii. p. 761—2. Sylb. p, 270. Klotz, vol. iii. p. 123

† vi. 636, 637. [Potter, vol. ii. p. 761—763. Sylb. p. 270. Klotz. vol. iii. p. 122. 123.]

‡ vi. 644. [Potter, vol. ii. p. 769, 770. Sylb. p. 273. Klotz, vol. iii. p. 133.]

§ vi. 671. [vi. 672. Potter. vol. ii. p. 799. Sylb. p. 285. Klotz, vol. iii. p. 170. The German is hardly an exact translation of the Greek. It is rather a condensation of the text of Clement. I have, therefore, followed the German. The word *verdauen*, to *digest* or *concoct*, I have translated by *assimilate*, which is equally applicable to vegetable and animal functions. See Prout's Bridgewater Treatise, part iii., especially p. 469.)—H. J. R.]

he will be able to digest the nourishment imparted to him, and become a garden olive tree." He beautifully illustrates the difference between the pure revelation of truth in Christianity, and those individual beams of truth which are dimmed by an intermixture of human imperfection, by a comparison drawn from the light artificially imprisoned in a burning lens, as contrasted with the pure and clear sunshine.* The Alexandrians were full of the great idea, which now, when Christianity *began to unfold* its essential nature to the thinking mind, for the first time revealed itself in a passing manner, and was unable as yet to become the principle which, carried out into every individual application, should be the life-giving principle of Christian theology, and of a Christian consideration of history, the idea which alone gives the right key to the contemplation of human nature and of history; namely, that Christianity is, as it were, the centre to all the rays of human imperfection† (*literally, one-sidedness;*) that it proves itself the religion of human nature, inasmuch as it reconciles with each other all the contending dispositions which meet each other in human nature; that it divides truth from falsehood in all human and imperfect systems, that treat of Divine matters; and that it teaches us to recognise in errors the truth, which being misunderstood, has formed the foundation of them. Such a light of the Spirit, *according to the idea of Clement,* ought Christianity to have lighted for the Gnostic, and thus ought he, standing on the ground of Christianity, through which he has attained the true centre for the religious nature of man, to be able freely and securely to separate truth and falsehood from each other in all the systems of Grecian philosophers and Christian heretics. Thus Clement says:* "As truth is one, for falsehood only has a thousand paths of error, in which truth is dismembered, just as the Bacchæ dismembered the body of Pentheus, thus the sects of the philosophy derived from the barbarians (*the Christian*) and of the Hellenic philosophy pride themselves upon that portion of truth, which each happens to possess, as if it were the whole truth, but all is enlightened at the rising of the dawn. As," he says, "eternal existence† represents that in *one* moment, which is broken by means of time into past, present, and future, so also is truth able to collect together the seeds which belong to her, even if they may have fallen into a strange soil. The Hellenic and the barbarian philosophy have in some sort received portions of eternal truth; they have received not Dionysius, as in that mystical legend, but the divine revelation of the eternal Logos, dismembered and divided into fragments. But he who gathers together again that which was torn asunder by them, and reinstates the Word in its perfection and unity, will without doubt, learn the truth."‡ This mode of view peculiarly distinguished the Alexandrians, as compared with the partial polemical views of other divines, and therefore, they alone were in a condition to appreciate, with less prejudice, the opinions of heretics, to judge about them with more justice, and in considering their systems, to separate not only the truth from the falsehood which appeared in them, but the

---

* ἡ μὲν ἑλληνικὴ φιλοσοφία τῇ ἐκ τῆς θρυαλλίδος ἔοικε λαμπηδόνι, v. 560, vi. 688. [Potter, vol. ii. p. 663. Sylb. p. 239. Klotz, vol. iii. p. 22. Now, I do not see any mention in this passage of *Brennglas*, though the part of the sentence which follows should be given also; it is this ἐν ἀνάπτουσιν ἄνθρωποι, παρὰ ἡλίου κλέπτοντες ἐντεχνῶς τὸ φῶς. It seems to me only a comparison of the artificial *and feeble light of a lamp*, which is, in fact, *originally stolen from the sun*, to the full clear light of day. The *Brennglas* is taken from vi. 688, (Potter, vol. ii. p. 817. Sylb. p. 292. Klotz, vol. iii. p. 191,) where a different simile is used, ὡς γὰρ που τὸ ἀπὸ τοῦ ἡλίου φῶς δι' ὑέλου σκεύους πλήρους ὕδατος μεθόδῳ ἡ τέχνη εἰς πῦρ, οὕτω καὶ ἡ φιλοσοφία ἐκ τῆς θείας γραφῆς τὸ ἐμπύρευμα λαβοῦσα ἐν ὀλίγοις φαντάζεται.—H. J. R.]

† [I understand by this a point in which all human dispositions which are apt to run into excess, each in one direction, and thus some in directions exactly opposite to each other, may meet and be reconciled and united; *e. g.* extreme liberality tends to prodigality, extreme prudence to inhumanity; Christianity alone gives the right direction of the heart which shall unite the two properly. I have thought it necessary to add this explanation, because I do not choose to incorporate a *paraphrase* with the text, and the literal translation hardly gives an adequate notion of the meaning to the English reader.—H. J. R.]

* i. 298. [Potter, i. p. 348. Sylb. p. 128. Klotz, vol. ii. p. 43.—H. J. R.]

† "Das ewige Seyn." In the Greek it is ὁ αἰών. —H. J. R.

‡ Strom. i. 298, as above. [Potter punctuates and explains the latter part of the sentence somewhat differently. It is thus: ὁ δὲ τὰ διῃρημένα συνθείς, καὶ ἑνοποιήσας τέλειον λόγον ἀκινδύνως εὖ ἴσθ' ὅτι κατόψεται, τὴν ἀλήθειαν. He, therefore, makes τὴν ἀλήθειαν in apposition with τέλειον τὸν Λ., but I apprehend Neander's is probably the more correct construction, for I think in the other case we should have τὸν τέλειον λόγον. Τέλειον is the predicate of a clause of the sentence.—H. J. R.]

important errors also from the unimportant.*

On the one side it may, indeed, also appear that Clement, far from supporting the Gnostic distinction between an *esoteric* and an *exoteric* Christianity made *one* life of faith in all Christians, and understood by Gnosis nothing but a well-informed knowledge and capacity of explaining the *one* faith, which was to belong to all Christians. It is certain, in accordance with the connected theory, which has been laid down above, and which may be proved by many passages of Clement, that this alone was his impression on the one side, but on the other side we find also indications, that he had no clear view of the bearing which different forms of religious belief and knowledge had to the essential character of the Christian life. Beautifully as he speaks in many passages of the *nature* and the *power of faith*, yet he was not always clearly conscious to himself of the full meaning of these declarations, and they did not become principles, logically carried out, of his dogmatical (doctrinal) opinions. There was mixed up with that idea of faith which Clement had deduced from the essential nature of Christianity, the idea which adhered to Clement from his former Platonism, namely, the idea of a mythical popular faith,† in which fancy and truth are intermixed, as contrasted with the pure religious knowledge of the philosophically educated, and this notion would have a close affinity with the Gnostic ideas of the relation of γνωσις to πιστις. By many explanations, which he gives, he appears to understand by πιστις only a very subordinate stage of subjective Christianity, and of the Christian life, a carnal faith, received upon authority and clinging to the letter, a faith which is still far removed from the true spirit and essence of Christianity, and which, as Clement represents it, is essentially more able to repress the external outbreaks of evil, than to produce true inward sanctification of the heart (although he well knew that on this latter the very essence of practical Christianity depends;) but γνωσις, on the contrary, is in his language, an inward, living, spiritual Christianity, a Divine life. If the mere *Believer* is impelled towards good by fear of punishment and hope of future happiness, the *Gnostic*, on the contrary, is animated toward all good by the inward, free impulse of love; he needs no outward grounds to persuade him of the Divine origin of Christianity, he lives in the consciousness and in the perception* of Divine truth and even already feels himself blessed by its means. If the mere *Believer* (πιστικος) acts on the dictates of uncertain feelings, and therefore, at times fails in doing that which is right, or does it, but not in the right way, the *Gnostic*, on the contrary, acts always under the guidance of an enlightened reason with clear Christian views and with a consciousness of their clearness.†

---

* [Anschauung. This word is variously used. It sometimes means merely contemplation, sometimes intuitive perception, sometimes the object of our perception. It is here applied to the *act*, and, therefore, may be rendered *perception*, as showing that the Gnostic has (in the view of Clement) as clear perceptions of Divine truth, as men usually have of those ideas, which we call ideas of sensation. See the Edinb. Rev. for Oct. 1832.—H. J. R.]

† Clement, Stromat. 518-9, [Pott. vol. i. p. 612, 615. Sylb. p. 222-3. Klotz, vol. ii. p. 338, 341.] 645. [Pott. vol. ii. p. 770-1. Sylb. p. 274. Klotz, vol. iii. p. 133-4.] 652. [Pott. vol. ii. p. 777-8. Sylb. p. 277. Klotz, vol. iii. p. 143.] where he says that the πιστις γνωστικη has already received in anticipation, what to others is still something future; through love, the future is to him already present; ιστιν αυτου δι' αγαπην ινεστως ηδη το μελλον; vi. 663, [Pott. vol. ii. p. 789. Sylb. p. 281. Klotz, vol. iii. p. 158,] where he divides *good* into that which is worthy of being pursued for its own sake, and that which is only a means to something higher. *Gnosis* belongs to the first class, because we shall attain nothing else by means of it, when it is attained, but only obtain the possession of itself, and be in the enjoyment of an uninterrupted immediate knowledge,* and we shall make our way to

---

* Hist. as in Strom. vi. 675. [Pott. vol. ii. p. 802. Sylb. p. 287. Klotz, vol. iii. p. 195.] The important distinction is made between οι περι τινα των εν μερει σφαλλομενοι and those οι εις τα κυριωτατα παραπιπτοντες. Clement also in vi. 647. [Pott. vol. ii. p. 773. Sylb. p. 275. Klotz, vol. iii. p. 138,] argues against the blind condemnation of all, which is said by heretical teachers, merely on account of the person by whom it is said, without weighing the matter itself, and this he does particularly with reference to the Montanistic prophets. " Nor must we on account of the person who speaks ignorantly, condemn before hand that which he says, which observation is applicable to those who now pass as prophets, but we must prove that which is said, whether it is conformable to the truth."

† δοξα των πολλων.

---

* Anschauung. See note above. The last clause of the sentence is thus in the German: dass wir uns in ununterbrochenen Anschauung befinden, und zu dieser und durch diese uns durchkämpfen; by which I only understand that *this state* becomes a means only to its own continuance, and not an introduction to a higher state. —H. J. R.

Where Clement speaks of the progressive enlargement of the Divine scheme for the education of man, and represents the Logos as the Θιιος παιδαγωγος, he says,* "All men belong to him, some of them with a consciousness of what he is to them, (κατ' ἐπιγνωσιν,) others without that consciousness; some as friends, some as faithful *servants*, and others merely as *servants*; it is the teacher, who leads the *Gnostic* by the revelation of mysteries, (the inward perception of truth,) the believer *by good hopes*, and the hard-hearted by corrective discipline, by appeals to the senses." Now here Clement's γνωστικος appears in many respects to resemble the πνευματικος of the Gnostics, and his πιστικος their ψυχικος, and in regard to their interior life they both appear to bear the same relation to each other, but there is, nevertheless, this great distinction, that amidst all the differences which they held to exist in the subjective Christianity of the two conditions, the Alexandrians maintained that there was the selfsame foundation of objective Christianity, of which they only admitted different conceptions, the one more spiritual and the other more sensuous, nor did they, like the Gnostics, make these two different subjective conditions dependent on an original and ineffaceable difference of human dispositions. It may, indeed, be said, that, nevertheless, the two different conditions of subjective Christianity which Clement distinguishes from each other, were really in existence in his day, and are again found in other times, inasmuch as they are founded in the very nature of man; and therefore, that it cannot be of so much consequence, by what name we distinguish the two conditions, nor can it make so great a difference whether we consider them as two different stages in the development of faith, and of the life under the influence of faith, or whether we accord the true spiritual life of faith only to Gnosis, as Clement has done in many passages. And yet this difference is by no means so unimportant, as it may seem at first view; but its foundations lie deeper and its consequences are more important. The cause that the Alexandrians conceived the thing in this way, lay partly in their own predominant turn of mind, and partly in the manner in which they viewed the faith of a large class of Christian people.

As far as the first is concerned, the contemplative and speculative turn of mind was far too predominant among the Alexandrians, and this prevented them from recognising in its full extent the independent practical power of faith in the reformation of the interior life, and they were still under the influence of that view, which proceeded from the Platonic School, and was natural, indeed, generally to the whole of the ancient world, namely, that the inward, spiritual, and religious life, in short, maturity in religion, could not exist without philosophical culture of the mind.*

As far as the second point is concerned, we must take into the account the manner in which they (the Alexandrians,) were often accustomed to meet with faith in a certain class of uneducated Christians, as a mere belief received upon authority, united with a sensuous Eudæmonism,† and a fear of hell, that presented to the mind only images of horror derived from the senses. They could not mistake the bettering influence of faith upon the life, even where it appeared to them under this form, when they compared what these men had become, as Christians, with what they had been as heathens; but they did not believe that they could perceive any traces of the ennobling influence of Christianity upon the whole inward nature of man, or of a divine spiritual life; and this sensuous Christianity was in contradiction to their spiritualized religious habits

---

* viii. 702. [Potter, vol. ii. p. 831-2. Sylb. p. 298. Klotz, iii. 209, and seqq.]

this and through this, [i. e. a state to which we attain through itself.—H. J. R.] *Faith* belongs to the second class, on account of the fear of punishment which arises from it, and on account of advantages, and the hope of reward; fear being a motive to the multitude to abstain from sinning, and the promises a motive to strive after obedience, through which the happiness of heaven is to be obtained.

* There is a remarkable passage in Clement, vi. 691, in which he distinguishes an inward perception, [Geistes-anschauung,] a learned knowledge or Gnosis and faith, from one another. The first, or νοησις, consists in an immediate connection of the Spirit with the highest origin of things, the mere ἐπιβαλλειν; γνωσις is distinguished from νοησις by the addition of βεβαιων λογων ἀποδεικτικω, the reception of the fundamental doctrines without the inward perception (anschauung) in regard to the practical exercise of them is Faith. (ἡ φερνησις:) ἐν τοις εἰς ὁληθειαν συντεινουσι γνωμην, και ανευ θεωριας παραδεξαμένη τον αρχικον λογον κατα την ἐν αὐτῇ ἐνεργειας τηρησιν πιστις λεγεται.

† Eudæmonism. The word in the original is Eudämonismus, which is a modern coinage. It expresses a notion of the Deity being pleased with man and rewarding him, especially in good that affects the body.—H. J. R.]

of thought. They might, therefore, be inclined to attribute a very low grade of the religious life to πιστις and to the κοινος πιστικος, and to consider the higher life of Christianity, of which they saw nothing in the κοινοι πιστικοι, as fruit due only to the γνωσις of the well informed and highly cultivated. It must, indeed, be avowed that they were very likely in this case to do injustice to those, who were in an entirely different condition as regarded both the turn of their mind, and the extent of its development, if they passed judgment upon the more hidden spiritual life of faith from the impure reflection of it in a habit of thought, neither thoroughly formed, nor as yet thoroughly penetrated by the leaven of Christianity.

The prejudicial consequences of this predominance of the contemplative and speculative turn of mind, and of this extremely sharp division of γνωσις from πιστις, show themselves in Clement in a variety of ways. Instead of bringing forward the *Gnosticos*, under the image of an humble-minded Christian, living in the constant conviction of the sinfulness that still adheres to him, and constantly advancing in holiness, he often appears in Clement under the form of a Neoplatonic Theosopher, living in contemplative self-sufficingness,* and unmoved by passions,† although, even hither the Christian element has again made its way, as may be seen by the circumstance, that the Gnostic cannot feel himself entirely blessed in contemplation alone, and living for himself and shut up in himself alone; but is represented as actuated by the desire of working actively for the benefit of others.‡

Hence also it happened, that instead of contenting themselves with a mere systematic (*lit.* organic) development of that which is known in faith, the Alexandrians wished to transcend the bounds of faith by their Gnosis, and lost themselves in the region of Theosophy, which desired to comprehend divine things; so that mistaking and overlooking the practical aim of Divine Revelation for the improvement and salvation of human nature, they endeavoured to find the solution of speculative inquiries in Scripture. When many came forward and opposed the speculative Gnosis with this just argument: "The wise man is persuaded that there is much which is incomprehensible, and his wisdom even consists in the very acknowledgment of the incomprehensibleness of the incomprehensible:"* Clement answered, "This is also common to those, who are able to see only a little way before them; the Gnostic apprehends that which appears to be inapprehensible to the rest of men, for he is persuaded that there is nothing which cannot be apprehended by the Son of God; whence it follows that there is nothing which cannot be taught [by him,] for he who suffered out of love to us, would debar us from nothing which could contribute to the instruction of Gnosis." One sees how indefiniteness here becomes the source and foundation of great error, for this declaration is true enough when understood of that only which it is necessary for man to know for his salvation, but not when applied to things, which serve only to the gratification of speculative and ill-directed curiosity.

The notions of Clement in these matters, are repeated in those of his great disciple Origen, only conceived in a peculiar manner, full of deep thought, and systematically worked out, but there is the same connection of the ideas of Gnosis and Pistis in relation, as well to different conditions of subjective Christianity, as to the different operations of a Divine scheme for the general instruction of man, which lets itself down to the varied wants which arise from the variety of these conditions of man. In his controversies with the heathen, who reproached Christians with their blind faith, Origen often declares it to be a peculiarity of Christianity as a revelation of a God who came for the salvation of *all* men, that it is able to attract even the multitude who are incapable of scientific investigation and knowledge, and in virtue

---

* [The word "self-sufficiency" is so constantly used in English in an idiomatic sense, as implying merely conceit and vanity, that I have used a word which, if not a current word, may be perhaps allowed.—H. J. R.]

† See F. 748. [See Potter, vol. ii. pp. 881-2, Sylb. p. 318. Klotz, vol. iii. p. 268.]

‡ Clement says, beautifully, on this point: "The Gnostic, who sees his own salvation in the advantage of his neighbour, may justly be called a living image of the Lord; not with regard to the circumstances of his outward form, but from similarity to that which he was in power, and from a resemblance to his preaching." Ὁ γνωστικος ιδιαν σωτηριαν ηγουμενος την των πελας ωφελειαν, ὡς αλμα εμψυχον εικοται· ὁν τω Κυριω λεγοιτο, ου κατα την της μορφης ιδιοτητα, αλλα κατα το της δυναμεως συμβολον και κατα το της κηρυξεως ὁμοιωμα.

---

* vii. 649. [Potter, vol. ii. p. 775. Sylb. p. 276; Klotz, vol. iii, p. 140. N.B. The reference in Neander should be vi. 649. not vii. 649.—H. J. R.]

of mere faith,* to work upon them to sanctification with divine power; and he appeals to the experience of very many, as a testimony to this efficacy of Christianity.† Those who had attained to faith at first only in this manner, might then become impelled of their own accord to penetrate constantly more and more also into the deeper sense of Scripture.‡ He makes πιστις the lowest stage of Christianity, which must, nevertheless, have an existence, in order, that "the simple, who give themselves up to holiness according to their power, may be able to attain salvation;" and above faith he places both *Gnosis* and *Sophia*. This last is that Divine Wisdom, which is imparted to the souls, who are, by God's grace, capable of receiving it, and who have sought to obtain it from God, by study of the Scriptures, and by prayer. Human wisdom, the wisdom that belongs to our world, is only a preparatory exercise of the soul, in order that it may become capable of attaining that which is the real aim and object of its existence, by means of cultivating its intellectual faculties.§

Origen, as well as Clement, in many places declares expressly in reference to the nature of faith, that it is a fact of the inward life, through which man enters into a real communion with divine things, and he distinguishes this living faith from a belief, resting on authority, which clings only to outward things. Thus, in explanation of John viii. 24,‖ he says, "That faith brings with it a spiritual communion with that on which we believe, and hence there is generated a kindred condition of the heart,¶ which must show itself in works. The object of our belief is received into the inward life, and becomes a forming and fashioning principle for it. In all the relations (ἐπινοιαις,) under which Christ becomes an object of faith, according to all these the believer receives Christ into his inward life; thus, for example, since Christ is called the power of God, power to all good actions cannot be wanting to him, who believes on Christ, as the source of divine power." Thus, in tom. xx., in Joh. c. xxv., he makes a distinction between a sensuous belief in miracles, and a faith in the truth. He compares John viii. 43, and 45, and says, that those sensuous Jews were impressed by the miracles, and would have believed on Jesus as a worker of miracles, but they were incapable of receiving Divine truth,* and never would have believed on Jesus as a preacher of deep truth; and he adds, "This may also be seen in many, who look with wonder on Jesus, when they consider his history, but who cannot have any farther faith in him, when a deep doctrine, which surpasses their comprehension, is unfolded, but begin to cavil at it, and say that it is false. Therefore, let us take heed, lest he say to us also, 'ye believe not me, because I declare the truth.'" Nevertheless, the relation to what is dependent on historical grounds, and the practical influence, which is inherent in the idea of faith, as conceived by St. Paul, is clearly thrown more into the back ground by Origen. That higher condition of faith was, in his notions, at the same time a condition in which Christianity was applied and conceived in a more spiritual manner—a condition in which truth was more immediately the object of interior perception; and this condition of faith so exactly accorded with his notion of the condition of Gnosis, that he often contrasts Gnosis with a mere historical belief. "Faith may exist without a definite conception of the thing believed."† He ascribes this Gnosis to those who devote themselves wholly to the contemplation of Divine matters, who after they have cleared their spirit from foreign elements, behold God with more godlike eyes. He finds also that such a Gnosis is contrasted with mere faith, in John viii. 31, 32.‡ For this distinction between Gnosis and Pistis he appeals also to 1 Cor. xii. 9; where, however, faith being represented as a gift of grace, can-

---

* ψιλη πιστις, πιστις ἀλογος.
† Compare *e. g.* c. Celsum, lib. i. c. 10.
‡ C. Celsum, lib. vi. Philocal. c. 15. μετα την ἀπαξ γενομενην εἰσαγωγην φιλοτιμησασθαι πρὸς το και βαθυτερα των κεκρυμμενων νοηματων ἐν ταις γραφαις καταλαβειν.
§ C. Cels. vi. 13. [Ed. Spencer, p. 283.] Origen maintains that St. Paul sets those graces, which are connected with knowledge, higher than the gift of working miracles. ἐπει τον λογον προτιμα των τερατων ἐνεργειων, δια τουτο ἐνηργηματα δυναμεων και χαρισματα ἰαματων ἐν τῃ κατωτερω τεθηεικε χωρᾳ παρα τα λογικα χαρισματα. c. Cels. iii. 46. [Ed. Spenc. p. 139.]
‖ Tom. xix. Joh. § 6. [See Origen, ed. Huet. vol. ii. pp. 284, 285.—H. J. R.]
¶ διακεισθαι κατα τον λογον και συμπεφυκεναι αὐτῳ.

* As if our Saviour had intended to say, καθ' ὁ μεν τερατα ποιω, πιστευετε μοι, καθ' ὁ δε την ἀληθειαν λεγω, οὐ πιστευετε μοι. [The reference in the text has not enabled me to consult the original passage. —H. J. R.]
† [Erkenntnisse is the German word here used, which I have translated "definite conception." See the Conversations Lexicon in verbo.—H. J. R.]
‡ See t. xix. in Joh. c. 1.

not be that historical belief of which Origen speaks as opposed to Gnosis, but where it is rather the designation of a peculiarly practical power of faith. Origen places the condition of Gnosis so far above that of faith, that he represents it, in speaking of this contrast, as a life of sight. "Those," he says, "who have received the charisma of Gnosis and Sophia, no longer live in faith, but in sight; the spiritually-minded, who already dwell no longer in the body, but even here below, are already present with the Lord. But those who do still dwell in the body, and are not yet present with the Lord, who do not understand the spiritual sense of Scripture, but cling wholly to its body (i. e. the letter, see below.) For how, since the Lord is the Spirit, should he not be far from the Lord, who does not understand the life-giving spirit and the spiritual sense of Scripture? such an one lives in faith."* He busies himself here very diligently in endeavouring to explain, after his own notions, what St. Paul says in utter contradiction to this view in 2 Cor. v., about the relation of faith to sight; and not without sophistical arguments involving a confusion of ideas, he contends against the just interpretation of most of the fathers, who maintain that even Paul speaks of himself, as one who still lived in faith, and had not yet arrived at living in sight. He makes the expression, "to dwell in the body," entirely equivalent to "living in the flesh, and according to the flesh;" and thus obtains as a result, that St. Paul said this, not in reference to himself and all spiritually-minded persons, but only in reference to those believers, who were still carnally-minded. He applies also (and in him the application is consistent) what St. Paul says (1 Cor. xiii.) of the perfect, to the genuine Gnostics, as contrasted with the mere believers, who are still in childhood, and still have only the mere partial knowledge.† This twofold condition, according to the notion of Origen, corresponds with the twofold condition of a spiritual and a fleshly Christianity.‡ He who is in the position afforded by a fleshly Christianity, abides only by the letter of Scripture, and by the historical account of Christ; he clings only to the outward appearance of the Divine, without raising himself up in spirit to the inward essence, which is revealed in it; he confines himself wholly to the earthly, temporal, and historical appearance of the Divine Logos; he does not raise himself up to the actual perception of the latter (the Logos) itself; he contents himself with the mere shell of the Christian doctrines, without penetrating to the interior kernel contained in them; he clings solely to the letter of Scripture, in which the spirit lies bound. The spiritual Christian on the contrary, in the temporal appearance and operations of Christ, sees the revelation and the representation of the eternal government and operations of the Divine Logos; with him, the letter of Scripture is only the covering of the spirit, and he knows how to detach the spirit from this covering. With him, all that is temporal in the form, under which Divine things are presented to us, is elevated into the inward perceptions of the spirit; with him the sensuous Gospel of the letter,* becomes spiritualized into the revelation of the eternal spiritual Gospel,† and it is the highest question to which his soul applies itself, to find the latter in the former, and to turn the former into the latter; and to understand Holy Scripture as the revelation of a continuous scheme of education, provided by the Logos for human nature, and of his uninterrupted activity for the salvation of man, a scheme of which the centre point is his appearance among men (which is the sensuous representation of his eternal and spiritual operation,)‡ and the aim of which is to bring back all fallen being to God. While he refers every thing to this one view, the whole volume of Holy Scripture becomes to him, by means of the Gospel, elevated and refined into Gospel. Hence, Origen believes by means of spiritual communion with the Logos, by the reception of the Spirit of Christ into the inward life alone,§ can any one attain to the true spiritual Christianity, and to the right spiritual understanding of the whole Scripture. Just then as the prophets *before the temporal advent of Christ* were partakers in spiritual communion with the Divine Logos,

---

* Origen. t. xiii. Joh. c. 52.
† In Matt. ed. Huet. frag. 213. He does not always remain consistent in this respect; in another passage (in Matt. 271,) he properly refers τελειον to eternal life.
‡ A χριστιανισμος πνευματικως and a χριστιανισμος σωματικως, a πνευματικα; and a σωματικως χριστιανιζειν.

* το ευαγγελιον αισθητον.
† του ευαγγελιου πνευματικου, αιωνιου.
‡ The επιδημια αισθητη, an image of the επιδημια νοητη του λογου.
§ The επιδημια νοητη του Χριστου.

and in virtue of that communion were enabled to foretell that advent, and the whole of Christianity beforehand, just as they, therefore, had the spiritual understanding of the Old Testament, and in some degree were Christians before the coming of Christ; so after the temporal appearance of Christ, there are among Christians, persons also, by whom this spiritual communion with the Divine Logos has not been obtained, and they, like the Jews of old, still cling to the outward covering; and the saying of St. Paul about the Jews before the appearance of Christianity, (Gal. iv.;) *viz.* "That they were still children, that the time appointed by the Father for them, had not yet arrived, and that they were still under guardians and governors," is still applicable to them, as being in a condition through which they must necessarily pass, in order to be prepared and made capable of receiving the true spiritual Christianity. "Every soul," says Origen, "which enters upon childhood, and proceeds on the road towards perfection, until the time destined for its perfection shall arrive, requires a teacher, and guardians, and stewards."*

Whatever portion of truth there may be in this expression of Origen, and however applicable it may be to the progress of the development of the Christian Church, yet it cannot be denied, that the meaning of historical Christianity, the intimate connection between historical and inward Christianity, appear to be obscured in his representation. We will now hear him speak in his own words,† "We must know, that the spiritual appearance of Christ, was communicated before his personal advent to the perfect and to those who were not in the condition of infants,—to those, who were no longer under schoolmasters and guardians, and to whom the spiritual fulness of time had appeared, namely, the Patriarchs, Moses, the Servants of God, and the Prophets, who had seen the glory of Christ. Now just as he himself, before his visible and bodily appearance, appeared to the perfect, thus also after his incarnation has been preached to those who are still in a state of childhood, because they are under guardians and stewards, and have not yet reached the fulness of time, to them have the harbingers of Christ appeared, namely, the ideas proper for the souls of children, of which (the ideas or notions) it may be justly said, that they are advantageous for the instructions of such souls. But the Son himself, the Divine Logos, in his majesty has never yet appeared to them, because he awaits that preparation which must take place beforehand among the men of God, who are to be capable of receiving his Godhead. We must also know, that as there is a law, which contains the shadow of good things to come, which good things are revealed (in Christianity) by the preaching of the true law; so also the shadow of the Christian mysteries is represented by that Gospel, which all, who read it, think they understand. *The* Gospel, on the contrary, which St. John calls an eternal Gospel, and which ought properly to be called the spiritual Gospel, sets clearly before the eyes of those, who understand it, every thing which regards the Son of God himself; the mysteries which were shadowed forth in his language, and the things of which his actions were the symbols. In conformity with what is here said, we must also suppose that, as there is an outward Jew, and an outward circumcision, so also there is an outward Christian and an outward baptism." Origen here scripturally points to spiritual communion with Jesus Christ, as the source of systematic and lively perception of that, which is only hinted at in Scripture; and what he said, was certainly just when taken as said in opposition to a blind and narrow-hearted zeal for an orthodoxy which adhered merely to the letter, and a conceited, unprofitable acquaintance with Scripture; but such declarations, if they were not sufficiently defined and limited, might easily favour a speculative habit of dealing arbitrarily with Scripture, which, under the pretence of a higher truth, mystified the simplicity of the Gospel, and did not recognise the depth which was united with that simplicity. As for instance when he says, "I believe, that the whole body of Holy Writ, even when understood very accurately, contains only a very small part of the elements of Gnosis, and a very brief introduction to it." Thus in his allegorical explanations of the conversation with the Samaritan woman, the well of Jacob is the symbol of the Holy Scripture, and the living water which Jesus gives, is the symbol of

---

* Comm. in Matt. 213. πασα ψυχη ερχομενη εις νηπιοτητα και οδευουσα επι την τελειοτητα, δειται μεχρις ενστη αυτη το πληρωμα του χρονου, παιδαγωγου και οικονομων και επιτροπων.

† Origen in Joh. tom. i. p. ix. [p. 8, 9. Ed. Huet, in which, however, the last sentence of this quotation is imperfect.—H. J. R.]

that, which transcends Scripture. "Scripture is then," he says, "the introduction, and after we have sufficiently understood that, we must raise ourselves up to Jesus in order that he may bestow upon us the fountain of water that bubbleth up into eternal life."*

In his mind this theory of two different stages of Christianity was closely connected with the theory of different forms of the Revelation of Christ, or of the Divine Logos, in relation to these two different conditions. The Gnostics, indeed, according to the different conditions of the spiritual world, by reason of the difference in the natures of men, were accustomed to divide† the revealing and the redeeming power of God among different hypostases; they acknowledged a Monogenes, a Logos, a Soter, an ἄνω and a κάτω Χριστος, a spiritual and a natural‡ Christ; but, on the contrary, Origen the unity of the being of Christ and of his Divine-human appearance; the one Christ is every thing to him, he only appears under different predicates, in different modes of conception, and in different relations to those, to whom he reveals himself, according to their different capacities, their different requirements; and hence he appears either in his heavenly dignity, or his human state of abasement. The thought often occurs in Origen, "that the Redeemer became all things to all men in a more Divine sense than St. Paul, in order to win all men."§ "The Redeemer," he says, "becomes much, or rather perhaps, every thing, according as the whole creation, which is to be released by him, happens to require him."‖ We must separate those predicates, which belong to the Divine word, in virtue of his nature, as the eternal Revealer of God for the whole spiritual world, and the source of all truth and goodness, from those, which he has taken upon him for the advantage of the fallen natures, which are to be redeemed by him, in relation to the different conditions in which those natures are found. "Happy are they," says Origen,* " who have made such progress, that they need the Son of God no longer as their physician that heals their sick, nor as the shepherd, nor as their redemption, but require him only as truth, as the Logos, as righteousness, and whatsoever he is besides to those, who from their own perfection are able to conceive him in the utmost splendour." Christianity in its historical and practical form, the preaching of Christ crucified, was reckoned by Origen only a subordinate condition, above which he placed the wisdom of the perfect, which acknowledged Christ no longer in the condition of a servant, but in his dignity as the Divine Logos, although he recognised the former condition as a necessary preparatory stage, in order to ascend from the temporal to the eternal Revelation of God, in order that a man being purified through faith in the crucified Redeemer, and sanctified by the following after the Son of God who appeared in human form, should be rendered capable of receiving the spiritual communications of his Divine Being. "If thou canst understand," says Origen,† "the differences in the Divine word, according as it is announced in the foolishness of preaching, or brought forward in wisdom to the perfect, then you will see in what manner the Divine word has the form of a servant to novices in Christianity .... but it comes in the glory of the Father to the perfect, who are able to say, 'we have seen his glory, the glory as of the only begotten Son of the Father, full of grace and truth;' for to the perfect the glory of the Word appears, as well as his being the only begotten Son of the Father, and his being full of grace and truth also, which they are unable to comprehend, who require the foolishness of preaching to induce them to believe." In another passage,‡ he says, "To those, who live in the flesh, he becomes flesh; but to those who walk no longer after the flesh, he appears as the Divine Logos, who was in the beginning with the Father, and he reveals the Father to them." He says of that preparatory stage of belief,§ "If any

---

* Tom. 13. Joh. p. 5 & 6. [Ed. Huet. vol. ii. p. 201, 2.—H. J. R.]

† See Part II.

‡ [*Pneumatischen* and *psychischen* are the German terms, which are here opposed as in St. Paul: the *pneumatical* meaning spiritual as belonging to the soul, and *psychical* meaning *natural* as required only to the *animal* soul or life of man.

The difference between the Gnostic view and that of Origen, may be shortly stated in one sentence. They believed in an *objective* difference in Christ's nature, and he only in a subjective.—H. J. R.]

§ Tom. 20. Joh. 28.

‖ Tom. 1. Joh. 22. Where, I think, instead of καθαριζυ, we must read καθ' ἁ χρηζη αὐτ.υ ἡ ἐλευθερουσθαι δυναμινη πασα κτισις.

* Joh. i. 22.

† In Matt. p. 290. Ed. Huet.

‡ Commentar. in Matt. p. 268.

§ In Joh. i. c. 11. [?]

one also belongs to the class of the Corinthians, among whom Paul will know nothing except the crucified Jesus, and whom he teaches to acknowledge only him who became man for our sakes, yet he may by means of the man Jesus become a man of God, by the consequences of his death may die to sin, and by consequences of his resurrection may rise up to a Divine life." So that Origen reverenced even that subordinate condition, and he desired that the Gnostics would let themselves down* to the weakness of those who were placed in it, and avoid giving them offence and occasions of bitterness. "Just as Paul," he says, " could not be of service to those who were Jews according to the flesh, if he had not, when he had good reasons for his conduct, caused Timothy to be circumcised, shorn his own hair, offered sacrifices, and became a Jew to Jews, in order to gain the Jews; so also he, who is inclined to be useful to many, cannot improve those who are still in the school of sensuous Christianity, by spiritual Christianity alone, nor lead them thus to a higher and better state, and he must, therefore, unite spiritual and sensuous Christianity together.† And where it is necessary to preach the sensuous Gospel, in virtue of which among carnal men he can know nothing,‡ but Christ crucified, he must also do this. But when they are grounded in the faith and continue to bring forth fruit in the Spirit, then must we bring forward to them the word, which, having appeared among men, has raised itself again to that, which it was with God in the beginning."§ Thus too, in his allegorical interpretation and application of Matt. xiv. 10,‖ after he has deduced from the passage, that a man must become a child to children, in order to gain children to the kingdom of Heaven, just as Christ, though he was in a Divine form, became a child, he says beautifully, " We must be well aware of this, in order that we may not, out of a presumption of wisdom and advancement, as great ones in the Church, despise the little ones, and children, but inasmuch as we know that it is said, 'Of such is the kingdom of Heaven,' we ought to become such men, that through us the salvation of children may be promoted. We must not only not hinder such from being brought to Christ, but we must do his will by becoming children with children, so that when those children arrive at salvation, through us, who have become children, we may be exalted by God, as men who have abased themselves." Origen here blames those, who, like the Gnostics, despised ordinary preachers and teachers, who were destitute of spiritual culture of the higher order, and who presented the simple Gospel in an unattractive form, just as if such persons did something unworthy of so great a Saviour and master.* "Even if we were arrived at the very highest and clearest perception [anschauung] of the Logos and of truth," says Origen,† "yet still we must not wholly forget the passion of Christ, for it is to that we owe our introduction into this higher life during our abode on earth."

With this twofold condition, namely, that of spiritual, and that of sensuous Christianity, the theory of a twofold condition of Scriptural interpretation and the theory of different senses of Holy Writ were closely connected, for spiritual Christianity brought with it a penetration into the spirit of Scripture, and an understanding of the eternal, spiritual Gospel, just as, on the contrary, sensuous Christianity abided by the letter of Scripture alone. The highest problem of Scripture interpretation was in his estimation the changing of the sensuous Gospel into the spiritual,‡ just as the highest aim of Christianity was to elevate itself from the earthly appearance of the incarnate Logos to communion with him and to the contemplation of his Divine nature. Thus he saw also in the whole body of Scripture a letting down of the overwhelming heavenly Spirit to the human form, which was incapable of containing it; a letting down of the Divine Teacher of man to

---

* Thus also Clement on the οἰκονομία of the Gnostic. Stromat. vii. p. 730. [Potter, p. 863, 864. Sylb. p. 310. Klotz, vol. iii. p. 246, 247.] Comp. the notions of Philo given above, vol. i. p. 73, &c.

† πνευματικως και σωματικως χριστιανιζων.

‡ [It is difficult to imagine a text more tortured in its application than this passage. It was written to show that the knowledge of Christ crucified, whereby we are led to righteousness and to heaven, transcends all other knowledge, which St. Paul casts away in comparison of it—it is applied to degrade that doctrine of Christ crucified, in comparison of other doctrines and revelations of the same Christianity.—H. J. R.]

§ Tom. i. in Joh. p. 9.

‖ In Matt. l. c. 374, 375.

* βλεπετω οὖν τις τίνας των ἐπαγγελλομενων κατηχησιν ἐκκλησιαστικην και διδασκαλιαν, πςοσφεροντα τα μωρα του κοσμου και τα ἐξουθενωμενα και τα ἀγενη.

† Tom. ii. Joh. p. 4. [?]

‡ το μεταλαβειν το αἰσθητον εὐαγγελιον εἰς το πνευματικον.

the weakness and the wants of men, and all Scripture was in like manner a revelation of the incarnation of the Logos. Thus he says,* "All which is here called Word of God, is a revelation of the Divine Word, which became flesh and emptied itself in relation to its heavenly nature, and hence we see the Word of God on earth when he became man, as a human Word, for the Word constantly becomes flesh in Scripture, in order to dwell among us.† But when we have lien on the breast of the Word that became man, and are enabled to follow him as he climbs up the high hill, (Matt. xvii.) then we may say, 'we have seen his glory,'"‡ He sets out from the principle of an analogy between the Holy Scripture as a work of God, and the whole creation which proceeds from the same God; a principle, which carried out in his lively and spiritual manner, would at once become fruitful for the right consideration of the twofold revelation of God. Thus he says, and the saying shows at once how thoroughly imbued he was with the notion that the Holy Scripture is the Word of God:§ "We need not think it strange, if in every passage of Holy Writ the superhuman nature of the thought does not strike the unlearned, for in the works of Providence, which extend over the whole universe, some of them show manifestly, that they are the works of Providence, while others as so concealed, as to give occasion to incredulity in respect to God who governs all things with inexpressible skill and power. . . . . But just as we do not dispute the doctrine of a Providence,‖ on account of those things of which we are ignorant, when once we are justly persuaded of his existence, so we cannot doubt of the Divine authority of the Holy Scriptures, which extends to every portion of them, because our weakness is unable in every case to come up to the hidden glory of their doctrines, which is clothed in inadequate language, for we have the treasure in earthen vessels." And in another passage he says:* "He who once admits that these Scriptures are the work of the Creator of the world, must be persuaded, that whatsoever phenomena in regard to the creation present themselves to those who attempt to give an account of it, the same will also occur to him who inquires about the Scriptures. There are now, for instance, in Scripture many things which human nature may find difficult, or be unable to explain, but we are not on that account, to accuse the Creator of the Universe; as for example, when we are unable to explain the cause why basilisks and other poisonous animals were created; for here it is the duty of a pious mind, taking into consideration the weakness of man, and how it is impossible fully to understand the creating wisdom of God, to reserve to God the knowledge of such things, and he will afterwards, when we are considered worthy of it, reveal to us that, about which we have doubted in reverence." How full he was of the belief in a Divine Spirit which breathed throughout the whole of Scripture, and how thoroughly persuaded he was that this could be received only with an humble and a believing heart, is beautifully expressed in the following words of Origen:† "We must believe that no title of Holy Scripture is deficient in the wisdom of God, for He, who proclaimed to man, '*Thou shall not appear empty before me*,' (Exod. xxxiv.,) will himself far less utter any empty word; for the prophets take what they say, out of his fulness; therefore, all parts are animated (*lit.* breathe) by this fulness, and there is nothing in the Prophets, the Law, or the Gospel, or the Apostolic Epistles which does not proceed from this fulness. The breath, therefore, of this fulness (πληρωμά, Pleroma,) descends on those who have eyes, to see the revelations of the Divine fulness, ears to hear it, and a sense to catch the sweet smelling savour, which proceeds from this fulness. But if, in reading Scripture, you meet with a thought which, so to speak, is a stone of stumbling and a rock of offence, blame yourself, be assured, that this stone of stumbling contains thoughts, by which that saying shall come to pass, '*He that believeth shall not be put to shame*, (Rom.

---

* See Philocal. c. 15.

† Similarly also Clement says, that the character of the Holy Scripture is a parabolical one, as also the whole appearance of Christ is a parabolical one—viz. the Divine in an earthly garb. παραβολικος γαρ ό χαρακτηρ υπαρχει των γραφων, διοτι και ό Κυριος ουκ ἀν κοσμικος, ὡς κοσμικος εἰς ἀνθρωπους ἠλθεν. Stromat. vi. 677.

‡ The ennobling of Scripture for him, who learns to understand its spirit by a living communion with Christ.

§ Philocal. c. i. p. 10. [p. 5. Ed. Spencer, 1658.—H. J. R.]

‖ ω χρεοκοπειται ή προνοια.

---

* Philocal. c. ii, p. 61. [p. 23. Ed. Spencer.— H. J. R.]

† L. c. c. i. p. 51. [p. 19, 20. Ed. Spencer.-- H. J. R.]

x. 11.) Believe first, and you shall then find much holy assistance and support under that which appeared to you an offence."

But however just this principle of Origen might be, yet in the application of it he was led astray by means of the false position, from which he viewed the spirit and the object of Holy Scripture, and of all Divine revelation through the Word; and this false position was intimately connected with his false conception of the relation between *faith* and *Gnosis* (πιστις and γνωσις.) In both respects he was led astray by the speculative point of view, which was too prevalent, inasmuch as he did not sufficiently distinguish the nature of a Christian system of faith, and a Christian philosophy from each other, and he did not keep sufficiently before his sight the essentially practical object of all Divine revelations, and especially of Christianity. He did not refer every thing to the one object, that affects all mankind—redemption, regeneration, sanctification, and the blessings resulting from them; but the practical object of man's improvement was, in his estimation, only a subordinate one, which was chiefly of use to the great mass of believers, who were incapable of receiving any thing of higher character. In his estimation, the highest object was the speculative, the communicating the most elevated truths to spiritual men who were capable of understanding them, i. e. to the Gnostics. These higher truths have reference chiefly to the following points:* " About God—about the nature of his only begotten Son, and the mode in which he is the Son of God—about the cause which impelled him to come down and take upon him the nature of man—about the effects of this incarnation, whom it affects—about the higher kinds of reasonable beings who have fallen from a state of happiness, and the causes of their fall—about the difference of souls, and whence this difference arises—what the world is, and wherefore it was created—why there is so much evil in the earth, and whether evil is found only there, or elsewhere also." As Origen made it the chief object to find explanations and answers to these inquiries; many parts of Scripture, if he abided by their natural interpretation, would naturally appear to him to be unfruitful towards that which he considered its essential object. All narratives embracing only earthly occurrences, all legislation bearing only on earthly relations, he explained as being only the symbolical guise of a higher history of the world of Spirits; and of higher laws which related also to that world. Thus the higher and the subordinate object of Scripture would be united together, and the revelation of the higher class of truth would be hidden in a literal form, adapted to the improvement of the general mass of mankind. "The multitude of genuine and simple believers," says Origen, " bears testimony to the usefulness, even of this inferior understanding of the Scriptures." Between these two kind of senses included in Scipture, Origen imagined an intermediate kind, an allegorical sense adapted for those who had not yet arrived at that higher state of spiritual perception; this was a general, moral, and instructive application of those passages of Scripture, which relate to individual cases, though this application was not of that elevated and profound class;* and he adduces as examples of this, the explanation of 1 Cor. ix. 9; and most of the allegorical interpretations of Scripture then commonly used, even in the instruction of the people. Thus, the triple sense of Scripture corresponded to the three parts of man's nature, which the theory of Origen acknowledged; that which is really Divine in man, the *Spirit*, which is directed towards the Eternal, and finds its proper life in the perception and contemplation of Divine things; the *Soul*, whose sphere of action is the temporal and the finite; and the *Body*. While Philo agreed with Origen in the essential and fundamental features of his view, he (Origen) sought also on the whole to preserve the objective truth of the literal and historical contents of the Scriptures,† which are given as the dress in which the spiritual revelations are communicated. And yet, he formed passages where the letter could not, in his opinion, be defended; because he was destitute of right hermeneutic principles, and of other necessary helps and aids; or because he did not know how to separate the divine from the human in the Holy Scriptures.

---

* Philocal. i. 28. [p. 11, Ed. Spencer.—H. J. R.]

* [As in the higher class of interpretation, which he imagined.—H. J. R.]
† το σωματικον των γραφων, το ενδυμα των πνευματικων.

As for Tertullian, whose powerful Christian realism made him hold fast the fundamental truth of a Christian Anthropopathism, although in the feelings of his heart, and in the conception of his spirit, he frequently had more than he was able neatly and clearly to express in his uncultivated and carnal modes of expression, he justly reproaches Marcion, who thus separated the attributes of God, with inconsistency in his belief about redemption: and says to him,† "Does not the forgiveness of sin presuppose the existence of sin in the eyes of God, who forgives sin?" and, on the contrary, he maintains, that the goodness of God cannot be separated from his righteousness; that principle, which sets every thing in order, and attributes to every one that which is his.‡ "The goodness of God has created the world, and his righteousness has duly arranged it." In opposition to Marcion, he shows the necessity of an Anthropopathism, which even Marcion himself, although unconsciously to himself, could not avoid; but he shows also how a just Anthropopathism must consist in this, that we should not let down the attributes of God to human sinfulness and imperfection; but by a restoration of the image of God in human nature, ennoble that which is human till it becomes a mirror of the Divine. He says to Marcion, "Those are extremely foolish, who judge that which is Divine according to that which is human. Why shouldst thou imagine God to be partly human, and not wholly Divine? . . . . . . [Moreover, while you acknowledge, that man became a living soul, being breathed into by God, and not God by man's operation,] it is perverse enough on your part, to let down God to the nature of man, instead of elevating man to the image of God . . . . . . Why do ye consider long suffering, mercy, and the mother of all *goodness itself*, to be something Divine. And yet, at the same time, all this is not in us in its perfection, because God alone is perfect."§ Tertullian recognises in every revelation of God a progressive condescension, the highest point and the object of which is the incarnation of God.‖ "Whatever you may collect together, which speaks of inferiority, or weakness, or any thing that is unworthy of God, I will give you a simple and consistent answer. God cannot enter into any association with man, without attributing to himself human sensations and affections; and thus by his condescension he softens the overwhelmingness of his majesty, which human weakness could not bear; and this is a condescension, which, however unworthy of the Deity, is necessary for man, and, therefore, worthy of God; because nothing is so worthy of God, as that which serves to the salvation of man* . . . . . God deals with man, as with one like himself, in order that man may act towards God as with a being like himself. God appeared in humility, in order that man might be raised to the highest pinnacle of greatness. If thou art ashamed of a God like this, I see not indeed how thou canst believe in a crucified God." It must be acknowledged that the latter charge of inconsistency did not apply to Marcion, because the same principle which induced him to oppose the anthropopathical conceptions of God belonging to the Old Testament, made him also an opponent of the doctrine of a crucified Deity.

The Alexandrian Fathers distinguish themselves peculiarly, in consequence of their philosophical culture, by endeavouring to eradicate entirely a carnal Anthropopathism out of the Christian system of doctrine; but it was also very easy for them to carry their notions too far in the contrary direction, and they were liable to lower the doctrine of the Divine attributes and involve it too completely in what is only subjective. Let us take as an instance the following beautiful passage of Origen, in which, notwithstanding all the beauty with which he speaks of God's education of man, he does not conceive with sufficient depth the sense of the Biblical expression of the 'wrath of God' against sin. Working upon the idea of Philo, as to the two systems in regard to Divine things, the *Humanizing*, and the *De-Humanizing* system, he says,‡ "When the Scriptures represent God, as God in his Divine Majesty,§ and do not involve in their consideration his dealings in relation to men, they declare

---

† Adv. Marc. ii. 26-7.   ‡ L. c. ii. 12.
§ [Tertull. Contr. Marc. ii. xiv. Ed. Rigalt.—H. J. R.]
‖ L. c. ii. 15.

* L. c. ii. 27.
‡ Hom. 18, in Jeremiam, § 6. [p. 169, and seq. Ed. Huet.—H. J. R.]
§ [θεολογωσι τον Θεον κατ' αὑτον, i. e. speak of him absolutely and not in relation to man.—H. J. R.]

that 'he is not like a man, for there is no end of his greatness.' (Ps. cxlv. 3.) And again, 'the Lord is a great God, a great king above all Gods.' (Ps. xcv. 3.) . . . . . . But when his dealings with the human race are interwoven with the subject, then God assumes the mind, the fashion, and the language of man; just as when we talk to a child of two years old, we lisp for the sake of the child; for if we maintain the dignity of mature age, in talking to children, and do not let ourselves down to their language, they are unable to understand us. Think, then, that God also acts in the same way, when he lets himself down to the race of men, and especially to those who are still in their [intellectual] childhood. See now, how we grown up men alter even the name of things, when we communicate with children, and how we call bread by some peculiar name, and also drinking we designate by some other term, because we make use of the language of children, and not of grown up persons . . . . . . If any one heard us talking thus, would he say 'This old man is become foolish ?' and thus also God speaks [with us] as with children. 'Behold,' says our Saviour, 'I and the children whom God hath given to me.' (Heb. ii. 13.) . . . . . . When you hear of the wrath of God, do not imagine that wrath is a passion to which God is subject. It is a condescension of language in order to convert and amend the child, for we ourselves put on a look of severity and anger towards children, not from feeling the passion ourselves, but designedly. If we preserve our mildness of aspect, and testify our love of the child, without changing our look, as the real interest of the child would require us to do, we spoil it utterly. Thus also God is represented to us as angry, in order to our conversion and improvement, while in fact he is not subject to anger; but thou wilt undergo the wrath of God, by drawing down upon thyself by thy wickedness, sufferings hard to be borne, when thou art punished by what is called the wrath of God." Origen spoke thus in one of his *Sermons*; and also in another passage in his commentary on Matthew, where he developes the same theory, he says,* "Much may be said to those, *who are not in a condition to be injured by it,*

about the goodness of God and the abundance of his grace, which he properly hides from those *who fear him.*"

The Alexandrians here also took a middle path between the Gnostics and the rest of the Fathers. While these maintained that there is no absolute retributive justice in God,* nay, set aside the whole notion of justice as contradictory to the nature of a perfect God, and opposed the God of justice to the God of goodness, the Alexandrians, on the contrary, made the notion of justice altogether into the notion of a Divine love, which educates rational beings in a fallen state, according to their several capacities and needs.† Thus they might say, that the distinction made by the Gnostics between a just and a good God, might be applied in a certain true sense, by attributing the epithet of "the just" peculiarly to Christ (the Divine Logos) as the educator and the purifier of fallen beings, the aim of whose education was that they might be rendered capable of receiving the goodness of their everlasting heavenly Father, and thus becoming blessed.‡

The *doctrine of a creation out of nothing* is closely connected with the peculiar character of the Christian doctrine regarding the Deity. In opposition to the notions of antiquity founded upon a religion, which consisted of a deification of nature, which either carried back a succession of causes and effects to a blind unconscious chaos, or at least made God only the fashioner of an inorganic, chaotic matter—in opposition to these notions, Christianity, which frees the con-

---

* [The sentence in Neander runs thus: 'Wenn diese eine absolute Gerechtigkeit in Gott setzten, ja den ganzen Gerechtigkeitsbegriff als einen des Wesen des volkommenen Gottes widersprechenden umstiessen, und den gerechten Gott dem guten entgegensetzten,' &c. 'While these acknowledged *an absolute* retributive justice in God, and even farther than this threw aside,' &c.

As the two parts of the sentence are contradictory of each other, I conceive that there is some mistake, and I have translated it as if *keine* stood in the place of *eine*.—H. J. R.]

† Α δικαιοσυνη σωτηριος.

‡ Clemens, Pædagog. lib. i. p. 118. καθ' ὁ μεν πατηρ νοειται ἀγαθος ἐν, αὐτο μενων ὁ ἐστι, κεκληται ἀγαθος, καθ' ὁ δε υἱος ἀν ὁ λογος αὐτου ἐν τω πατρι ἐστι, δικαιος πρεσηγορευται. And Origen t. i. in Joh. p. 40, speaking of the difference between the Θεος ἀγαθος and the δημιουργος δικαιος.

(ταυτα δε οιμαι μετ' ἐξετασεως ἀκριβους βασανισθεν δυνασθαι λεγεσθαι ἐπι του πατρος και του υἱου, του μεν υἱου τυγχανοντος δικαιοσυνης, του δε πατρος τους ἐν τῃ δικαιοσυνῃ του υἱου παιδευθεντας μετα την Χριστου βασιλειαν εὐεργετουντος.

---

* p. 378, Ed. Huet. [The phrase '*who fear him,*' of course alludes to those whose religious character is imperfect; who have not arrived at the point where they may cast away fear.—H. J. R.]

sciousness of God's existence from every thing like a connection with the deification of nature, presented the doctrine of the Creation as the object of a faith which raised itself over the whole circle of causes and effects in the world cognisable by sense [literally, *the appearance-world,*] up to the free author of all existence. The characteristic circumstance here, and that which is of practical importance, is this; that the incomprehensible was maintained to be incomprehensible, and that which alone can be of any interest or importance towards affecting our religious faith here, was separated from all the uncongenial elements of poetry and speculation, by which it had been contaminated in the old Oriental systems of religion. Christianity was here destined to purify the religious faith as it had been already revealed in the Old Testament, from all the strange additions it had received by intermixture with the Platonic and the Oriental systems. Thus in the Epistle to the Hebrews, chap. xi., it is proclaimed as an object of faith, that things visible came not from things visible, but that the world was created by the Almighty power of God. This was negatively expressed in the doctrine of a Creation out of nothing,* a conclusion which was altogether misconceived by the Gnostics,† when they opposed to it the old saying, (ex nihilo nil fit,) " from nothing, nothing can come," because this doctrine has an antithetical force only against the supposition of matter, which should limit creation; and in this doctrine it is not Nothing but the Supreme, absolute Being = GOD which is declared to be the formation of all existence. It must, however, be confessed, that this conclusion was intended to exclude also a view, which declared all existence as a kind of development of nature proceeding from God, subjected God to a necessity arising from the course of nature, and went near to destroy the notion of the absolute dependence of creation on the Creator. But we have already remarked that those Oriental Theosophists, the Gnostics, were unable to content themselves with this negative conception of the incomprehensible Being. They wished to explain it, and to make that intelligible and perceptible to our ideas, which the doctrine of the creation out of nothing only presented as an object of faith.

* κτισις εκ του μη οντος
† See above, Part ii.

Hermogenes, who lived probably at Carthage, about the end of the second and the beginning of the third century, agreed with the Gnostics in their controversy against this portion of the Church doctrine. He was essentially distinguished from the Gnostics by the turn of his mind, which was more of a Western cast, for he was more addicted to Grecian speculation than to Oriental intuition [Anschauung,] and hence also his system, which did not, like the Gnostic systems, set the powers of the imagination to work, was not able to obtain so much acceptance as theirs, and in fact we do not hear of any sect of Hermogenians. Nor did he, like the Gnostics, sketch out for himself a peculiar system of esoteric religious doctrines, but he departed from the Church doctrine only in one point, which was, however, a point necessarily very influential on the whole system of religion. He was a painter, and probably a very determined opponent of the Montanism which was spreading over the north of Africa; the artist was as little suited to the Montanistic sect, as they were to the artist. Perhaps also, Hermogenes,* while he opposed the harsh and gloomy character of the Montanists, went into the other extreme of laxness in his estimation of what is Christian and what unchristian; he appears to have had no scruple in representing the objects of the Heathen mythology in the way of his art, because he considered them as mere objects of

* The obscure words of Tertullian, from which we are enabled to derive this account, are as follows. Pingit illicite, nubit assidue, legem Dei in libidinem defendit, in artem contemnit. The first sentence might be understood so as to convey the notion that Tertullian looked on painting itself as something heathenish and sinful, but such a judgment could not be confidently affirmed even of the Montanistic hatred of art in Tertullian, and no proof in favour of such an explanation is to be found in his writings. Neither do the words " he despises the law of God in reference to his art" favour this interpretation, for one cannot think of any passage of Scripture, which Tertullian can have considered as an entire prohibition of painting; but probably Tertullian comprised the old Testament under the expression " Lex Dei," and alluded to the prohibition of idolatrous images: and the sense would then be, " he despises the authority of the Old Testament by the manner in which he plies his art, and yet he will make its authority available to him to defend a second marriage, against the Montanists, who maintained that the authority of the Old Testament in this respect was superseded by Christianity, and by the new revelations of the Paraclete."

art, independently of any reference to religion at all.

Hermogenes controverted the emanation doctrine of the Gnostics, because it transfers sensuous images to the Being of God, and because the idea of the holiness of God was irreconcilable with the sinfulness of a nature which emanated from him. But he also controverted the doctrine of a creation out of nothing, because, if the world had had no other source than the will of God, it would have corresponded to the nature of the perfect and Holy God, and therefore, would of necessity have been perfect and holy; nothing imperfect nor evil could have found place in it, for in a world whose only source was God, whence could any thing arise which was uncongenial to the nature of that God? Hermogenes, no doubt, here partly followed, as the Gnostics did, a subjective rule of too limited a nature in his estimation of the different creatures according to the different grades of being, and partly he omitted to take into consideration what is included in the very idea of Creation. In respect to moral evil he was as little inclined as the Gnostics to throw himself back upon the distinction between *willing* and *permitting* on the part of God, and he also with justice abandoned the ground, that evil is necessary as the foil to good, in order that the latter may be known by the contrast; because this position denies the self-existence and independence of good, and the very nature of evil would be destroyed, if it were considered as something which is necessary to the harmony of the whole. But Hermogenes fell into the very error which he desired to avoid; because he still deduced the existence of evil from a necessity inherent in nature. According to his theory, all that is imperfect or evil in the world originates from this cause, that God's creation is limited in consequence of the eternal existence of inorganic matter. From all eternity two principles have existed; the one, the active, and the forming and fashioning (the plastic,)—namely, God; and the passive, the undeterminate in itself,* and the formless—namely, matter. This latter is an infinite chaotic mass in constant motion, in which all opposite qualities are present undeveloped and run into each other, full of wild impulse, without law or order, and like the motion of a cauldron that boils up in every direction.* This infinite chaos, thrown as it was into endless and irregular motion, could not at any point be laid hold of by a single act, brought to a stand-still, and compelled to subject itself to be formed and fashioned. It was only through the relation of his nature to that of matter, that God could work upon this mass; as the magnet by some inherent necessity attracts iron;† as beauty exerts a natural force of attraction on all that approaches it, so God exerts a fashioning influence on matter by his mere appearance, and by the superior power of his Divine Being.‡ According to these principles, he could not, with any consistency, maintain a beginning of existence to the creation, and, in fact he does not appear to have assumed any such beginning, as we may judge from the grounds which he alleges for his doctrine on this subject; namely, that since dominion is a necessary attribute of God, there must always have been matter for him to exercise that dominion upon. In accordance with this view he maintained an eternal influence of God upon matter, which consisted, according to his system, in the victorious plastic power. From what has been said, it follows, that we must not conceive that in his system chaos was a separate thing existing by itself, and that the influence of this Divine plastic power had begun at some particular instant, whereas [according to his system,] it can exist only in connection with this organization, which is imparted to it [by God,] and they can be separated only in idea. From the resistance of this infinite matter, which was to be fashioned by degrees in all its separate parts, against the fashioning power of God, which could only penetrate it successfully by degrees, he deduced all that is imperfect and evil. Thus the old chaos manifests itself in all that is hateful in nature, and all that is morally evil in the spiritual world."§

That Hermogenes should maintain a

---

* ['Das in sich selbst unbestimmte;' 'without power or purpose to throw itself into any definite state or form."—H J. R.]

* Inconditus, et confusus, et turbulentus motus, sicut ollæ undique ebullientis.

† We here recognise the painter.

‡ Non pertransiens materiam facit Deus mundum, sed solummodo apparens et adpropinquans ei, sicut facit qui decor, solummodo adparens, et magnes lapis solummodo adpropinquans.

§ [i. e. Physical deformity and moral evil are the phenomena which give testimony to the existence of this Chaos, and they are its manifestations.—H. J. R.]

progressive formation of matter, co-existing with an eternal creation, was an inconsistency, because no progressive development can be imagined without a beginning. His inconsistency would be still more striking, if the account of Theodoret is accurate, by which he is made to hold a final aim of this development. He maintained in fact then, (if this account be true,) like the Manichees, that at last all evil would resolve itself into matter, from which it originated, and then also that a separation would take place between that part of matter, which is capable of organization, and that which offered an obstinate resistance to it.* Here the teleological and moral element, which adhered to him from his Christianity, and did not suit this heathenish natural view of evil, rendered him inconsistent.†

Irenæus and Tertullian maintained, the former against the Gnostics, the latter against Hermogenes, the simple Christian doctrine of the creation, without permitting themselves to enter upon speculations concerning it.

Origen was distinguished also in this respect from these Fathers by a system peculiar to himself, of which we must develope the fundamental features, as far as they are connected with the doctrine of the creation. In accordance with the character of *his* Gnosis (see above,) he founded his system on the belief generally prevalent in the whole Church, and thought that his speculative inquiries, which stepped beyond this, might be very consistently united with it. He declared himself in favour of the doctrine of a creation out of nothing, as far as the free action of Divine power, unlimited by any condition inherent in pre-existent matter, was indicated by this doctrine; and this he did, not merely with acquiescence, but out of hearty persuasion.* He also acknowledges a definite beginning to the limited and definite world now in existence; but with regard to what preceded it, he conceived that Scripture and the faith of the Church left him fully at liberty to speculate. And here then he found those general grounds for opposing any beginning of creation, which are sure to strike any thinking mind, which is unwilling to be satisfied with a *mere belief* in the incomprehensible. How can it happen that if creating is suitable to the nature of God, any thing which is suitable to that nature, should ever have been wanting? How should the qualities, which reside in the being of God, omnipotence and goodness, fail to have been always active? The transition from inaction to creation cannot be conceived without the notion of *change;* to which the Being of God is not liable.

Origen was also an opponent of the emanation doctrine, as it was conceived by the Gnostics; because it appeared to him to transfer sensuous representations to the being of God, and by the supposition of an unity-of-substance (the ὁμοούσιον,) between God and the natures that emanated from him, appeared to abolish the proper distinction between the Creator and the creation. But he assumed a system of emanation spiritually conceived and abjuring all sensuous images, a spiritual world of a kindred nature with God, and which beamed forth from him from all eternity, above which he is, however, immeasurably exalted, and in all these Spirits, was there the partial revelation, the partial reflection of the Glory of God,† as the Son of God is the collected revelation of the Glory of God.

Origen here conceived the idea of an absolute dependence without any beginning in time;‡ a causation, in which the existence of the creation, as a thing which

---

* Theodoret does not say this expressly, but such a doctrine is necessarily implied in that, which, according to his account, Hermogenes held. Theodoret's words (Hæret. fab. i. 19,) are these: τον δε διαβολον και τους δαιμονας εις την υλην αναχθησεσθαι.

† Theodoret ascribes to Hermogenes also the doctrine, that Christ deposited his body in the sun. A question would arise here, whether Theodoret has not confused his doctrine with some others like it; and in what way his words are to be understood. Perhaps, Hermogenes taught that Christ, when he raised himself into his heavenly existence, left behind him in the sun the garb which he had taken from the material world. And yet it is difficult to attribute confidently so entirely fantastic an opinion to Hermogenes, and the matter must be left in obscurity for want of evidence. Perhaps also, some meaning of Psal. xix. 4, with a *messianic* interpretation according to the version of the LXX. may have led the way to this notion.

* See Præfat. Libb. π ἀρχ. p. 4. ibid. lib. ii. c. i. § 4. Lib. iii. c. 5.—Commentar. Genes. init.
† π. αρχ. lib. i. c. 2. § 6. In Joh. t. 20. c. 16. T. 13. c. 25. T. 32. c. 18. ὁλης μεν ουν της δοξης του Θεου απαυγασμα ειναι τ.ν υιον, φθανειν μεν τοι γε απο του απαυγασματος της ὁλης δοξης μερικα απαυγασματα επι την λοιπην λογικην κτισιν.
‡ ['Ohne ein zeitliches werden,' literally 'without a temporal *becoming* or coming into existence.' In the next clause of the sentence ('as a thing,' &c.) the original is 'als etwas seinem Wesen noch nicht in sich selbst ruhendes,' 'as something according to the laws of its nature not reposing on itself;' i. e. not self-dependent, or self-existent.—H. J R.]

could not have a self-existence, was founded from all eternity.‡ What he says of the continuous regeneration of the pious, and of the generation of the Son of God, may be applied in the sense in which he uses it to this also; because the Divine Logos stands in the same relation to the rest of the spiritual world as its source of Divine light, as God stands in to him. He says, Jerem. Hom. ix. § 4. [p. 106. ed. Huet. H. J. R.] "I will not say that the righteous is born of God once for all; but that he is constantly born of him in every good action. And if also I lay down to you in reference to our Saviour, that the Father did not beget the Son and then cease, but that he always begets him, I should also maintain something similar in respect to the righteous. Let us then see who is our Saviour? The reflected image of [God's] glory. Now the image of glory is not produced once for all, and then ceases to be produced; but as long as the light is efficient in creating the image itself, so long is the image of the glory of God constantly created. If, therefore, thou hast the spirit of adoption (sonship,) God constantly begets thee in that same sonship, in every act and in every thought, and thus thou art forever being born as a son of God in Jesus Christ."†

Bishop Methodius, the adversary of Origen, whose theory of creation was controverted by the bishop in his work concerning *creatures*, was by no means his equal in respect to a spirit of speculation.‡ He had not a sufficient power of speculative perception, justly to conceive the ideas of Origen, and he represented what he did not understand as foolish and impious. While he himself compares the relations in which God stands to his creatures with the relation between a human workman and the works of his hands, he makes against the system of Origen objections, which could not justly lie against it. How little able he was to understand that great man, whom in his blind zeal he calls a Centaur, appears by the following argument, which he casts in his teeth; viz. that if the transition from noncreation to creation implies a change in God, the transition from creation to noncreation equally implies a change. Now God must have ceased to create the world, when it was finished, and thus a change in God would clearly be implied. He did not observe, that with Origen the conception of the upholding of the world was the conception of a continuous creation, and he did not consider, that just exactly by such a representation of creation, as is contained in his own argument, a self-existence would be attributed to creatures which is inconsistent with the idea of them as creatures. He made another objection, which although more directed against an inaccurate expression of Origen, than against what he really meant, was more correct; and it was this, that the idea of God's perfection actually implied, that it is a thing, whose foundation is in itself; that it is dependent on nothing besides, and limited or conditioned by nothing whatever.*

The doctrine of Origen relative to creation is intimately connected also with his peculiar conception of *the omnipotence of God*. It happened to him in this matter, as, indeed, in many other respects, that, being entangled in the ideas of the philosophical school, from which his learning and his education were derived, he set out from those ideas, as if they were acknowledged truths. Thus he set out from the principle, *that an infinite line cannot be conceived by any mind*, into which the Neo-platonic school allowed itself to be deluded, by their attempt to measure an absolute reason by the limits of finite human thought.† From this Origen drew the conclusion; that we must not, in order to enhance the Divine omnipotence, make it *infinite*, because then it would be unable to comprehend itself.‡ Thus also God could create only

---

* Methodius represents faithfully the expressions of Origen, when he ascribes to him the doctrine of a γενητον ἀει γενεσεως ἀρχην οὐκ ἰχον, and of an ἀναρχος κρατων του τεχνηματος.

† Thus tom. i. in Joh. p, 32, we must not imagine that any limitation of time is indicated, but ὁ συμπαρεκτεινων τω ἀγεννητω και ὁσιω ζωη, ἐν' οὑτως εἰπω, χρονος ἡμερα ἐστιν αὐτω σημερον, ἐν ἡ γεγεννηται ὁ υιος.

‡ Extracts from the book of Methodius found in Photius, Cod. 235.

* το αὐτο δι ἑαυτου ἐνυπιν πληρωμα ὸν και αὐτο ἐν ἑαυτω μενιν, τελειν εἰναι τουτο μονον δεξασθειν.

† [N.B. The word here is *Bewusstseyn*, which will express that wherein our knowledge or our capacity of entertaining ideas resides, as well as our consciousness of those ideas. In *popular* language, *understanding* would come the nearest; but it is so desirable to keep the distinction between *reason* and *understanding*, as definite as possible, that I would rather use *thought* or *comprehension* instead of it.—H. J. R.]

‡ το ἀπειρον ἀπεριληπτον, and in Matt. Ed. Huet. p. 305, he says expressly: ἀπερα γαρ τη φυσει οὐχ οἱα τε περιλαμβανεσθαι τη πρατων πεφυκυια τα γινωσκμενα γνωσι.

a definite and not an infinite number of beings endued with reason, because otherwise they could not be embraced by his providence. We recognise also in this error of Origen the leaning which he had in the matter of religion. This doctrine is of great importance to his whole system (as will be seen below) when taken in connection with his theory, that, since the number of reason-gifted beings is definite, and is always the same, therefore, it is only from the change of will and intention among them that all other changes can proceed.

The peculiar nature of Christianity reveals itself in the recognition and worship of God, not merely as the Creator, but also as the Redeemer and Sanctifier of human nature, in the belief that God, who has created human nature pure, has redeemed it when it became estranged from him by sin, and continues to sanctify it, until it shall have attained in an eternal life to an untroubled and beatified communion with him in perfect holiness. Without this faith and knowledge, there is no lively worship of God, no worship of God in spirit and in truth, because a lively worship of God cannot exist without communion with him, and because this communion cannot be shared by man, as long as he is estranged from God by sin; as long as that, which separates him from God, is not removed; and because the worship of God in spirit and in truth, can only proceed from a soul which has been sanctified so as to become a temple of God. This doctrine of *God the Creator*, the *Redeemer* and the *Sanctifier* of human nature, is the essential import of the doctrine of the *Trinity*, and therefore, since in this latter doctrine the essence of all Christianity is contained, it could not but happen, that, as this doctrine proceeded out of the depths of Christian consciousness, it should be considered as the chief doctrine of Christianity, and that even in the earliest Church the essential import of the faith should be annexed to the doctrine of the Father, the Son, and the Holy Ghost.* This doctrine again is nothing else than the doctrine of God, who has revealed and imparted himself to sinful man in Christ; every thing here reverts to the doctrine of God's being in Christ, for the working of God in human nature redeemed by him, presupposes the inward relation, into which God has entered with human nature through Christ, and all is here only the continuation and the consequence of that [relation;] and therefore, this doctrine is nothing else but the perfect development of the doctrine about Christ, which the Apostle Paul, 1 Corinth. iii., calls the foundation of all Christianity, the development of that which Christ himself designates as the essential import of his doctrine; "This is Eternal Life that they should know thee, that thou alone art the true God, and Jesus Christ whom thou hast sent." But the speculative doctrine of the Trinity is carefully to be distinguished from this its essential Christian import, and men might agree in the latter, and yet differ from each other in their conceptions of the former. The former only set itself up as an human attempt to bring into just harmony with the unity of the Divine Being, the existence of God in Christ, and through Christ in the faithful, as it is represented in Holy Scripture, and out of that Holy Scripture formed an image of itself in the inward life and the inward perceptions of the faithful. But it was an evil, that, in this attempt, men did not rightly divide the speculative and dialectic element from that essential and practical foundation; the consequence of which was, that men transplanted that doctrine from its proper practical ground, in which it is rooted in the centre point of Christianity, into a speculative region foreign to it, which might give an opportunity of mingling with it much extraneous matter, and again might lead to setting Christianity, contrary to its peculiar character, on a speculative instead of a practical foundation; and the consequence of this again was, on the one hand, that men, overprizing the importance of speculative differences, tore asunder the bond of Christian communion, where there was yet an agreement in what is practical and essential; and on the other hand, that men stinted the *free development* of the Christian doctrine by the attempt to *attain an uniformity of speculative* conceptions.*

---

* This is literally translated; perhaps the meaning would be more nearly expressed as follows,—that the acknowledgment of the doctrine of the Father, Son, and Holy Ghost was considered to comprise the essentials of the Christian Faith. The original is "dass .... der wesentliche Glaubensinhalt an die Lehre vom Vater, Sohne, und Heiligen Geist angereiht wurde."—H. J. R.

* [We must also be careful that in endeavouring to reconcile contending views we do not depart from the great truth which is contained in the acknowledgment of the Athanasian Creed, that

It is self-evident from what has been said, that the development of this doctrine must first proceed from speculations on the manner, in which the Divine nature in Christ was in relation with the Godhead of the Father. Providence had then so exactly managed things in this respect, that in the Spiritual world in which Christianity first made its appearance, many notions, at least apparently of a kindred kind, were afloat, in which Christianity could find a point on which to attach the doctrine of a God revealed in Christ, or which it might appropriate to itself as general, intelligible forms, in which it might envelope that doctrine. In a discourse preserved to us by the Apostle John, Christ himself has expressed with Divine confidence the consciousness of his oneness with God, an incomprehensible fact of his consciousness (Matt. xi. 27,) without founding his declaration on any of the then notions of his age, but rather in opposition to the limited representations, current among the Jews, of the Messiah as a man, who proceeded from the ordinary development of human nature. But the Apostles Paul and John, united with the doctrine of God revealed in Christ, the idea that was already in existence in the Jewish theological schools, of a revealer of God elevated above the whole creation, the perfect image of the hidden Divine Being, from whom [the Word] all the communication of life from God proceeded, the image of the invisible God, the Word, in whom the hidden God reveals himself, the First-born before all creation—and they confirmed and established this idea and applied it to Christ. John, in particular, by the brief introduction prefixed to his Gospel, induced those among his contemporaries who sought after a knowledge of Divine things, who busied themselves with speculations on the self-revelation of God in his own express image—the Word that expressed his hidden nature, or the revealing and creating Reason—to give a lively, an historical and a practical meaning to this idea, by applying it to the appearance of Christ, instead of constantly restraining it to the regions of speculation. By this means, the development of the doctrine of Christ's Divinity was placed in connection with that speculative idea, which was already to be found current, although under a different form, among the Jewish Theologians, the Oriental Theosophists, and the Platonic Philosophers.

But in the conception of this doctrine there existed already among the Jews *two different views*. One party considered the Divine Logos as a Spirit, which existed in an independent personality, although in the most intimate union with the Divine First Cause,* while another party rejected this notion of an Hypostasis, as inconsistent with strict Monotheism, and they conceived to themselves, under the name of Logos, nothing but the Reason, which is either hidden in God and only engaged in contemplation,† or else reveals itself both after the manner of thought, which manifests itself in human speech, and also by its efficient operation in the work of creation,‡—the Reason, which cannot be divided from God, and which either concentrates itself in him or beams forth from out of him.§

---

each person is acknowledged "by himself to be both God and Lord, and yet that no one should for a moment believe that there be 'three Gods or three Lords.'" We must take care that we do not explain the Divinity of the Son as the mere indwelling of the Father in Jesus Christ; or believe that the Son is the mere manifestation of the Father; or we shall fall into Sabellianism or Patripassianism at once. The evil which Neander wishes to obviate seems to be the attempt to *explain* this great truth *speculatively*, and creating differences in consequence of such attempts. However wrong such attempts may be, in opposing them we must still be careful to maintain that great Catholic truth, the Trinity in Unity, and the Unity in Trinity, which is founded on the Scriptures and must be received by faith, though our finite faculties are unable to explain its mysteries. —H. J. R.]

* [Literally, Urwesen. Original Being. It is impossible to express the idea with metaphysical accuracy; if we speak of *first*, we give the idea of being prior to the *Word*, which is yet held to be eternal. I use the word First cause, therefore, relatively to other Beings, as it is used in common parlance, not as expressing priority of existence in the Father relative to the Son, or Word.—H. J. R.]

† The λογος ενδιαθετος. [I recommend those English readers who wish for clear statements on this subject, to consult Newman's "Arians of the Fourth Century," especially ch. ii. § 3 and 4.—H. J. R.]

‡ λογος προφορικος. [The same Reason, therefore, was conceived under two different conditions. It received the name of λογος ενδιαθετος when considered as residing in God, and delighting itself in contemplation, and that of λογος προφορικος when considered as emanating forth from Him and revealing God by spoken words or by the acts and the works of creation.—H. J. R.]

§ See Clementin. Homil. 16. c. xii. Τῃ δε σοφιᾳ, ωσπερ ιδιω πνευματι ου συνεχαιρει, ηνωται μοι ως ψυχη τω Θεω, εκτεινεται δε απ' αυτου ως χειρ δημιουργουσα το παν, κατα εκτασιν και συστολην η μονας δυας ειναι νομιζεται.

PATRIPASSIANS.

While the former was the predominant mode of conception [as to the Logos] in the doctrines as exhibited by the Church, the other mode of conception made its appearance not unfrequently during this season in opposition to the Church doctrine, and this opposition served again, on the other hand, to promote the systematic formation and development of the former view.

Those who embraced the latter mode of conception, in their controversy against the Church Doctrine of the Trinity, and in their religious leaning, were in agreement in one respect, namely, that it was of the utmost importance to them, firmly to maintain the doctrine of the Unity of God,* and to avoid every thing which bore even the appearance of Polytheism.† But in the manner in which they applied this theory to Christ, they varied widely from each other, according as they happened to be peculiarly interested in maintaining merely the principles of the *Monarchia*, or were at the same time filled with a belief in the Divinity of Christ, and although they controverted the doctrine of an independent personality of the Logos, yet had a lively interest in maintaining the Divinity of Christ; in fact, according as they were under the direction of a dialectic and critical understanding, or of an inward and practical Christian disposition. The former, together with the Church doctrine of the Trinity, controverted also that of the Divinity of Christ, though they were nevertheless content to admit his godly nature [Göttheit, divinity; Göttlichkeit, godly nature or godliness] in a certain sense; that is to say, they taught that Jesus was a man, like all other men, but that from the very first he had been animated and influenced, more than all other prophets and messengers of God, by that Divine Power, the Reason or Wisdom of God, and that, on this account, he was to be called the Son of God. They were distinguished from those, who embraced entirely Ebionite sentiments, by not admitting that this connection of God with Christ began at any one definite moment of his existence, but they conceived it to be coeval with the development of the human nature of Christ.

The others, on the contrary, in regard to the doctrine about Christ, were still more strongly opposed to this class of Monarchianism than to the opinion adopted by the Church; not only a leaning towards the doctrine of the Monarchia, in which even a Jew might join with them, but also a leaning towards some of the peculiar features of Christianity, made them hostile to the doctrine of the Church. Not only did the manner, in which the doctrine of the Unity of God was conceived in the Church doctrine, fail to meet their Monotheistic views, but also the manner, in which the Divinity of Christ was there understood, was unsuited to their peculiar Christian class of feelings and wants. While the Logos, who became man in Christ, was usually represented as a Being, different in person from God the Father and subordinate to him, although in the most intimate connection with him, they thought this a disparaging representation of Christ, and such a distinction between Christ and the Supreme God was offensive to their belief about Christ; to them he was the one, Supreme God himself, who in a way that he had never done besides, had revealed himself in human nature, and had appeared in a human body. It was only inasmuch as God was to be named after two different considerations [or relations, ἐπίνοιαι]—the hidden Being, as he was before the creation, the Father—and in so far as he revealed himself, the Son of the Logos—it was only in virtue of these considerations that Christ as the most perfect revelation of God the Father, was called the Son of God. They maintained that their doctrine was most eminently calculated *to dignify Christ.** They were called *Patripassians*,

---

* The μοναρχία, the doctrine of the μόνη ἀρχή, whence this party obtained the name of Monarchians.

† It was their term of distinction, the watchword of their party. Tertullian c. Praxeam, c. iii. Monarchiam tenemus. Origen, in Joh. t. ii. § 2. τὸ πολλοὺς φιλοθέους εἶναι εὐχομένους ταράσσον, ἀναβουμένους, ἀναγορεύται δύο θεούς.

* τί οὖν κακὸν ποιῶ, δοξάζων τὸν Χριστόν; said Noëtus, an adherent of this theory, when he was accused before a Synod. Hippolyt. c. Noët. c. ii. And Origen, in Matth. p. 420. ed. Huet, says, οὐ νομιστέον εἶναι ὑπὲρ αὐτοῦ (τοῦ Χριστοῦ) (*that they are on his side*) τοὺς τὰ ᾄδην περὶ αὐτὸν φρονοῦντας, φαντασίᾳ τοῦ δοξάζειν αὐτὸν, ὅποι εἰσὶν εἰ συγχέοντες πατέρα καὶ υἱὸν ἐννοίαν καὶ τῇ ὑποστάσει ἕνα διδόντες· εἰ καὶ τὸν πατέρα καὶ τὸν υἱὸν, τῇ ἐπινοίᾳ μόνῃ καὶ τοῖς ὀνόμασι διαιροῦντες· τὸ ἓν ὑποκείμενον (the one Divine Subject.) And Origen, probably, had this in his mind, when, like the Gnostics, he separated those who knew no higher God than the God of the Old Testament, the Demiurgos, from those, who elevated themselves above him (the Demiurgos) to the knowledge of the Supreme God, and like Philo also, separated those who knew God only in his mediate revelation the

PATRIPASSIANS.—NOETUS.

because they were accused of attributing the sufferings of Christ to the Father.*

The first name which occurs among the Patripassians is that of Praxeas, of Asia Minor, the native region of the doctrine of the Monarchia. Having made a confession of faith under torture, during the persecution of Marcus Aurelius, he afterwards travelled to Rome, where Eleutheros was bishop (see above,) and there he brought forward his doctrine without receiving any obstruction, which perhaps, arose from the Church doctrine not having as yet been so accurately defined, that the contradiction to it by the doctrine of Praxeas could at once make any impression; it may have been the case, that by his zeal for the Divinity of Christ against the other party of Monarchiani, the Theodotians, which had perhaps, arisen at Rome by that time, Praxeas, who must have been favourably looked upon in virtue of having been a *Confessor*, won still greater favour for himself, and thence, therefore, that men were more easily induced to overlook other points of difference. He appears afterwards to have betaken himself to Carthage, where he found followers, but where the contrast between his doctrine and that which was predominant attracted more observation. He wrote and published an explanation which was looked upon, at least by his opponents, as an express recantation; but we cannot very accurately determine the state of the case, because it may have happened that Praxeas defended his doctrine only against consequences with which it was unjustly charged, and misrepresentations of it. Tertullian, who would not be favourably disposed towards Praxeas, as an adversary of Montanism, wrote against him, and his book is the only source from which we can learn the doctrine of this person with any certainty.

But, if we take Tertullian as our guide, we might take two different views of his doctrine. From some places it would appear that Praxeas had taught the doctrine of the Patripassians, in the manner in which we have before represented it. He acknowledged the doctrine of a Divine Logos in a certain sense, he applied the name of *Son of God* not merely to Christ after his appearance in the form of man, but he recognised from the time of the creation of the world a difference between the hidden invisible God, and that [God] who revealed himself outwardly as well in the Creation, as in the Theophaniæ [appearances of the Deity] of the Old Testament, and lastly in a human body in Christ. In the latter respect he was called the Logos or the Son; by extending his agency in a certain manner beyond himself and thus begetting the Logos, he made himself into a Son to himself.* On the contrary, in other passages, it appears as if he had denied every distinction in regard to the Divine Being, and had applied the name of Son of God only to the human nature of Christ.† We may suppose, either that Tertullian has not always entered justly into the tenour of the ideas of Praxeas, or else, that among the adherents of this latter, different conceptions of his system had arisen, because men of uncultivated understanding, whom this doctrine suited, could not enter into those subtle distinctions.

Noëtus, also, who appeared at Smyrna during the first half of the third century, and was excommunicated for his unchurchly theory, belongs *to this class* of Patripassians. Theodoret gives, as well as Hippolytus, the most characteristic traits of his doctrine,‡ and he observes, with justice, that Noëtus did not bring forward any new invented doctrine of his own, but that others§ had made up such a system before his time. According to this system, there is one God the Father, who is invisible when he will, and appears (reveals himself) when he will; he is visible and invisible, begotten and unbegotten.

Λογῳ, from those who elevate themselves above all mediate revelation to the intellectual perception of the Divine Being, who are the υἱοὶ τοῦ Θεοῦ; and this is the manner in which Origen arranges the two classes of men.

1. οἱ μὲν Θεὸν ἔχουσι τὸν τῶν ὅλων Θεόν, ἄνθρωποι οἰκεῖοι τῳ πατρί, μερίδος ὄντες αὐτοῦ, 2. οἱ ἱστάμενοι ἐπὶ τὸν υἱὸν τοῦ Θεοῦ, τὸν Χριστὸν αὐτοῦ, οἱ ἐπὶ τὸν σωτῆρα φθάσαντες καὶ τὸ πᾶν ἐν αὐτῷ ἱστάντες. In Joh. t. ii. § 3. [Ed. Huet. p. 49. In the above quotation μερίδος ought clearly to be μερίδες. The words are not exactly copied throughout.—H. J. R.]

* Origen expressly distinguishes between these two classes of Monarchiani, particularly in Joh. t. ii. § 2, and t. ii. Joh. § 18, t. x. § 21. c. Cels. l. viii. c. 12. On the obscure passage Commentar. in Tit. f. 695, t. iv. Ed. de la Rue, see below.

* See Tertullian, c. 10. 14. 26.
† See c. 27.
‡ Hæret. fab. iii. c. 3.
§ Among whom he mentions two men who are unknown to us, Epigonius and Cleomenes.

ORDER FROM YOUR FAVORITE BOOKSELLER OR CALL FOR OUR FREE CATALOG

***That Old Time Religion: The Story of Religious Foundations*, by Jordan Maxwell and Paul Tice.** This book proves there is nothing new under the sun — including Christianity. It gives a complete rundown of the stellar, lunar, and solar evolution of our religious systems; contains new, long-awaited, exhaustive research on the gods and our beliefs; includes research by Dr. Alan A. Snow, famous Dead Sea Scrolls scholar, on astrology in the Dead Sea Scrolls. Dr. Snow has been referred to by Sydney Ohmarr as the "world's greatest authority on astrology and the Dead Sea Scrolls." Includes 3 chapters by Paul Tice, a well known Gnostic minister. This book is illustrated, organized, and very comprehensible. Educate yourself with clear documented proof, and be prepared to have your belief system shattered! **ISBN 1-58509-100-6 • 220 pages • 6 x 9 • trade paper • $19.95**

 ***Jumpin' Jehovah: Exposing the Atrocities of the Old Testament God*, by Paul Tice.** Was Jehovah a criminal? Was he psychotic? In the realm of the gods, was Jehovah just a renegade punk gone wild? Paul Tice has collected all the dirt on this shady historical character. Once you read this book, your views on God will never be the same again. Jehovah is stripped bare of all his fabricated "godliness" and we discover in this book an entity with no sense of ethics, forgiveness or compassion. Jehovah delighted in roasting people alive and tormenting his followers in a variety of creative ways. Tice takes us from the very beginning, when this crafty character first came on the scene, and shows us how he conned and bullied his way to the top of the godly heap. Jehovah then maintained his standing through threats and coercion—and when that didn't work, he did what any mentally deranged god would do: he just moved in and killed people. Basic theological questions are explored like: Was Jehovah really a god, or a demon? Why did Jehovah never promise a heaven or any kind of reward to his followers? Does any entity who murders thousands of devoted followers deserve to be worshipped? What are the differences between a false god and a true one? Jehovah has stopped punishing people in terrible ways, so it's probably safe to buy this book. **ISBN 1-58509-102-2 • 104 pages • 6 x 9 • trade paper • $12.95**

***The Book of Enoch, A Work of Visionary Revelation and Prophecy, Revealing Divine Secrets and Fantastic Information about Creation, Salvation, Heaven and Hell*, translated by R. H. Charles.** *The Book of Enoch* was considered one of the most important books in early Christianity and was used widely. R. H. Charles, who translated the book, said, "the influence of *1 Enoch* on the New Testament has been greater than that of all the other apocryphal and pseudepigraphical books put together." One of the main influences from the book is its explanation of evil coming into the world with the arrival of the "fallen angels". Enoch functions as a scribe, writing up a petition on behalf of these fallen ones, to be given to higher powers for judgment. Enoch was apparently chosen for this duty because he was of a different nature than the angels. It appears that Christianity later adopted some of its ideas and philosophies from this book, including the Final Judgment, the concept  of demons, the Resurrection, the origins of evil, and the coming of a Messiah and Messianic Kingdom. This makes *The Book of Enoch* of immense importance, not only to the study of Christianity's origins, but to the possible reality of strange, otherworldly visions or visitations. If this book was so important to Christian beginnings, why was it removed from the canon and banned? Enoch had found and experienced God face to face, something which Gnostics always strive for. The Church opposed Gnostics—to them, they were heretics. Only now, after many centuries, are people rediscovering this book's value, along with its important counterpart, *The Book of the Secrets of Enoch*. Both of these important books are now shedding new light on Christian origins and otherworldly "encounters." See also the longer version of *Enoch*, below. **ISBN 1-58509-019-0 • 152 pages • 5 1/2 x 8 1/2 • trade paper • $13.95**

ORDER FROM YOUR FAVORITE BOOKSELLER OR CALL FOR OUR FREE CATALOG

Of Heaven and Earth: Essays Presented at the First Sitchin Studies Day, edited by Zecharia Sitchin. ISBN 1-885395-17-5 • 164 pages • 5 1/2 x 8 1/2 • trade paper • illustrated • $14.95

God Games: What Do You Do Forever?, by Neil Freer. ISBN 1-885395-39-6 • 312 pages • 6 x 9 • trade paper • $19.95

Space Travelers and the Genesis of the Human Form: Evidence of Intelligent Contact in the Solar System, by Joan d'Arc. ISBN 1-58509-127-8 • 208 pages • 6 x 9 • trade paper • illustrated • $18.95

Humanity's Extraterrestrial Origins: ET Influences on Humankind's Biological and Cultural Evolution, by Dr. Arthur David Horn with Lynette Mallory-Horn. ISBN 3-931652-31-9 • 373 pages • 6 x 9 • trade paper • $17.00

Past Shock: The Origin of Religion and Its Impact on the Human Soul, by Jack Barranger. ISBN 1-885395-08-6 • 126 pages • 6 x 9 • trade paper • illustrated • $12.95

Flying Serpents and Dragons: The Story of Mankind's Reptilian Past, by R.A. Boulay. ISBN 1-885395-38-8 • 276 pages • 6 x 9 • trade paper • illustrated • $19.95

Triumph of the Human Spirit: The Greatest Achievements of the Human Soul and How Its Power Can Change Your Life, by Paul Tice. ISBN 1-885395-57-4 • 295 pages • 6 x 9 • trade paper • illustrated • $19.95

Mysteries Explored: The Search for Human Origins, UFOs, and Religious Beginnings, by Jack Barranger and Paul Tice. ISBN 1-58509-101-4 • 104 pages • 6 x 9 • trade paper • $12.95

Mushrooms and Mankind: The Impact of Mushrooms on Human Consciousness and Religion, by James Arthur. ISBN 1-58509-151-0 • 180 pages • 6 x 9 • trade paper • $16.95

Vril or Vital Magnetism, with an Introduction by Paul Tice. ISBN 1-58509-030-1 • 124 pages • 5 1/2 x 8 1/2 • trade paper • $12.95

The Odic Force: Letters on Od and Magnetism, by Karl von Reichenbach. ISBN 1-58509-001-8 • 192 pages • 6 x 9 • trade paper • $15.95

The New Revelation: The Coming of a New Spiritual Paradigm, by Arthur Conan Doyle. ISBN 1-58509-220-7 • 124 pages • 6 x 9 • trade paper • $12.95

The Astral World: Its Scenes, Dwellers, and Phenomena, by Swami Panchadasi. ISBN 1-58509-071-9 • 104 pages • 6 x 9 • trade paper • $11.95

Reason and Belief: The Impact of Scientific Discovery on Religious and Spiritual Faith, by Sir Oliver Lodge. ISBN 1-58509-226-6 • 180 pages • 6 x 9 • trade paper • $17.95

William Blake: A Biography, by Basil De Selincourt. ISBN 1-58509-225-8 • 384 pages • 6 x 9 • trade paper • $28.95

The Divine Pymander: And Other Writings of Hermes Trismegistus, translated by John D. Chambers. ISBN 1-58509-046-8 • 196 pages • 6 x 9 • trade paper • $16.95

Theosophy and The Secret Doctrine, by Harriet L. Henderson. Includes **H.P. Blavatsky: An Outline of Her Life,** by Herbert Whyte, ISBN 1-58509-075-1 • 132 pages • 6 x 9 • trade paper • $13.95

The Light of Egypt, Volume One: The Science of the Soul and the Stars, by Thomas H. Burgoyne. ISBN 1-58509-051-4 • 320 pages • 6 x 9 • trade paper • illustrated • $24.95

The Light of Egypt, Volume Two: The Science of the Soul and the Stars, by Thomas H. Burgoyne. ISBN 1-58509-052-2 • 224 pages • 6 x 9 • trade paper • illustrated • $17.95

The Jumping Frog and 18 Other Stories: 19 Unforgettable Mark Twain Stories, by Mark Twain. ISBN 1-58509-200-2 • 128 pages • 6 x 9 • trade paper • $12.95

The Devil's Dictionary: A Guidebook for Cynics, by Ambrose Bierce. ISBN 1-58509-016-6 • 144 pages • 6 x 9 • trade paper • $12.95

The Smoky God: Or The Voyage to the Inner World, by Willis George Emerson. ISBN 1-58509-067-0 • 184 pages • 6 x 9 • trade paper • illustrated • $15.95

A Short History of the World, by H.G. Wells. ISBN 1-58509-211-8 • 320 pages • 6 x 9 • trade paper • $24.95

The Voyages and Discoveries of the Companions of Columbus, by Washington Irving. ISBN 1-58509-500-1 • 352 pages • 6 x 9 • hard cover • $39.95

ORDER FROM YOUR FAVORITE BOOKSELLER OR CALL FOR OUR FREE CATALOG

History of Baalbek, by Michel Alouf. ISBN 1-58509-063-8 • 196 pages • 5 x 8 • trade paper • illustrated • $15.95

Ancient Egyptian Masonry: The Building Craft, by Sommers Clarke and R. Engelback. ISBN 1-58509-059-X • 350 pages • 6 x 9 • trade paper • illustrated • $26.95

That Old Time Religion: The Story of Religious Foundations, by Jordan Maxwell and Paul Tice. ISBN 1-58509-100-6 • 220 pages • 6 x 9 • trade paper • $19.95

Jumpin' Jehovah: Exposing the Atrocities of the Old Testament God, by Paul Tice. ISBN 1-58509-102-2 • 104 pages • 6 x 9 • trade paper • $12.95

The Book of Enoch: A Work of Visionary Revelation and Prophecy, Revealing Divine Secrets and Fantastic Information about Creation, Salvation, Heaven and Hell, translated by R. H. Charles. ISBN 1-58509-019-0 • 152 pages • 5 1/2 x 8 1/2 • trade paper • $13.95

The Book of Enoch: Translated from the Editor's Ethiopic Text and Edited with an Enlarged Introduction, Notes and Indexes, Together with a Reprint of the Greek Fragments, edited by R. H. Charles. ISBN 1-58509-080-8 • 448 pages • 6 x 9 • trade paper • $34.95

The Book of the Secrets of Enoch, translated from the Slavonic by W. R. Morfill. Edited, with Introduction and Notes by R. H. Charles. ISBN 1-58509-020-4 • 148 pages • 5 1/2 x 8 1/2 • trade paper • $13.95

Enuma Elish: The Seven Tablets of Creation, Volume One, by L. W. King. ISBN 1-58509-041-7 • 236 pages • 6 x 9 • trade paper • illustrated • $18.95

Enuma Elish: The Seven Tablets of Creation, Volume Two, by L. W. King. ISBN 1-58509-042-5 • 260 pages • 6 x 9 • trade paper • illustrated • $19.95

Enuma Elish, Volumes One and Two: The Seven Tablets of Creation, by L. W. King. Two volumes from above bound as one. ISBN 1-58509-043-3 • 496 pages • 6 x 9 • trade paper • illustrated • $38.90

The Archko Volume: Documents that Claim Proof to the Life, Death, and Resurrection of Christ, by Drs. McIntosh and Twyman. ISBN 1-58509-082-4 • 248 pages • 6 x 9 • trade paper • $20.95

The Lost Language of Symbolism: An Inquiry into the Origin of Certain Letters, Words, Names, Fairy-Tales, Folklore, and Mythologies, by Harold Bayley. ISBN 1-58509-070-0 • 384 pages • 6 x 9 • trade paper • $27.95

The Book of Jasher: A Suppressed Book that was Removed from the Bible, Referred to in Joshua and Second Samuel, translated by Albinus Alcuin (800 AD). ISBN 1-58509-081-6 • 304 pages • 6 x 9 • trade paper • $24.95

The Bible's Most Embarrassing Moments, with an Introduction by Paul Tice. ISBN 1-58509-025-5 • 172 pages • 5 x 8 • trade paper • $14.95

History of the Cross: The Pagan Origin and Idolatrous Adoption and Worship of the Image, by Henry Dana Ward. ISBN 1-58509-056-5 • 104 pages • 6 x 9 • trade paper • illustrated • $11.95

Was Jesus Influenced by Buddhism? A Comparative Study of the Lives and Thoughts of Gautama and Jesus, by Dwight Goddard. ISBN 1-58509-027-1 • 252 pages • 6 x 9 • trade paper • $19.95

History of the Christian Religion to the Year Two Hundred, by Charles B. Waite. ISBN 1-885395-15-9 • 556 pages. • 6 x 9 • hard cover • $25.00

Symbols, Sex, and the Stars, by Ernest Busenbark. ISBN 1-885395-19-1 • 396 pages • 5 1/2 x 8 1/2 • trade paper • $22.95

History of the First Council of Nice: A World's Christian Convention, A.D. 325, by Dean Dudley. ISBN 1-58509-023-9 • 132 pages • 5 1/2 x 8 1/2 • trade paper • $12.95

The World's Sixteen Crucified Saviors, by Kersey Graves. ISBN 1-58509-018-2 • 436 pages • 5 1/2 x 8 1/2 • trade paper • $29.95

Babylonian Influence on the Bible and Popular Beliefs: A Comparative Study of Genesis I.2, by A. Smythe Palmer. ISBN 1-58509-000-X • 124 pages • 6 x 9 • trade paper • $12.95

ORDER FROM YOUR FAVORITE BOOKSELLER OR CALL FOR OUR FREE CATALOG

Biography of Satan: Exposing the Origins of the Devil, by Kersey Graves. ISBN 1-885395-11-6 • 168 pages • 5 1/2 x 8 1/2 • trade paper • $13.95

The Malleus Maleficarum: The Notorious Handbook Once Used to Condemn and Punish "Witches", by Heinrich Kramer and James Sprenger. ISBN 1-58509-098-0 • 332 pages • 6 x 9 • trade paper • $25.95

Crux Ansata: An Indictment of the Roman Catholic Church, by H. G. Wells. ISBN 1-58509-210-X • 160 pages • 6 x 9 • trade paper • $14.95

Emanuel Swedenborg: The Spiritual Columbus, by U.S.E. (William Spear). ISBN 1-58509-096-4 • 208 pages • 6 x 9 • trade paper • $17.95

Dragons and Dragon Lore, by Ernest Ingersoll. ISBN 1-58509-021-2 • 228 pages • 6 x 9 • trade paper • illustrated • $17.95

The Vision of God, by Nicholas of Cusa. ISBN 1-58509-004-2 • 160 pages • 5 x 8 • trade paper • $13.95

The Historical Jesus and the Mythical Christ: Separating Fact From Fiction, by Gerald Massey. ISBN 1-58509-073-5 • 244 pages • 6 x 9 • trade paper • $18.95

Gog and Magog: The Giants in Guildhall; Their Real and Legendary History, with an Account of Other Giants at Home and Abroad, by F.W. Fairholt. ISBN 1-58509-084-0 • 172 pages • 6 x 9 • trade paper • $16.95

The Origin and Evolution of Religion, by Albert Churchward. ISBN 1-58509-078-6 • 504 pages • 6 x 9 • trade paper • $39.95

The Origin of Biblical Traditions, by Albert T. Clay. ISBN 1-58509-065-4 • 220 pages • 5 1/2 x 8 1/2 • trade paper • $17.95

Aryan Sun Myths, by Sarah Elizabeth Titcomb, Introduction by Charles Morris. ISBN 1-58509-069-7 • 192 pages • 6 x 9 • trade paper • $15.95

The Social Record of Christianity, by Joseph McCabe. Includes *The Lies and Fallacies of the Encyclopedia Britannica,* ISBN 1-58509-215-0 • 204 pages • 6 x 9 • trade paper • $17.95

The History of the Christian Religion and Church During the First Three Centuries, by Dr. Augustus Neander. ISBN 1-58509-077-8 • 112 pages • 6 x 9 • trade paper • $12.95

Ancient Symbol Worship: Influence of the Phallic Idea in the Religions of Antiquity, by Hodder M. Westropp and C. Staniland Wake. ISBN 1-58509-048-4 • 120 pages • 6 x 9 • trade paper • illustrated • $12.95

The Gnosis: Or Ancient Wisdom in the Christian Scriptures, by William Kingsland. ISBN 1-58509-047-6 • 232 pages • 6 x 9 • trade paper • $18.95

The Evolution of the Idea of God: An Inquiry into the Origin of Religions, by Grant Allen. ISBN 1-58509-074-3 • 160 pages • 6 x 9 • trade paper • $14.95

Sun Lore of All Ages: A Survey of Solar Mythology, Folklore, Customs, Worship, Festivals, and Superstition, by William Tyler Olcott. ISBN 1-58509-044-1 • 316 pages • 6 x 9 • trade paper • $24.95

Nature Worship: An Account of Phallic Faiths and Practices Ancient and Modern, by the Author of Phallicism with an Introduction by Tedd St. Rain. ISBN 1-58509-049-2 • 112 pages • 6 x 9 • trade paper • illustrated • $12.95

Life and Religion, by Max Muller. ISBN 1-885395-10-8 • 237 pages • 5 1/2 x 8 1/2 • trade paper • $14.95

Jesus: God, Man, or Myth? An Examination of the Evidence, by Herbert Cutner. ISBN 1-58509-072-7 • 304 pages • 6 x 9 • trade paper • $23.95

Pagan and Christian Creeds: Their Origin and Meaning, by Edward Carpenter. ISBN 1-58509-024-7 • 316 pages • 5 1/2 x 8 1/2 • trade paper • $24.95

The Christ Myth: A Study, by Elizabeth Evans. ISBN 1-58509-037-9 • 136 pages • 6 x 9 • trade paper • $13.95

Popery: Foe of the Church and the Republic, by Joseph F. Van Dyke. ISBN 1-58509-058-1 • 336 pages • 6 x 9 • trade paper • illustrated • $25.95

Career of Religious Ideas, by Hudson Tuttle. ISBN 1-58509-066-2 • 172 pages • 5 x 8 • trade paper • $15.95

ORDER FROM YOUR FAVORITE BOOKSELLER OR CALL FOR OUR FREE CATALOG

Buddhist Suttas: Major Scriptural Writings from Early Buddhism, by T.W. Rhys Davids. ISBN 1-58509-079-4 • 376 pages • 6 x 9 • trade paper • $27.95

Early Buddhism, by T. W. Rhys Davids. Includes ***Buddhist Ethics: The Way to Salvation?,*** by Paul Tice. ISBN 1-58509-076-X • 112 pages • 6 x 9 • trade paper • $12.95

The Fountain-Head of Religion: A Comparative Study of the Principal Religions of the World and a Manifestation of their Common Origin from the Vedas, by Ganga Prasad. ISBN 1-58509-054-9 • 276 pages • 6 x 9 • trade paper • $22.95

India: What Can It Teach Us?, by Max Muller. ISBN 1-58509-064-6 • 284 pages • 5 1/2 x 8 1/2 • trade paper • $22.95

Matrix of Power: How the World has Been Controlled by Powerful People Without Your Knowledge, by Jordan Maxwell. ISBN 1-58509-120-0 • 104 pages • 6 x 9 • trade paper • $12.95

Cyberculture Counterconspiracy: A Steamshovel Web Reader, Volume One, edited by Kenn Thomas. ISBN 1-58509-125-1 • 180 pages • 6 x 9 • trade paper • illustrated • $16.95

Cyberculture Counterconspiracy: A Steamshovel Web Reader, Volume Two, edited by Kenn Thomas. ISBN 1-58509-126-X • 132 pages • 6 x 9 • trade paper • illustrated • $13.95

Oklahoma City Bombing: The Suppressed Truth, by Jon Rappoport. ISBN 1-885395-22-1 • 112 pages • 5 1/2 x 8 1/2 • trade paper • $12.95

The Protocols of the Learned Elders of Zion, by Victor Marsden. ISBN 1-58509-015-8 • 312 pages • 6 x 9 • trade paper • $24.95

Secret Societies and Subversive Movements, by Nesta H. Webster. ISBN 1-58509-092-1 • 432 pages • 6 x 9 • trade paper • $29.95

The Secret Doctrine of the Rosicrucians, by Magus Incognito. ISBN 1-58509-091-3 • 256 pages • 6 x 9 • trade paper • $20.95

The Origin and Evolution of Freemasonry: Connected with the Origin and Evolution of the Human Race, by Albert Churchward. ISBN 1-58509-029-8 • 240 pages • 6 x 9 • trade paper • $18.95

The Lost Key: An Explanation and Application of Masonic Symbols, by Prentiss Tucker. ISBN 1-58509-050-6 • 192 pages • 6 x 9 • trade paper • illustrated • $15.95

The Character, Claims, and Practical Workings of Freemasonry, by Rev. C.G. Finney. ISBN 1-58509-094-8 • 288 pages • 6 x 9 • trade paper • $22.95

The Secret World Government or "The Hidden Hand": The Unrevealed in History, by Maj.-Gen., Count Cherep-Spiridovich. ISBN 1-58509-093-X • 270 pages • 6 x 9 • trade paper • $21.95

The Magus, Book One: A Complete System of Occult Philosophy, by Francis Barrett. ISBN 1-58509-031-X • 200 pages • 6 x 9 • trade paper • illustrated • $16.95

The Magus, Book Two: A Complete System of Occult Philosophy, by Francis Barrett. ISBN 1-58509-032-8 • 220 pages • 6 x 9 • trade paper • illustrated • $17.95

The Magus, Book One and Two: A Complete System of Occult Philosophy, by Francis Barrett. ISBN 1-58509-033-6 • 420 pages • 6 x 9 • trade paper • illustrated • $34.90

The Key of Solomon The King, by S. Liddell MacGregor Mathers. ISBN 1-58509-022-0 • 152 pages • 6 x 9 • trade paper • illustrated • $12.95

Magic and Mystery in Tibet, by Alexandra David-Neel. ISBN 1-58509-097-2 • 352 pages • 6 x 9 • trade paper • $26.95

The Comte de St. Germain, by I. Cooper Oakley. ISBN 1-58509-068-9 • 280 pages • 6 x 9 • trade paper • illustrated • $22.95

Alchemy Rediscovered and Restored, by A. Cockren. ISBN 1-58509-028-X • 156 pages • 5 1/2 x 8 1/2 • trade paper • $13.95

The 6th and 7th Books of Moses, with an Introduction by Paul Tice. ISBN 1-58509-045-X • 188 pages • 6 x 9 • trade paper • illustrated • $16.95

www.ingramcontent.com/pod-product-compliance
Lightning Source LLC
Chambersburg PA
CBHW031650040426
42453CB00006B/256